The Agile Workforce and Workplace:

Flex Primer for the New Future of Work

by
Karol Rose
and
Lori Sokol, Ph.D.

The Agile Workforce and Workplace:
Flex Primer for the New Future Work

Published by:

Working Mother Media
2 Park Avenue
New York, NY 10016
212.219.7470
workingmother.com

Copyright © 2011 by Working Mother Media. All rights reserved.

No part of this book may be reproduced in any form or by any means without written permission from Working Mother Media.

For additional copies, contact Working Mother at 212-219-7470 or visit www.workingmother.com

Printed in the United States of America

ISBN 978-0-9833060-3-0

Contents

WELCOME
Letter from Mike Kaufmann, Cardinal Health — vii
Letter from Richard T. Clark, Merck — ix
Letter from Alison Quirk, State Street — xi

FOREWORD
J.T. (Ted) Childs, Jr. — 1

INTRODUCTION
Karol Rose and Lori Sokol, Ph.D. — 5

CHAPTER 1: At a New Tipping Point — How Did We Get Here? Where Are We Going? — 9
    Flex In-Depth: State Street — 29
    References — 31

CHAPTER 2: The Role of Flexible Work in Attracting, Engaging and Managing Diverse Talent — 35
    Worksheet: Flexible Work and Diversity and Inclusion — 44
    Best Flex Practices: Hands-On Tips for Integrating Flex and Diversity — 48
        Kodak — 48
        Royal Dutch Shell — 48
        Pitney Bowes — 49
        PepsiCo — 50
        McKesson Corporation — 51
        The Timken Company — 51
        Procter & Gamble — 52
        Walmart — 52
    Tip Sheet: Attracting, Engaging and Managing Diverse Talent — 54
    References — 55

CHAPTER 3: Flexible Work and Technology — 57
    Worksheet: Flexible Work and Technology — 66
    Flex In-Depth: Cisco — 70
    Tip Sheet: Flexible Work and Technology — 74
    References — 75

CHAPTER 4: Flexible Work and Business Continuity and Disaster Planning — 77
    Worksheet: Business Continuity Strategy — 86
    References — 88

CHAPTER 5: Flexible Work and Business Facilities Planning — 89
    Flex In-Depth: British Telecom — 97
    Sample: Home Office Safety Self-Assessment Checklist — 99
    Tip Sheet: Flexible Work and Facilities Planning — 102
    References — 103

CHAPTER 6: The Connection Between Employee Wellness and Flexible Working — **105**
    Worksheet: Flexible Work and Health and Wellness Strategy — 113
    Flex In-Depth: Cardinal Health, Inc. — 115
    Flex In-Depth: GlaxoSmithKline — 117
    Flex In-Depth: Prudential — 119
    Flex In-Depth: Wells Fargo — 121
    Tip Sheet: Connecting Health, Wellness & Flexibility — 124
    References — 126

CHAPTER 7: Flexible Work and Legal/Compliance Issues — **127**
    Tip Sheet: Tips for Flexible Work and Legal/Compliance Issues — 139
    References — 140

CHAPTER 8: Trends in Flexible Work — **141**
    Tip Sheet: Trends in Flexible Work — 158
    References — 159

CHAPTER 9: The Process: How to Plan, Implement and Manage Flexibility — **161**

CHAPTER 10: Assessing the Value of Flexible Work — **185**
    Flex In-Depth: First Tennessee — 190
    Sample: Assess Your Organization — 194
    Flex In-Depth: Ernst & Young — 206
    Tip Sheet: Assessing the Value of Flexible Work — 210
    References — 211

ABOUT THE SPONSORS — **213**
ABOUT THE AUTHORS — **214**
ABOUT THE WORKING MOTHER RESEARCH INSTITUTE — **215**

At Cardinal Health, we make healthcare more cost-effective so our customers can focus on their patients. Our ability to deliver on this promise depends upon the unique contributions, ideas and perspectives of our more than 30,000 employees worldwide. That's why we consider a diverse and inclusive culture a true business imperative.

Like our partners at Working Mother, Cardinal Health is committed to work/life integration. We know that it's not just the right thing to do; it drives business results. By identifying what employees value and giving them the tools and resources they need, we will foster an engaging and supportive culture that allows people to do their best work.

As the executive sponsor for Cardinal Health's Women's Initiative Network (WIN,) an employee resource group of over 4,000 women and men, I know that our focus on work/life integration will make Cardinal Health a better, stronger company.

Cardinal Health is proud to sponsor the Working Mother Work Life Congress and the *Flex Primer*. Both are essential to the needs of working mothers, both on the job and outside of work. We take great pride in our partnership with Working Mother and look forward to continuing our collaboration in the years ahead.

Here's to an outstanding 2011 conference!

Warm regards,

Mike Kaufmann
CEO, Pharmaceutical Segment
Cardinal Health

Dear Readers,

Merck is proud to sponsor the Working Mother Research Institute's *Flex Primer*. Our mission is to discover, develop and provide innovative products and services that save and improve lives around the world. We believe that our ability to deliver on that mission is linked to many things, including employees who are engaged, productive and focused on making decisions every day to help the world "Be Well".

At Merck, we take a comprehensive and holistic view of work-life integration. We know people are managing multiple responsibilities in the home and in the workplace, so we offer a broad array of programs to meet the needs of our colleagues at all stages of life. Helping employees successfully integrate their personal and work lives enhances their commitment to the company. It also increases their engagement and productivity, and helps to make Merck more agile and competitive. Over the years we've learned that work-life integration is in the eye of the beholder, so we offer a portfolio of options for our employees. Examples include:

- Global Flexible Work Arrangements policies
- Back-up care in the U.S. for both children and elders
- Adoption assistance
- Parental leave for both birth and adoption
- College preparation, financing and applications support

Beyond creating an environment which fosters successful work-life integration, we've learned that building and maintaining a culture of innovation is accomplished by fostering diversity of thought in our workforce. Part of Merck's broader diversity strategy also addresses the role of employees who have a variety of backgrounds and interests.

This primer will be a valuable resource for evaluating and further refining company and organizational programs and policies.

We wish each of you success as you build a healthy and productive work-life culture for your organization.

Be Well,

Richard T. Clark
Chairman
Merck

State Street is proud to sponsor *The Agile Workforce and Workplace: A Flexibility Primer for the New Future of Work*. Talent management is a key component of corporate strategy, and it is currently becoming a top priority among C-suites across the globe. We believe that the power of our organization comes from our people. Organizational sustainability is dependent on meeting our employees' diverse needs in ways that also address business needs. We have found that by creating a more flexible work environment, we can address business and personal needs simultaneously, and produce positive outcomes for both.

Having a strategic focus — and aligning our internal stakeholders in facilities, IT and HR — has enabled State Street to dramatically enhance our flexible work initiative. As a global organization, we are working hard to expand our flexible work efforts across all 26 countries where we are located by identifying appropriate ways to adapt to regional, cultural and local requirements. We recognize that creating a more agile workforce and workplace is not a quick fix program, but rather a culture change process that takes time and commitment from every level of the organization.

We are very pleased to support Working Mother Media and authors Karol Rose and Lori Sokol for their thought leadership publication that can serve as a guide for the business community, and stimulate new ideas and approaches that can accelerate the implementation and expansion of flexible work throughout all organizations. As this book demonstrates, the research is clear: creating a more flexible work environment and work force is good for our employees, our business — and its benefits extend beyond that to the greater community and environment. There can be no doubt, the agile workforce and workplace is the 'new future of work.' We look forward to sharing the State Street journey and learning with others as we all explore new, more effective ways for flexible work to work in our organizations.

Sincerely,

Alison Quirk
Executive Vice President, Global Human Resources
State Street

FOREWORD

"The subject of workplace flexibility was born in the early 1980's. Its birth was not due to the vision of enlightened, caring management. It was an employee relations example of 'necessity is the mother of invention.'"

This necessity was caused by the seventies migration of women from homes to the American workplace. It was caused because we were confronted with the follow-on social upheaval in America's homes. It affected women and men. It was not about flexibility. It was about intra family negotiation — a process that began with women being professional, but often in the lower paying of the two jobs in their families. The negotiation was not about flexibility, but who would deal with the chores — not doing the dishes, or taking the garbage out. Who would handle those chores that required someone to be at home: going to school to pick up a sick child; who would let the plumber in; who would take an animal to the vet; who would take a car to be serviced. Low salaried person loses the negotiation.

As women, however, have achieved jobs of equal, and frequently more responsibility than their partners, and the accompanying earnings power, their negotiating posture has improved. With that improved posture in the eighties, the subject of "Workplace Flexibility" — alternative approaches to employee uses of time — has become a meaningful business topic. Initially, the flexibility tools were used by, and seen as beneficial to, women. As women gained more equality in the intra family negotiation, and as a new generation of men became more supportive of their wives who work, and sought more involvement in the lives of their children, men and women found flexibility tools not to be a benefit, but a necessity.

While the flexibility subject began as a U. S. "women's issue," it is now the core of a global debate with governments and national policy leaders. In March of 2010, President and Mrs. Obama hosted The White House Forum on Workplace Flexibility. Following that seminar, U. S. Secretary of Labor, Hilda Solis, launched a multi-city National Dialogue on Workplace Flexibility.
In November of that year, The Alfred P. Sloan Foundation sponsored "Focus on Workplace Flexibility," a day-long discussion addressing the importance of this subject, and including the participation of senior government, business and military leaders. In February of this year, a critical project partnership was formed between the Families and Work Institute, our premier work-life research engine, and The Society for Human Resource Management, our premier human resource membership organization. The purpose of this partnership, "Moving Work Foreword," is "to help businesses become more successful by transforming the way they view and adopt workplace flexibility."

In June 2009, the Japanese Diet passed an amendment on childcare leave. The law addresses working hours for employees with children, and leaves of absence.

In both cases, the nation is treating flexibility as a critical tool of national workplace competitiveness. Issues get addressed in time — when it is their time. Today is the time for

Foreword

the flexibility debate. If talent management is the core HR objective, then flexibility is the cornerstone of that goal, the key HR challenge of this management generation.

Throughout the thirty years of our evolving flexibility journey, only a handful of organizations, and people, have been involved as creditable thinkers. Karol Rose is one of those people, and I have known her throughout that journey. "The Agile Workforce and Workplace" looks at the flexibility challenge through multiple lenses: talent, technology, facilities, the law, employee health and evolving workplace trends; and it explores how organizational leaders in those areas are changing the way flexible work is done and the speed at which it is being adopted in their organizations. We need our leaders — business, government and institutional — to be innovative in both their thinking, and their execution, in addressing the flexibility needs of their people. They must be driven by pursuit of the "What is possible?" question, and not satisfied with "what was, or is."

This book is about helping them to have the mindset today to pursue the "What is possible?" question to facilitate tomorrow's behavior — not because they are curious, but because they understand that doing so is a strategic, survival necessity, and because they realize that we have only scratched the surface in our flexibility dialog. When posing that question becomes part of our ongoing DNA, then the real driver will not be asking, but what we do with the answers. Those answers will be driven by yet-to-be-achieved technology accomplishments that will both increase the demands that are possible to make of employees, and the ability of those employees to respond. If the outcome is a management / employee partnership, the yield will be competitive advantage for businesses, institutions and nations. This book is about getting into the head of someone who has traveled this journey, and understanding how she has used her focus on flexibility to interpret, and respond to each generation of change; and how we must use that journey to have the insight and ability to respond to future, inevitable changes.

The focus on mindset is the table setter for a companion focus on mind tolerance — how do we develop the mindset to have the mind tolerance to competitively respond to those flexibility changes yet to occur, sparked by those future technical innovations? Each generation of worker, and manager, gets comfortable with its tools, its gimmicks, and establishes the workplace tolerances for its generation of doing business. The challenge comes when technology gives a future generation new tools. Management will want / demand the benefits of those tools, but anchored in their generation of workplace practices — the how, where and when of doing work. Karol is a thinker who has lived through the evolution of this issue, and can constructively help us prepare for such challenges, and she, along with her co-author, Lori Sokol, does it masterfully in this discussion of yesterday's and today's workplace, and marketplace, and in so doing, tomorrow's everyplace.

The flexibility discussion is an ongoing workplace debate. And flexibility is winning, but not easily, and the slowness of our progress does competitive harm. Even when a flexibility driven solution is the right, even common sense outcome, it meets with the resistance of the "old ways." Karol's thinking helps to place a spotlight on that debate, and bring clarity to our focus to help us reach, recognize, and execute common sense solutions.

In the framework of that focus, I think that we must do five things to leverage flexibility as a tool to unleash the talent of our global workforce.

Foreword

First, we must redefine the terminology — flexibility is not an accommodation or a favor. It is the linchpin in the employee / management partnership. And, it is the key tool in the pursuit of productivity, morale and retention — it is distinctively not a barrier to the achievement of those goals — it is the enabler to our being able to do so. Achieving those goals is critical to enabling our employees to contribute to our winning, whatever the field of competition — business, government or institution. If losing is not an option, then embracing flexibility as a workplace tool is a necessity.

To quote my old boss at IBM, SVP of HR, Randy MacDonald, "We have seen profound changes in the workplace since we began this journey over 30 years ago. In this new world, work is something that one does, and not necessarily a place one goes. In IBM, we have found that providing employees flexibility often enables them to achieve higher levels of connection and communication with their dispersed and increasingly global colleagues and clients."

Second, we must get comfortable with the goal of this specific workplace tool, and both discuss, and communicate that goal. Work / Life Balance, as the goal, did not work because it was not achievable. The "scales of justice" concept is not applicable in this debate, and chasing an elusive, impossible-to-achieve "balance" is very frustrating to employees, and an inhibitor to business performance. While different terms have emerged, I am firmly committed to the concept of "Life / Work Integration." For me, it simplifies the goal: help people integrate their personal life and working life, so they can have a life.

Third, we must understand that the flexibility discussion is about all workers, not just women. To quote Ellen Galinsky, President of the Families and Work Institute, "Let's not make assumptions about men at home, the way we have about women at work."

Fourth, we must treat flexibility as a strategic survival and negotiating tool in the global marketplace. As such, we must treat it with respect. It is like money — it is our new workplace currency. Our people have three things to give: their talent, energy, and time. Control over their "time" is up for negotiation. With workplace demands ascending, and resources to compensate declining, flexibility is the currency of exchange: talent, and energy in exchange for how, where and when they are deployed. We must act like flexibility is the coin of the international workplace realm. People have told us that they are "time poor" — they don't have time to spend the money they make; and they will, increasingly, leave an employer not for more money, but for more control over, and respect for, their time.

The fifth thing we must do to unleash the talent of our people, is to understand that a commitment to flexibility does not involve expecting less excellence or commitment from our people. It involves managing people by focusing on results — not on where, when or how the work gets done, but rather by allowing flexibility to enable the people to control the where, when and how, while still meeting our excellence and commitment expectations. When we do so, flexibility will be the launch-pad for employee energy and workplace spirit.

Understanding the context of that employee energy and workplace spirit is the thread upon which "The Agile Workforce and Workplace" is built. Karol's participation in the evolution

Foreword

of flexibility, from its inception thirty years ago as a response to the needs of women, to a competitive tool that is central to today's global dialogue about attracting and retaining talent, is captured in this book. It is less a "how to do," and more a "how to develop and maintain the proper mindset and mind tolerance" to manage today's and tomorrow's talent in a competitive, unforgiving and global marketplace."

— J.T. (Ted) Childs, Jr.
Principal, Ted Childs LLC
Retired Vice President,
Global Workforce Diversity, IBM

INTRODUCTION

Today's workforce is increasingly made up of knowledge workers who are diverse and often working virtually. At the same time, work itself requires more customized, creative, 24/7, global solutions. For organizations to be successful in today's environment they must embrace the concept of a more agile workforce and agile workplace, which some are finding challenging.

The concept of agility is not new. What's changed are the needs of both employees and businesses for more flexibility in how, when, where, and how much work is done, and the internal stakeholders who are defining and shaping the way organizations are responding. However, these stakeholders often work in silos that don't encourage sharing and coordination of effort. There is a significant opportunity to "connect the dots" across internal stakeholders in order maximize the value, impact and speed of adoption of flexibility for both individuals and organizations. It is for these reasons that this book was written: to describe these changes and to provide examples of the ways new organizational stakeholders (including those in the fields of diversity, legal, facilities, technology, business continuity and health/wellness) are using flexible work to create more agile workforces and workplaces.

Each chapter in the book includes interviews with leaders in major organizations and thought leaders in areas related to flexible work. We also include original research conducted with the Working Mother Research Institute specifically for this book as well as other current research and relevant information.

This book can be used in a variety of ways. While it's possible to read the chapters in order, some may choose to explore chapters that focus on topics of special interest. In either case, the reader may want to start with the first chapter, which provides the context for the issues explored in future chapters.

Chapter 2 examines the way diversity and inclusion leaders are using flexible work to achieve their business objectives. As today's workforce becomes more diverse and dispersed, these leaders recognize that while it is necessary to continue to address discrimination issues related to gender, sexual orientation, ethnicity, age and disabilities, it is no longer sufficient to limit their focus to these topics. In order for organizations to attract, engage and retain the diverse talent they need to be competitive, inclusion leaders must become more involved in the way flexibility is understood and implemented.

In Chapter 3 we document the ways in which technology has become one of the most significant catalysts for the development of the agile workforce and workplace and how it will continue to influence growth and development of flexible work for the foreseeable future. While technology enables work to be done anywhere at any time, for too many employees this translates into not only working everywhere, but also all the time. This presents unique challenges as well as opportunities for technology leaders who are re-thinking the way they can leverage technology to more successfully support the agile workforce and workplace

Introduction

The fourth chapter focuses on flexible work and business continuity and the fact that companies are discovering that preparing employees and managers to work from multiple locations can be a very effective approach to business sustainability. While it may be impossible to predict what kind of business interruption a company may experience, the truth is that every company is at risk of some kind of emergency occurring at some point in time. Those responsible for an organization's disaster and business continuity plans work in partnership with human resources and information technology to support a variety of flexible work options — specifically, the ability for employees to work some or all of the time from another location — as they create a smooth transition where work is uninterrupted, or at least work can resume quickly during a crisis.

We address issues related to facilities planning in Chapter 5 by exploring the changes that have occurred in the way organizations plan for and use their physical space and the impact of those changes on the people side. There was a time when facilities managers in organizations were mainly charged with finding new space to expand operations, but today that role has changed as facility managers are being asked to find ways to reduce or eliminate office space in an effort to save costs. In some cases, as space is eliminated, employees are being pushed out of their offices and told they must work from home, whether they wanted to or not. In such situations, companies frequently find that what they save on real estate costs, they lose in productivity, morale, and even retention. This can be a direct result of employees feeling they lack choice and control over where they work as well as whether they have been given the support they need to work from a remote location all the time.

The relationship between access to flexibility and employee health is examined in Chapter 6. When it comes to employees' health and wellness, common sense is not always common practice. We all know that when we feel that we have control over our work and our life, both benefit and we tend to feel better, less stressed, more rested and focused. It is what we call work-life "effectiveness," because when work is effective, life benefits, and when life works, work benefits. It is imperative that employees have the flexibility they need to manage work and life most effectively, as the ability to have control over how, when, where and how much work is done has been shown to positively impact employee health outcomes. The challenge for health and wellness professionals is to acknowledge that fact and to create approaches that leverage flexible work in order to achieve improved health outcomes for the good of employees and the organization.

Chapter 7 looks at important legal issues that impact the use of flexible work and the substantial legal implications of how, when, and where work is done globally. The rapid growth of flexible work makes it essential that employers understand and mitigate legal exposure associated with how it is executed.

The next two chapters look at flexible work trends and also offer a process for successfully implementing initiatives to create a more agile workforce and workplace. In Chapter 8, we describe a range of issues of major significance to organizations as they extend their understanding and use of flexible work to address business needs, while in the Chapter 9, we provide a roadmap for organizations to create a more agile workforce and workplace.

For many years flexibility was viewed as a special privilege for a select few employees. But today flexible work is becoming part of an organization's overall approach to culture change. To create a

Introduction

successful flexible work initiative requires a comprehensive plan involving a number of key internal stakeholders that include those in diversity/inclusion, technology, facilities, business continuity, legal and health and wellness. We have found that when leaders see the results of a well designed, implemented and managed flexible work initiative targeted to address their concerns, they 'get it'. For organizations focused on the need to improve business performance and shareholder value, get the best work from current employees and compete successfully for future talent, flexibility is not only a powerful business tool, but also a key component of successful management practice. This shift to business vs. personal outcomes for flexible work — which is in large part being driven by the new stakeholders discussed in this book — is significant as it positions flexibility not as "nice to do," but rather a "must have" for any size organization in every industry.

This book is the result of the contributions of so many colleagues and organizations who generously shared their ideas, work and time, but we'd be remiss if we didn't especially acknowledge the thought leadership provided by Dr. Sandy Burud, whose wisdom and knowledge are reflected throughout this work.

It is our hope that this book will encourage a new, cross-functional dialogue among key internal stakeholders who are in a position to accelerate and enhance the adoption and use of flexible work practices that are essential to create the agile workforce and workplace of today and tomorrow.

— Karol Rose & Lori Sokol
September 2011

Chapter 1

At a New Tipping Point — How Did We Get Here? Where Are We Going?

The concept of flexible work is not new. People have worked in shifts or part-time for ages. In the late 1980s, as women entered the workforce in record numbers and work/family issues became prevalent, requests for flexible work arrangements came primarily from working mothers. As the workforce became more diverse — not just in gender but in age groups dealing with various life stage stressors — a larger number of employees wanted to be able to work flexibly to manage their work and personal needs, and the late 1990s saw technology advances create more opportunities for employees to work from anywhere. Working in a traditional office was no longer a necessity for many, and add to that the fact that even local businesses were becoming part of the global economy. All these factors — changing employee demographics, innovative technology and global business operations — resulted in increased needs and opportunities for flexible work. Heading into the 21st century, employers now see that flexible work can actually be good for business.

In Chapter 1, we will explore the following:

- ✔ How flexible work has evolved in organizations and why
- ✔ What flexible work looks like today
- ✔ The history of flexible work in organizations
- ✔ The new business case for flexible work
- ✔ Who are the new flexible work stakeholders in organizations
- ✔ What do these changes mean for flexible work in organizations in the future
- ✔ Some of the challenges for the future of flexible work
- ✔ When to change

The Evolution of Flexible Work

The changing nature of work and the changing composition of the workforce have shaped the way flexible work is organized and delivered in companies. Flexible work has evolved from an accommodation that addressed the needs of some employees to a business-driven effort that is often used to retain talent or reduce costs.

The key to creating a more flexible culture is having guidelines in place and a manager who can translate them into practice. Employees, too, play a critical role in the process, and given the right tools, can assess their own needs and make an effective choice regarding the right type of flexibility that will meet their short- and long-term goals.

One of the greatest challenges for organizations as they consider and plan for a more flexible culture is that there are many moving parts involved in the process, from internal factors that impact the overall business to external factors, including the economy and environmental issues. Successfully implementing and supporting a flexible, agile work environment is a complex process that requires senior leadership support as well as a process that cascades information down and across the enterprise and demonstrates WIIFM (What's in it for me) at every level.

The chart below highlights how flexibility works in organizations that rely on an ad hoc program, that offer some flexibility programs, and one that embraces it on all levels.

Roadmap to A Flexible Culture

Ad Hoc Flexibility	Structured Flexibility	Culture Of Flexibility

Increasing Use/Promotion of Flexibility

Description

Ad Hoc Flexibility	Structured Flexibility	Culture Of Flexibility
• Individual accommodation	• Flexible work arrangements defined with specific rules • Limited use of occasional flex	• Results-based environment with less focus on work schedule and place • Any place, anytime work supported across organization

Challenges

Ad Hoc Flexibility	Structured Flexibility	Culture Of Flexibility
• Inconsistent application — compliance risks • Lack of awareness • Limited impact on recruitment & retention	• Rigid flexibility becomes norm • Managers are linchpin • Supporting guidelines required to ensure appropriate application • Compliance	• Alignment with all stakeholders in enterprise • Aligned systems and management processes • Integration with leading performance indicators

As you look at the chart above, it's important to understand the dramatic workforce changes that have impacted how work is done today. Flexibility isn't just an employee accommodation; it's also an essential business practice. It's a holistic way of operating — one that positions a business for success. The shift of much of our workforce from manufacturing to the global knowledge industry has fundamentally changed how businesses must operate to survive. Driven by such factors as the global economy, the recession, a volatile world in which disaster preparedness is a necessity, an increasing comfort with technology, and changes in how people view working mothers and older workers, these shifts affect people in every industry and job title. They include:

1. **Mobility, not centralization, is now key.** No longer is it necessary for everyone to be in the same room in order to get work done, and in fact, it's necessary for people to operate out of various geographical locations. Technology now permits anytime/anywhere work, and customers expect that workers will be dispersed geographically, in order to lower costs, improve efficiency and speed service.

2. **Customization and versatility have replaced standardization and synchronization as the way to do business.** The now outmoded production environment required standardization (everything done in the same way), with consistent employee input required for consistent output. But today, versatility (just-in-time delivery of information or goods — on the client's schedule) is the means to success. Currently, 85 percent of people are in knowledge- and service-based positions (e.g., designers, technicians) that rely on customized, non-standardized responses.

3. **Encouraging distinctly human abilities has become essential.** In the production environment, people were secondary to machines. Machine production relied on an almost mechanical input from workers, and those workers were interchangeable and replaceable. Employee compliance was more important than creativity, which actually threatened production. In today's knowledge environment, innovation is the name of the game, featuring new ideas, new ways of thinking and breakthroughs (from the production line on up). These very human talents — knowledge, creativity and relationships — are the primary goods being sold, as well as the competitive differentiators that lead to happy customers, growth and efficiency. Business practices must support, not squelch, learning and knowledge sharing, initiative and individual differences that are the source of new ideas and genuine connection.

4. **The employee, not the supervisor, is the best judge of how to do the work.** In both knowledge and service work, the employee knows better than the manager how to accomplish the work most efficiently. Knowledge is highly specialized and it changes quickly; it has a short shelf life. Any knowledge worker who doesn't know more than his/her supervisor has not been learning quickly enough! Hierarchies worked in the industrial environment because managers had previously done the job they supervised. That is no longer the case. And, in the case of service workers, who are face-to-face with the customer (whether an investment banker or a bank teller), they are the best judge of what that customer wants and how to deliver it.

5. **Retaining and engaging employees is more critical because of the nature of their contribution.** When knowledge workers leave a company, they take training and skills built up over time with them. For that reason, it's important to protect the investment you have made in that employee. Knowledge workers know they can earn a living in ways other than regular employment — as an entrepreneur or freelancer — and in order to retain them, employers must pay attention to what they need. On the service side, engagement takes on new importance as the employee who loves their organization and its products or services is more apt to make their customer love it, too.

6. **Intensified competition requires pushing decisions down.** E-business and globalization are just two of the changes that have intensified competition, making rapid response a must. Customers now have many more places from which to buy and, subsequently, they demand increased value and quicker response time. Organizational nimbleness and efficiency requires pushing more decisions into the hands of employees and eliminating layers of approval. Being more selective about whom you hire and granting more authority to employees is essential in order to deliver value to customers.

7. **An atmosphere of mutuality for employees and management is now vital.** If you are giving employees more autonomy, their interests must be aligned with those of the organization so they will act in its best interest. That means the organization also has to do what is in employees' best interests. What they get out of the deal — which includes the overall impact on their quality of life — must be commensurate with their investment of time, knowledge and energy. When the deal is mutual, discretionary effort and knowledge sharing increase and collaboration happens more readily.

8. **Assessment of performance, and how you measure it, has changed.** Many managers assess an employee's performance by seeing them work. Yet, in a knowledge environment, the ability to concentrate can require being away from others, not with them. Also, the most important work results — like good ideas and solid relationships with customers — are qualitative, not quantitative. For example, it's less important to note how many customers the technician helped and more important to know how satisfied they were. Judging performance by how much time someone invests no longer works. In fact, long work hours can exhaust employees and make them less effective. Concrete, rather than line-of-sight, measures of performance must be adopted.

9. **Most employees lead more complex lives and require a new way of working.** Most employees, by a margin of 3 to 1, are "dual-focus" workers, managing work and personal time simultaneously. The core workforce is no longer made up of "Ozzies" — men with a full-time partner at home to attend to life's tasks. Both men and women at all levels and in all kinds of jobs can no longer focus exclusively on work, even when they are at work. Control over their time and the ability to take a temporary time out in small or large increments to deal with these responsibilities without a major hit to their career is now essential.

10. **Employee well-being is now directly related to business performance.** Employees' mental and physical health directly affects their performance. Their work

requires their intellect and emotion, and employers must guard employees' overall well-being. Employees in general are closer to customers than ever before; it is often the only real contact customers have with the organization. If employees are exhausted, distracted, disconnected or disgruntled, customers feel it. Disregarding the state of mind of an employee, or compromising their effectiveness through overwork, can be organizational suicide. Increasing employees' sense of control contributes to both their health and performance.

11. **Business practices must be reinvented to follow a flexible human capital approach.** All of these conditions demand that business practices from previous eras — the standardized work day and week, centralized work sites, one-size-fits-all people practices, and hierarchical management — be replaced with a new model of flexible human capital management. This new model creates an atmosphere where employees have greater autonomy and greater responsibility for achieving results. Flexibility — defined as giving employees more choice and control over how, when, as well as where they work and the ability to customize a career path — is core to this approach. It replaces out-moded ways of measuring performance, such as time spent in the office, with a clear discussion of what businesses actually need. It uses technology and other tools to integrate, rather than separate, the personal and professional sides of employees' lives, while at the same time enhancing their physical and mental well-being.[1]

Flexible work creates the mobility, nimbleness, versatility, customization and personalization needed for success with customers and other stakeholders, as well as with employees. It is not possible to do one without the other. When you have employees whose jobs fit both their complex lives and their complex work, everyone can work toward the same goal: the highest possible performance.

Flexible Work Today

Flexible work has certainly come a long way. Just consider that in 1986, when *Working Mother*'s first list of Best Companies for Working Mothers was published, it featured only 30 companies and flexible work was just beginning to show up on the radar. Today, the list includes 100 companies; members of the Top 10 list all offer significant flexible work initiatives.

According to Ted Childs, principal of Ted Childs LLC, a New York-based workforce diversity consulting firm, one of the primary lessons learned over the last 25 years is that "flexibility works, and it can be a powerful manager/employee tool to achieve business results, not a barrier to them." Kathie Lingle, director of the Alliance for Work-Life Progress (AWLP), an Arizona-based organization promoting the integration of work, family and community objectives, goes further, saying that over the years we've learned that flexible work can be "the most subversive, culture-rattling initiative that takes place in the workplace [because] it is not about programs or what appears on the surface. It is about the culture, which can be very hard to change." Today, Lingle says, flexibility is a struggle over control. "Managers don't want to give it up and employees want more of it — and it takes the right kind of leadership to make it clear that rigid, inequitable behavior is not acceptable."[2]

Companies that lead on workplace flexibility also know that one size does not fit all. "Requiring all employees to work from home is as unproductive as not allowing *any* employees to work from home," says Patricia Lewis, vice president of Human Resources, Electronic Systems at Lockheed Martin Corporation. Sandy Burud, Ph.D., principal, flex employment services of FlexPaths, a flexible work software and solutions company based in New Jersey, agreed, noting that a one-size mentality does not work for work-life practitioners, either. "The biggest lesson we've learned over this quarter of a century is that flexible work must move out of its HR silo and be driven by different stakeholders," she says, "and it must have the support of the leaders."

The definition of flexibility has evolved over the past 25 years. Initially, it was considered a one-way street, an accommodation typically granted only to high-performing employees — most often women — at the last moment to avoid losing them. And in nearly all cases, flexibility was granted almost exclusively to help working mothers manage their childcare needs. Today, as Ellen Galinsky, president of the Families and Work Institute (FWI), a New York-based nonprofit research organization, points out, flexible work is now seen as a business issue that involves "when, where and how much people work and must work for both the employer and the employee." And it is important to note, too, says Burud, that flexibility has shifted from a program-focused practice where managers dictated when, where and how work is done, to a broader corporate mindset. "Real flexibility now requires that employees and teams contribute to the decision,' she says.

Diane Burrus, senior consultant of WFD Consulting, a Boston-based consulting firm, adds that flexibility must "involve management and work practices that are focused on results no matter when or where they are achieved," including:

- **Flexible work arrangements,** such as working an alternative schedule and/or from a remote location; formal, long-term arrangements are usually governed by policies and guidelines.
- **Informal, occasional, day-to-day flexibility,** such as the ability to change a work schedule or location daily to meet business and/or personal needs while meeting business requirements.
- **Career flexibility,** such as creating alternative career paths that enable people to adjust the pace of workload and advancement according to life cycle needs without being penalized in long-term career goals and opportunities.

A Short History of Flexibility

While the need for more flexibility is not a women's issue, in most organizations flexible work policies were initiated by women. In 1985, more than 54 percent of women age 16 years or older were in the workforce and more than half of these women had a child under the age of 1. The number of working mothers had more than doubled in the workforce since 1970, and already 55 percent of married couples were part of two-earner families. In the 1980s, women represented the fastest-growing segment of the American workforce, and companies were beginning to focus on the unique needs of working mothers and working families.

Before the 1980's, there was little flexibility in terms of work hours. Most employees had rigid start and stop times. By 1985, several companies had begun to offer flextime (adjusting the start and stop time of the work day), while only a few (Control Data and IBM) allowed employees to work from home. Realizing women were in the workforce to stay, these leading companies set the stage for programs — parental leave, telecommuting, flextime, part time work and job sharing — that have become hallmarks for the best companies today.

Workforce 2000, a document prepared by the U.S. Department of Labor by the Hudson Institute and published in June 1987 indicated, "if the United States is to continue to prosper in its continuing shift from a manufacturing to a service economy in the 21st century, it must make reconciling the conflicting needs of women, work and families a top priority... Demand for daycare and more time off from work for pregnancy leaves and child-rearing duty will increase, as will interest in part-time, flexible and stay-at-home jobs".[3]

By 1990, more companies had begun to embrace working from home (AT&T and Aetna), job sharing (Steelcase) and extended leaves of absence (Allstate, Hewitt Associates, U.S. West, Merck and IBM). Paternity leave also made its first appearance in companies, with Lost Arrow, NCNB and HBO leading the way. In 2000, 36 percent of the Working Mother 100 Best Companies offered paternity leave for fathers; in 2005, 48 percent did; and in 2010, 75 percent did. In 1990, more than half of the companies on the Top 75 list (52 percent) offered flextime to their employees.

By 2000, companies that had previously offered only leaves of absence were now beginning to offer the opportunity for mothers to "phase-back" into the work place after childbirth. Daily flexible schedules were expanded to flexible *weekly* schedules, now called compressed work weeks. But working parents weren't the only ones pushing for the right to have a life. Generations X and Y were now routinely asking companies about their health care and flex benefits and expecting to be able to work flexibly.

After 20 years of focusing on flexible work, things had changed significantly. Not only were companies viewing flexibility as a business imperative, but a whole new generation of flexibility programs were in place. Where flexibility was once viewed as a slight change in start and stop times, it was now seen as flexibility in where work was done. Additionally, the time component of flexible work began to change, moving from flexibility in a single day (flextime) or a week (compressed work week) to an even longer view — one of career flexibility. This new generation of thinking, led by companies such as Booz Allen Hamilton, Allstate, Deloitte and IBM,[4] allowed employees to take charge and design work plans that fit their life needs.

Deloitte took the notion a step further by developing a "career customization" approach, allowing employees to dial their careers up or down. In 2005, this leading-edge thinking about flexibility helped paved the way for even more innovation and the introduction of new terms such as "on-ramps" and "off-ramps." Flexibility was no longer a single event, but a systemic tool for companies to manage talent. Flexibility morphed from a focus on *managing work schedules* to a focus *on managing one's career*.

The New Business Case for Flexible Work

Today, it is more broadly recognized that flexible work practices enable employees to vary a work schedule or location, work a reduced schedule or take time out of a career path without penalty. These practices are a shift from how work was done in the Industrial Age — when a machine-driven economy prospered with a homogeneous workforce working 9 to 5 at a central location, full-time without interruption throughout a career. In contrast, today's Knowledge/Informational Age thrives with a diverse workforce of individuals working autonomously on different schedules and from different places, exiting and re-entering employment.

These flexible work practices achieve goals vital to America's businesses and our economy, as well as contributing to the well being of employees and their families. Consider the research evidence.[5] In order to grow, be profitable, and deliver value to customers and shareholders, employers must do the following:

1. Reduce Overhead Costs:

Facilities: Businesses can trim office space and facilities and utilities costs by promoting telework, flexible schedules and remote work.
- For every 100 employees who work full-time from home or virtually, a typical business saves more than half a million dollars in space costs.[6]
- IBM saves more than $1 billion a year in facilities costs through its mobile work initiatives.[7]
- AT&T saves $25 million a year in facilities costs (and $65 million in improved productivity and $15 million in retention). At AT&T, 25 percent of managers telework at least twice a week and have no reserved office space; 10 percent are totally virtual. Half of all employees telework some of the time.[8]
- Sun decreased office space by 30 percent and saved $69 million in facilities costs in 2005.[9]
- Unisys cut office space by 90 percent.[10]

Medical: When employees have the flexibility they require, they have fewer stress-related health issues; their employers have lower medical costs.
- Large numbers of employees — 26 percent to 40 percent — find their jobs highly stressful.[11]
- Stress is directly related to high health care costs. Health care expenditures are 50 percent greater for workers with high stress.[12]
- People who can work flexibly also sleep and exercise more and engage in more stress management activities.[13]
- Employees who can work flexibly have a greater sense of control and lower stress (30 percent lower according to Bristol-Myers Squibb research);[14] lower-wage workers that work flexibly have 55 percent less stress.[15]

Staffing: Companies with flexible work options attract and keep employees despite job opportunities with higher compensation.
- 87 percent of full-time professionals look for flexible hours in a new job; 39 percent would accept a job that paid up to 10 percent less if they had more flexibility.[16]

- SAS Institute, a software firm with a flexible culture but midlevel pay and no stock options, consistently has 5 percent turnover in an industry that averages more than 20 percent.[17]
- By retaining employees, employers save the equivalent of 150 percent of the annual salary of a salaried employee and 75 percent of an hourly employee in recruitment costs and downtime,[18] which amounts to $785,500 saved by retaining 10 employees (five salaried and five hourly) at a salary of $80,000 and $50,000 respectively.
- Merck reduced overtime by 50 percent by granting employees greater authority to organize their work and their work schedules.[19]
- By using at-home reservations agents, JetBlue cut the cost of booking a flight by 20 percent.[20]

2. Prepare for continuity of operations in an emergency or disaster:
Emergencies are common and the interruption of business operations is costly.
- In 2008, there were 75 major declared disasters, according to federal statistics,[21] as well as many smaller incidents that halted business operations.
- One in five U.S. businesses suffered a disaster than caused operations to cease for a time.[22]
- 43 percent of companies that go through a severe crisis never open their doors again and another 29 percent fail within two years.[23]
- The companies that survive still suffer reduced productivity and earnings, as well as damaged customer relationships.[24]

Experienced flexible teams can minimize the lost productivity. When work teams are experienced and equipped at working virtually and managers can manage from a distance, business operations can often continue with little interruption.
- 71 percent of employees in companies with a telework program can continue work if the office is closed due to a storm or disaster vs. 17 percent in companies without telework.[25] Firms with stable and trained teleworkers are poised for a speedier rebound afterwards.[26]
- At Intel, when a broken pipe in an office building dislocated 500 employees, there was virtually no loss of productivity as employees were equipped with wireless laptops and adept at working remotely or from home.[27]
- JPMorgan Chase's telework aptitude enabled it to continue operations during the Northeast Blackout of 2003 and the SARS outbreak in Asia in 2003, minimizing the impact of the events.[28]

Disaster preparedness costs are lower for companies with experienced, trained and well-equipped teleworkers and remote workers.
- By preparing remote workers and setting up the security and IT systems in advance, disaster preparedness costs can be reduced, such as the cost to purchase spaces at off-site recovery centers.[29]
- JPMorgan Chase estimates annual savings in the millions from using telework as a proactive business continuity strategy; 40 percent of its investment banking staff telework.[30]

3. Increase earnings, satisfy customers and deliver value to shareholders:
Companies that use flexible work have higher customer satisfaction and return to shareholders.
- Companies with more flexibility in work arrangements capture the skills and knowledge of a wider range of talent, and have a 3.5-percent increase in shareholder value.[31]

- *Fortune*'s "Best Companies to Work For" have earned twice the market return for seven years.[32]
- Working Mother 100 Best Companies report customer satisfaction ratings one to seven points higher than other companies, which translated into a 3 percent to 11 percent increase in market value, or $22,000 per employee, in 2002 dollars.[33]
- First Horizon National Corporation, a financial services company, has 7 percent higher customer retention rates in departments where managers allow greater flexibility, with 95 percent customer retention overall. Less frazzled employees lead to happier customers, who were also more profitable. After adopting flexibility as the core to its "Employees First" culture, FHNC had earnings nearly double that of its peers for four straight years, and was consistently rated most profitable U.S. bank by *Forbes*.[34]
- An in-depth study at Xerox by MIT researchers found that when people work flexibly — not all in the same place at the same time — managers are forced to be clearer in setting goals/expectations. In response, managers and teams must plan ahead and communicate better, which ultimately result in stronger team performance.[35]
- Cisco credits teleworking efforts with achieving $195 million in increased employee productivity in 2003. Employees are working rather than commuting; Cisco finds them more focused on completing the task at hand.[36]
- Siemens, Compaq, Cisco, Merrill Lynch, Nortel and American Express have each reported a 10 percent to 50 percent increase in productivity from telework.[37]

4. Recruit and Retain the Best Talent: Flexible work options attract and retain critical talent across generation, gender and position.
- One fifth of exempt employees and 15 percent of hourly employees have considered leaving their employer for greater flexibility; 17 percent have seriously considered it and 9 percent have taken action.[38]
- 81 percent of mid-level and senior women who work flexibly credit that option (including the option to work less than full time) as *the* reason they were able to stay in their job.[39]
- At AT&T, one-third of teleworkers said in 2001 if they no longer could work from home, they would look for another job or quit.[40]
- First Tennessee National Corporation fills open positions 40 percent faster than the industry average by promoting its flexible culture.[41]
- Among hourly workers, 26 percent without flexibility predict they will leave their job in two years, compared with 17 percent who had flexibility; 22 percent of men without flexibility plan to leave in two years, compared to 18 percent of men who have it.[42]
- 83 percent of hourly workers say the opportunity to work flexibly impacts whether they will stay with their employer. It is even more important for female and younger hourly workers.[43]
- 95 percent of employees at Discovery Communications chose to work at the company in part because they could work flexibly. At Bristol-Myers Squibb, 30 percent of women and 12 percent of men hired in the last three years were influenced to join the company by the access to flexibility.[44]
- For 75 percent of woman in law firms, a commitment to family and personal life is a barrier to advancement. Only 9 percent of women in corporate legal departments believe that working flexibly will not affect their advancement.[45]
- 85 percent of employees are retained by home-based call centers, compared to 10 percent to 20 percent retained at conventional call centers.[46]

5. Reduce their carbon footprints: Telework and remote work enables the business to reduce its carbon footprint through saving on office space (cited earlier).
- A company gains an estimated 2,400 lbs. of carbon offset credits for every 100 employees not traveling to work.[47]

6. Reduce energy consumption: From expanded telework alone (not including reductions in commuting through flexible work schedules, such as a compressed work weeks) the following energy savings occur:
- People commuting to work in personal vehicles consume 44 billion gallons of gasoline a year.[48] Increasing the number of full-time equivalent teleworkers by 10 percent would reduce consumption by 4.4 billion gallons per year. The EPA reports that 40 percent of jobs are suited for telework,[49] but only 14 percent take advantage of it.[50]
- AT&T teleworkers drove 110 million fewer miles in 2001 and avoided the consumption of 5 million gallons of gasoline.[51]
- Besides fuel savings on travel, when people work from home it reduces the amount of energy used in commercial buildings — a difference of 3,000 to 4,400 kWh per year.[52]

7. Reduce harmful emissions: Flexible work options that reduce or eliminate commuting time can limit the emission of harmful chemicals into the atmosphere.
- Commuters in private vehicles release 424 million tons of carbon dioxide into the atmosphere a year,[53] 23 million tons of carbon monoxide, 1.8 million tons of volatile organic carbons and 1.5 million tons of oxides of nitrogen.[54]
- At AT&T, teleworkers avoided commuting 100 million miles, which reduced carbon dioxide emissions by 45,000 tons, or 1.8 tons per teleworker.[55]
- An estimated 3.5 billion square feet of saved commercial space would save 35 million metric tons of greenhouse gases. The avoidance of construction of these buildings would save another 36.4 million metric tons of greenhouse pollution.[56]

8. Increase employment level: Many groups could be employed who are not now, if they could work less than full time, from home or off-site, or on flexible schedules — women who have taken time out of employment, workers whose jobs are being sent overseas, boomers due to retire, the disabled and others.

Women A half-million college-educated women who have taken time out to care for family are ready to return to work but remain unemployed because they are unable find jobs that give them the flexibility to handle both personal and work responsibilities.

Laid-off workers By using flexible work options such as voluntary unpaid leaves and voluntary reductions to part-time (temporarily or permanently), companies like Charles Schwab and others have cut labor costs without resorting to wholesale layoffs.

Retirees American Express, the University of North Carolina and others use phased retirement options (working less than full time) to keep mature workers employed.[57]

Off-shored workers "Homeshoring" (a.k.a. working at home) can replace offshoring through increased telework and flexible work. To that end, companies such as JetBlue Airways, Alpine Access, PHH Arval and LiveOps use home-based work to employ U.S. agents in customer care jobs.[58]

Disabled Workers The Substance Abuse and Mental Health Services Administration, a division of the U.S. Department of Health and Human Services, guides employers on the use of workplace flexibility for people with mental illness.[59] National disability and illness-related organizations that promote flexible work arrangements include the American Cancer Society, National Multiple Sclerosis Society, National Mental Health Association, United Cerebral Palsy, and United Spinal Association.

Some important statistics to consider include:
- 63 percent of disabled individuals not working would prefer to be working.[60]
- 12 percent of disabled adults who are not working require flexible or reduced hours.[61]
- The EEOC and Office of Personnel Management recommend flexible work arrangements as reasonable accommodations for individuals with disabilities.[62]
- The U.S. Department of Labor's Job Accommodation Network recommends flexible work arrangements for more than 80 percent of the impairments it covers.[63]

9. Increase productivity:
- $1 trillion (7.2 percent of GDP) is wasted annually in time and vehicle expenses commuting.[64]
- AT&T research found almost one hour more spent each day on productive work by teleworkers than workers in a traditional office. The quality of work was also better, with virtual office managers more often rated as the best by comparison.[65]

10. Improve public health:
- With an already dispersed workforce that is working remotely — from home or in other less concentrated locations — infectious diseases are not transmitted as readily.[66]
- The ability to cope with bioterrorism threats and public health outbreaks is greater when employees and managers are equipped to work virtually or from more locations. For example, during the SARS outbreak in Hong Kong, JPMorgan Chase split up employees, sending a third to work from home and the rest to work from other sites. As a result, only two workers in Hong Kong were infected.[67]

11. Manage the demand for social services:
- Increasing the use of workplace flexibility can reduce the demand for social services, such as certain types of child and elder care, enabling workers to manage more of their family care.
- Reducing employees' stress and improving their health can lessen the strain on the already overburdened health care system.

The New Stakeholders
In response to the broad range of business drivers for flexible work, new internal stakeholders have emerged. These stakeholders include company leaders in technology, real estate, diversity/inclusion, business continuity and health/wellness, among others. In many cases, these new stakeholders do not realize their role in promoting flexible work, but rather, are determining the best ways to do their jobs. They may be operating independently or are becoming part of a collaborative team that is specifically charged with designing and implementing a coordinated flexible work initiative intended to achieve targeted business outcomes. For example, a task force to explore the possibility of eliminating office space may include IT, real estate and HR. In the past, this effort might have been conducted entirely by real estate planners without taking into consideration the human needs involved. Today, however, it is more likely that HR and

IT would work together to assure that remote workers are appropriately connected and are included in the process. These partnerships are one of the defining changes in the way flexible work is being designed, implemented and managed in organizations today. This will be explored in more detail throughout this book.

The Future of Flexibility

Given the focus on business results and the role of various internal stakeholders in the way flexible work is being delivered, there are clear implications for organizations as they look to the future. Today, companies are reporting that their culture is designed to encourage and legitimize flexible work. As first reported in the Working Mother/FlexPaths study, *Mastering the Art of Flexibility*, companies included in the 2009 Working Mother 100 Best Companies list noted that:

- Their leaders promoted or used flexible work practices themselves, and future leaders were drawn from a pool that includes people who work flexibly (94 percent).
- They include flexibility in their corporate objectives, mission, and vision and value statements (87 percent).
- Flex is an explicit part of their company's external employment branding (95 percent) and internal employment branding (91 percent).

The winning companies also noted that flexible work served as a strategic business imperative as documented by:

- 94 percent reporting flexibility as essential to the business strategy versus an accommodation designed to benefit employees.
- 94 percent connecting flexibility to organizational change.
- 86 percent connecting flexibility to sustainability and environmental strategies.
- 75 percent connecting flexibility to disaster planning.
- 74 percent connecting flexibility to facilities planning.
- 98 percent including flexibility in hiring practices.
- 91 percent including flexibility in diversity & inclusion practices.
- 90 percent including flexibility in leadership development practices.
- 87 percent including flexibility in training practices.

Drivers of such dramatic results are numerous, says Lingle of AWLP. To start, she says, "The workforce itself has changed markedly in 25 years, and the speed of change continues to accelerate." Additionally, she says, "life is far more complicated; global connections are more obvious and inescapable; and economic, political and social forces harsher and more unforgiving."

Lingle notes, too, that increasingly robust research studies and thousands of reports from organizations across all sectors over the past 25 years all lead to the conclusion that employers that embrace flexibility in a holistic way perform better in a number of measurable ways than those that don't. Says Lingle, "Workplace flexibility is proving itself over time to be such a critical element of organizational functioning that we now realize we are only on the verge of understanding how it mediates and interacts with other people strategies to loosen up the organizational arteries, thus maximizing the probability that an employer will be able to zig and zag with agility, land on its feet and meet the next big challenge."

Challenges Still Remain

However, even after 25 years of progress, there are still flex tools and techniques whose full potential is unrealized. Emerging practices that can take it to the next level include:

- **Manager Rewards/Accountability** Holding managers accountable for making flexible work a success is not yet common practice. Less than half of the 2009 100 Best Companies (48 percent) noted that they evaluate, reward or select managers based on their ability to support flexible work, while less than one-quarter (23 percent) reported that whether managers promote flex is a factor in their compensation.
- **Technology** New technology tools are not yet fully leveraged. Only half of the 2009 Best Companies use technology to handle flex requests (53 percent), only half track its use (55 percent), and less than three-fourths (72 percent) report having systems that ensure consistent and fair application of flex.
- **Impact Metrics** Although nearly all of the 2009 Best Companies consider flex essential to their business strategy, only 50 percent measure the impact of flexible work practices on business performance. More, but still less than three-fourths (72 percent), measure the impact on talent goals.

In many organizations, flexibility retains a stigma that is hard to shake. Cali Yost, CEO and Founder of Work + Life Fit, says her 2008 research, *CFO Perspectives on Work-Life Flexibility*, shows that 62 percent of the 100 chief financial officers at companies with at least 5,000 employees in organizations with flexibility policies feel their management team views flexibility as an informal perk. Only one-third feel their executive leaders believe flexibility is a business strategy to manage talent, resources and work flow. This disconnect between the perception that flexible work achieves business results and the reality of low usage rates perpetuates the myth that flex may be good for employees, but not for business. "Unbelievably," says WFD consultant Diane Burrus, "there is still concern from leadership/management in some organizations that increasing employees' access to flexibility will have a negative impact on productivity. The fact that the business case for flexibility is well documented needs to be shared with these leaders and they need to be shown how flexible work and management practices can be utilized to address their business challenges."

Work-life consultant Ted Childs noted too, that, "One of the challenges that persists is that of non-supportive managers, particularly middle managers or older, locked-in-time managers. The way to change that is to tell the business-case story and highlight success stories of employees who have used flexibility tools to help them respond to their work obligations; and highlight managers who have been supportive of their employees doing so to help other managers see a different picture."

Kathie Lingle agreed, adding, "Once men get it the turning point will occur. They represent the other half of the workforce, their work-life conflict is on the rise, and their health is on the decline along with their education and earnings. Their time is not far off."

There is a new recognition of the importance of viewing flexibility as a business tool versus individual accommodation, says Burrus. These companies realize that flexibility is not something just for women or working mothers because men value flexibility, too. Flex also increasingly has a role in attracting, retaining and motivating a multigenerational workforce — even occasional flex is highly valued by employees. As the economy improves, both employers and employees are facing new challenges in today's environment when it comes to flexible work — challenges that some see as positive, while others find them less encouraging.

Childs agrees: "Leaders are becoming more aware that they're at a competitive disadvantage — losing talent or being beaten by more flexible, agile competitor teams — when they don't encourage and support flexible work." Yost, meanwhile, describes the situation this way: "Employees are waking up post-recession to a workplace and career reality that is almost unrecognizable. What little job security there was is gone. They are going to have to chart their own course personally and professionally much more so than at any time in the past. While this has the potential for unlocking tremendous opportunity, many employees are scared of losing their jobs and are hanging on for dear life. Heads are down and people are working harder, faster, longer." Yost notes that one of the challenges is that "employees don't realize that they play a primary role in making flexibility succeed. Organizations can't give the answers, but they can create the environment in which the conversation and innovation can take place."

"In the meantime," Burrus says, "employers are juggling many of their own post-recession concerns, including the question of how to maximize productivity with fewer people, how to retain and engage critical talent to ensure success in the economic recovery, how to ensure organizational and individual agility and resilience and the ability to anticipate and adjust to rapid change, and how to ensure innovation — all the while considering ways to address increasing workload, stress and burnout.

"In some cases," Burrus continues, "this situation has had a negative impact on flexible work, as employers express concerns about productivity and competitiveness and the feeling that more face time is needed in this stressful time. Nevertheless, progressive organizations have used this economic downturn as a reason to look at flexibility more creatively — for example, as a tool to avoid layoffs and retain valuable employees, expand their ability to recruit remote talent, and reduce overhead costs."

When to Change

Change is difficult — whether on a personal or organizational level. One of the challenges is that it's hard to determine the right time to move in a different direction, to try something else. This is especially true when the mentality is "If it ain't broke, don't fix it." But the truth is that organizations need to be led to change — otherwise the changes that happen may not be the right ones to sustain and grow the enterprise. This is especially true when it comes to flexible work, which requires culture change to have an impact on business outcomes. One way to look at the importance of controlling the change is to consider the Sigmoid Curve.

Sigmoid Curve

The paradox of change, as the famed organizational development author Charles Handy described it, is that at the point where we need to be changing and switching to the technology or routines that will take us to the future, all the messages from our environment are sending us the exact opposite message: Look how great we are, folks can't get enough of what we are doing, there is no end in sight!

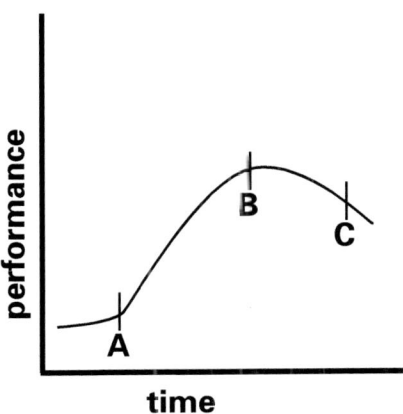
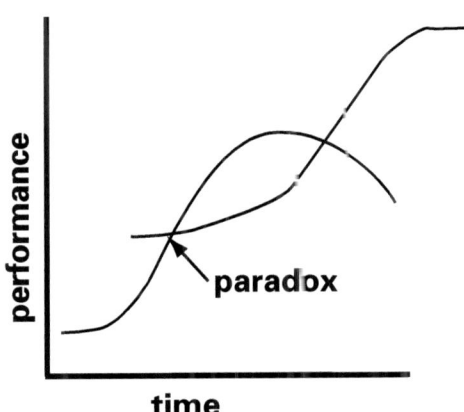

The task of leaders in flexible work is to not only sense the need for the second curve, but also to get others to share our understanding of the need for change and to develop a sense of urgency for a radically different future when people still want to revel in the success and comfort of the present. The paradox of success — what got you where you are won't keep you where you are — is a hard lesson to learn.[68]

Looking at the Working Mother 100 Best Companies over the past 25 years, we can see a number of trends in flexible work that may, in fact, forecast developments that will be necessary in order to move ahead in the next 25 years, including:
- How changes in the way organizations and individuals approach flexible work are linked to social and economic changes.
- Increasing commitment to flexibility as a common response to environmental, economic and business continuity pressures.
- The need for the business case for flexible work to be clearly articulated and personalized for each organization.
- Women leading the way toward more flexible organizations, with men increasingly joining the discussion.
- An expanding "flex community" that includes government, the private sector and academia.
- Incorporating flexible work as an infrastructure issue. It is as critical to an effective society as good schools, good roads, good business, good families and good communities.

We've learned a great deal over the last quarter of a century about the role and effectiveness of flexible work, but there's a great deal more to do.

Marching Orders: The Future of Flexibility

We've clearly reached a tipping point in the evolution of flexible work and a new standard has been set for companies that want to attract, engage and keep the best talent. That means that going forward, when companies say they have the systems in place to enable people to work flexibly, they must make sure all essential employees have access to flexibility. It is interesting to note, for example, that among the 2010 Working Mother Best Companies, while 96 percent say that employees' requests for flexibility are considered through an equitable process, less than half (42 percent) have an intranet or extranet site to allow employees to request a flexible work option and be notified of approval or denial of their request, and just over half (59 percent) have a technology-based mechanism for tracking the use of flexibility. The issue of the haves and have-nots also needs to be addressed. Even at the Working Mother 100 Best, there remain significant differences among employee groups as to who can use various flex options. For example, less than one-third (29 percent) of full-time, non-exempt employees at the 2010 Working Mother 100 Best Companies worked from home occasionally, compared to 60 percent of full-time, exempt employees.

Sandy Burud of FlexPaths argues that employers must do more to investigate and remove remaining barriers to flexible work, looking even beyond their existing workforce to talent that has never applied or turned down an offer. Companies need to examine the role flexible work or flexible career choices played in those decisions. Two important questions companies need to ask are:
- Do employees agree that if they work flexibly they will have equal access to advancement, development and quality assignments?
- Do managers have the attitude, competencies and wherewithal to manage dispersed and flexible talent well?

It is time for honest self-examination because the driving force behind flex has changed. The new reality — and this is no small matter — is that leading companies are no longer simply allowing flexible work because it helps employees. They are promoting flex for business reasons that may be even more urgent or powerful from a financial perspective. These reasons include the need to reduce their facilities footprints, or to be able to continue operations at full speed during an interruption or disaster. With this shift to a business necessity, it becomes essential that organizations eliminate anything that may hold employees back from working flexibly.

Last year, the Society for Human Resource Management (SHRM) commissioned a study by the Economist Intelligence Unit of C-suite executives, asking what the biggest threat was to their organizations' success. The answer: attracting and retaining top talent. They then conducted a study of HR executives, asking them about the best way to attract and retain top talent. The most frequent response — 58 percent — was workplace flexibility. At the press conference, Hank Jackson, the interim president and CEO of SHRM, said that this ranked even higher than compensation.

"If you think that this is one of those nice things to do for over-stressed employees, you're wrong. This is the next business imperative," says Jackson. "This is the next revolution in boosting productivity because empowering people to do their best at all stages of their lives, regardless of their industry, background or culture, leads to innovation, a higher quality of work, more employee commitment and, yes, higher productivity."

As the reality of the potential for flexible work to support business objectives becomes clear, new internal players such as disaster planners, facilities/real estate, diversity/inclusion, IT and others offer an opportunity to shift the momentum for flexible work — and may actually determine where the push for it originates. HR is now partnering with IT, risk management, facilities and others on making the business case for flex and in the design, development, facilitation and implementation of flexible work. In the future, it may be that HR won't be inviting these players into the conversation as much as coordinating with them as equal partners, creating an even more powerful focus on flex as a business solution.

Transforming a culture from one where work is done at the same time in the same place to anytime/anywhere work is no small undertaking, especially in a context of employment laws created for the once-traditional centralized, synchronized, standardized workplace — and often, where senior management may still have that mind set. As anytime/anywhere work becomes the norm, a range of new legal issues will arise that will need to be sorted out and regulated differently.

In the near term, however, how best to monitor the fair and consistent application of flex will continue to be a challenge. As more companies create systemic ways of coaching, tracking, educating and documenting flexible work, the transformation to flexible, dispersed and asynchronous work (i.e. working in different places at different times) will force teams to reinvent how they function and ultimately improve processes and output dramatically. It will also force teams to plan ahead more, establish better objective measures of results and be clearer in their communications.

These changes will improve the experience of employees, as well as boost their health and well being — and will generate enormous value back to the business. For businesses that sell knowledge or service, as most businesses do today, the state of their people is directly related to earnings and growth. Ideas and personalized service are the differentiators and the most innovative ideas come from the minds of people who are rested and clearheaded. Similarly, employees who feel respected and valued give better service. These are the hallmarks of a flexible work environment that recognizes both the business's and individual's needs.

The strength of the flexible cultures in organizations today is remarkable and it is clear that having a great employment brand requires meeting a new standard. It is no longer enough to simply offer flexible ways of working, innovative as that once was. Flexible work must now be part of a culture that recognizes and demonstrates trust and respect for all employees. It should be one where working flexibly is the new normal, supported by the communication, structures and systems that allow it to thrive. As Jeff Henderson, CFO of Cardinal Health, says, "We have to throw out the notions of the past. Flexible work today will be very different than it was in the past. We don't want to recreate what happened earlier, but, rather, reinvent flexible work for today's and tomorrow's workforce and workplace."

In addition to the new flex stakeholders in areas like diversity, technology and real estate, Kathleen Christensen, program director of the Workplace, Workforce and Working Family Programs at the Sloan Foundation, predicts that others like those focused on aging and corporate social responsibility may be the future drivers of flexible work in organizations. The fact that flexible work has found its place in corporate America now sets the stage for a more sophisticated dialogue, with a new set of issues, internal stakeholders and opportunities. While some may feel that we've arrived at a "destination," we've actually only begun the journey. The next evolution of flexible work will be an incredibly exciting and transformational time for both organizations and for employees.

FLEX IN-DEPTH: State Street

One Company's Journey To A Manager-Initiated Process

Challenge/Situation

Change is constant in the business environment. Advances in technology, workforce demographics, government regulations and employee engagement are pushing the global working culture to become more accommodating of flexible work arrangements. Clearly, there is evidence that flexible work arrangements are a "win" for employees, assisting in balancing work and personal commitments, reducing the length and costs of commuting. There is even more evidence that flexible work arrangements are beneficial to employers and to the community at large.

Who Was Involved

State Street, a Boston-based financial services firm, created an executive committee on flexibility, and from that work, the formal Flex Work Program was developed. Over time, it was decided that Flex should be more aligned with the company's business strategy, and the program's success would be achieved through a partnership between HR, IT, Real Estate and Procurement. Flex work is now led by the Flex Program Office and milestones are achieved through the support of a cross-functional working group, with work streams focused on Policy, Training, HR Business Partners, Communications, Real Estate, Procurement, IT, Finance and Business Transformation.

Process

Through the work streams listed above State Street built the foundation from which to execute Flex. With a robust communications strategy and training, State Street built awareness and adoption across its global locations. Its dedicated Flex Program Office's sole focus on continuing to evolve and deploy the program elements is key to its successful implementation.

Solution

Initially, the program was grassroots — an employee approached a manager to request a flexible work arrangement. The program in that form was slower to catch on, but did achieve some traction. By shifting the program to a top-down approach, State Street is moving much more rapidly and has set clear and measurable goals around implementation and plans.

Results

The employee approach seemed to cause some conflict for managers who felt that the rollout wasn't equitable in all areas. A shift from an employee-initiated to a manager-initiated approach allows managers to be proactively in tune with what is feasible from a business perspective. A manager-initiated approach is now in progress, and State Street continues to gather information to enhance the program as it evolves.

Measurement/Metrics

The Flex project management office has agreed to several key metrics, which quantify the level and success of Flex work. These metrics include:
- FlexTrax measures the requests, approvals and declines that are indicative of management adoption.
- Flex Center utilization reports on reservation data that measures and quantifies the demand from a location perspective.
- Engagement Survey data measures the link between successful flex work arrangements and the perception of flex work with employee engagement levels.
- Flex Work SharePoint serves as an information resource for employees, allowing the company to measure visitors in order to quantify awareness and interest in the program.

Most recently, State Street completed a year-over-year engagement survey, which indicated that more than 65 percent of the workforce understand they could participate in the flexible work program, and 31 percent of employees are on some type of formal flex work arrangement.

REFERENCES: CHAPTER 1

1. Copyright 2004 by Davies-Black Publishing, a division of CPP, Inc. Adapted from Leveraging the New Human Capital: Adaptive Strategies, Results Achieved, and Stories of Transformation, S. Burud and M. Tumolo. All rights reserved.
2. This section adapted from Working Mother 25th Anniversary Research *What Really Works: Lessons Learned from 25 Years of Workplace Flexibility Leadership* By Karol Rose, Principal Advisory Services, FlexPaths
3. Current Labor Population Survey, US Department of Labor; http://www.bls.gov/cps/wlf-table2-2008.pdf
4. Current Labor Population Survey, US Department of Labor; http://www.bls.gov/cps/wlf-tables19.pdf
5. Workforce 2000, Hudson Institute 1987
6. Over one hundred studies that have examined the business impacts of flexible work practices are reported in *Leveraging the New Human Capital*, Burud and Tumolo, 2004.
7. Calculation assumes 30 square feet per employee at $168 per square foot — the national cost average according to a study by Old Dominion University Center for Real Estate and Economic Development, 2005 *Market Survey*.
8. Brad Allenby and Joseph Roitz, "Implementing the Knowledge Economy: The Theory and Practice of Telework," Batten Institute Working Paper, 2003, p. 44.
9. (2003) Brad Allenby and Joseph Roitz, "Implementing the Knowledge Economy: The Theory and Practice of Telework" Batten Institute Working Paper, 2003, p. 44–45
10. Arnold, in Fuhr and Pociask, *Broadband Services: Economic and Environmental Benefits*, 2007, p. 19–20.
11. (2007) Balaker, p. 24, in Fuhr and Pociask, Broadband Services: Economic and Environmental Benefits.
12. Studies by Yale, Northwestern Life, and Families & Work Institute, cited in *Stress at Work*, NIOSH, 2007.
12. Journal of Occupational and Environmental Medicine, cited in Stress at Work, NIOSH, 2007.
13. Study by Wake Forest University School of Medicine cited by WFC Resources, 2008.
14. Corporate Voices for Working Families, *Business Impacts of Flexibility*, 2005.
15. WFD, 2009, p. 11.
16. Study by Lee Hecht Harrison, cited by Koeppel, *New York Times*, October 10, 2004.
17. Burud and Tumolo, *Leveraging the New Human Capital*, 2004.
18. Phillips, *Personnel Journal*, 1990.
19. Casner-Lotto, Holding a Job, Having a Life, 2000.
20. (2003) Brad Allenby and Joseph Roitz, "Implementing the Knowledge Economy: The Theory and Practice of Telework" Batten Institute Working Paper, 2003, p. 44.
21. FEMA, retrieved from http://www.fema.gov/news/disaster_totals_annual.fema, 2009.
22. AT&T and Partnership for Public Warning, 2004, cited in *Exploring Telework as a Business Continuity Strategy*, ITAC, p. 3.
23. Cerullo and Cerullo, 2004 cited in *Exploring Telework as a Business Continuity Strategy*, ITAC, p. 3.
24. Veritas, 2004 cited in *Exploring Telework as a Business Continuity Strategy*, ITAC, 2004, p. 4.
25. CDW-G, Telework Report, 2008.
26. *Exploring Telework as a Business Continuity Strategy*, ITAC, 2004, p. 7.

27. *Exploring Telework as a Business Continuity Strategy*, ITAC, 2004, p. 8.
28. *Exploring Telework as a Business Continuity Strategy*, ITAC, 2004, p. 29.
29. Fuhr and Pociask, p. 9.
30. *(2007) Fuhr and Pociask, p. 9.*
31. Watson Wyatt, Human Capital Index, 2001-2002.
32. Edmans, *Does the Stock market Fully Value Intangibles?* 2008
33. Simon, *Happy Employees, Happy Customers*, Cornell University, 2002.
34. Burud and Tumolo, p. 347.
35. (2004) Sandy Burud, Mary Tumolo, Leveraging the New Human Capital: Adaptive Strategies, Results Achieved, and Stories of Transformation, Davies-Black, p. 347.
36. Boston College Center for Work & Family, Workplace Flexibility Case Studies. Retrieved from http://wfnetwork.bc.edu/template.php?name=casestudy#AFLAC
37. Brad Allenby and Joseph Roitz, "Implementing the Knowledge Economy: The Theory and Practice of Telework" Batten Institute Working Paper, 2003, p. 35.
38. WFD, New Career Paradigm, 2008, p. 9.
39. Catalyst, *Flexible Work Arrangements III: A Ten Year Retrospective of Part-Time Arrangements for Managers and Professionals*, 2000.
40. Brad Allenby and Joseph Roitz, "Implementing the Knowledge Economy: The Theory and Practice of Telework" Batten Institute Working Paper, 2003, p. 25.
41. Burud and Tumolo, p. 343.
42. WFD and Corporate Voices for Working Families, Innovative Workplace Flexibility Options for Hourly Workers, 2009, p. 94.
43. WFD and Corporate Voices for Working Families, 2009, p. 94.
44. Corporate Voices for Working Families, Business Impacts of Flexibility, 2005, p. 10.
45. Catalyst, *Women in Law*, 2000.
46. Stephen Loynd, VoIPdesk Helps Chart the Future: Homeshoring Brand Ambassadors and the Shifting of the Customer Management Landscape," IDC, 2006, p. 5, in Fuhr and Pociask, p. 22.
47. Calculation from www.home2office.com.
48. Assumes fuel efficiency of 21 miles per gallon, EPA in Fuhr & Pociask, 2007, p. 24.
49. According to a survey conducted by Rockbridge the potential for telecommuting could reach 25% participation. Cited in Fuhr and Pociask, 2007, p. 24.
50. CDW-G, Telework Report, 2008.
51. Brad Allenby and Joseph Roitz , p.51.
52. Romm, p. 35. Cited in Fuhr and Pociask, 2007, p. 21.
53. Environmental Protection Agency, cited in Fuhr & Pociask, p. 24.
54. Retrieved from http://www.telcoa.org/id134.htm, cited in Fuhr & Pociask, p. 24.
55. Allenby and Roitz, p. 34.
56. Romm, p. 35, cited in Fuhr and Pociask, 2007, p. 20.
57. Boston College Center for Work & Family, Workplace Flexibility Case Studies. Retrieved from http://wfnetwork.bc.edu/template.php?name=casestudy#AFLAC .
58. Martha Frase-Blunt, "Call Centers Come Home," *HR Magazine*, January 2007, pp. 84–89, cited in Fuhr and Pociask, 2007, p. 23.
59. *Workers With Disabilities: The Role Of Workplace Flexibility*, Workplace Flexibility 2010, 2008, p. 3.

60. Source: 'Workers With Disabilities: The Role of Workplace Flexibility', Workplace Flexibility 2010.
61. Loprest and Maag, *Barriers To And Supports For Work Among Adults With Disabilities: Results from the NHIS-D, 2001*. Cited in *Workers With Disabilities: The Role Of Workplace Flexibility*, Workplace Flexibility 2010, 2008.
62. http://www.opm.gov/disability/8-03_employeeguides.asp and
63. http://www.eeoc.gov/facts/accommodations-attorneys.html .
64. http://www.law.georgetown.edu/workplaceflexibility2010/documents/WF2010DisabilityFactSheet.pdf
65. SAMSHA National Mental Health Information Center, 2006.
66. Fuhr and Pociask, 2007, p. 23. The calculation: "The average U.S. worker commutes 15 miles and 26.4 minutes one-way to their job, amounting to 918 billion miles traveled and 1.7 billion minutes lost each year. The travel time wasted is equivalent to the annual paid hours of 17.2 million production workers. In terms of dollars, the lost wages and cost of the vehicle (including gas, depreciation, insurance and maintenance) would be nearly $1 trillion."
67. Harvard Business School Press, 1994
68. http://www.bretlsimmons.com/2009-06/the-sigmoid-curve-and-the-paradox-of-change/#ixzz1Ezl4A2Pt

Chapter 2 | The Role of Flexible Work in Attracting, Engaging and Managing Diverse Talent

Diversity and Inclusion

Diversity and flexible work issues are becoming more enmeshed as the workforce becomes more diverse and dispersed.

Diversity and inclusion leaders recognize that while it is necessary to continue to address discrimination issues related to gender, sexual orientation, ethnicity, age and disabilities, it is no longer sufficient to limit their focus to these issues. There is a growing acknowledgement that in addition to these traditional considerations, diversity and inclusion functions must also consider an employee's needs for a flexible work situation. An employee's need for flexibility may be related to any of the diversity considerations, such as age or disability, but the connection between diversity and inclusion and flexibility goes well beyond that.

In order for organizations to attract, retain and engage diverse talent — people who want flexibility in how, when and where work is done — diversity and inclusion leaders must influence the way flexibility is understood, developed and implemented in organizations today.

Dr. Shirley Davis, diversity and inclusion officer for the Society for Human Resource Management (SHRM), says she believes there is increasing recognition on the part of human resources and diversity and inclusion leaders that the current workforce is transient, global and composed of multiple generations. Diversity and inclusion leaders will need to establish the link between their more traditional focus on race and gender issues to include flexible work when establishing employment policies and practices.

In Chapter 2, we will explore the following questions:

✔ Why is diversity and inclusion becoming a leader in developing, promoting and managing flexible work?

✔ Why is the key issue all about the talent?

Diversity and Inclusion

✔ What are the benefits of including flex as part of diversity and inclusion?

✔ What are some of the challenges diversity and inclusion leaders face related to flexible work?

✔ How can you leverage diversity and inclusion to make flex real?

Connecting Flex With Diversity and Inclusion

Business leaders have long said that employees are their most important asset. In today's information economy, and with the growing need for skilled knowledge workers, this statement is more relevant than ever. In a 2010 study by SHRM, C-suite leaders said that the most important issue organizations face today is attracting and retaining talent. And, when SHRM asked HR leaders what would most help achieve that goal, they overwhelmingly responded "flexibility."

Margaret Regan, president and CEO of The Future Work Institute, a consulting firm that advises corporations on diversity and new ways to work, says that flexibility is unique to the individual because the future of work is about "my job, my way" — the very essence of diversity — with a focus on total flexibility for everyone. She predicts that today's multigenerational workforce will drive the awareness and the need for a more agile work environment. While Boomers are still trying to come to terms with these changes, Gen Y already expects total flex. It is second nature to them, and there is no single workplace, as far as they're concerned. They know they can work anytime and anywhere.

Depending upon which segment of the workforce we consider, the ability to offer flexible workplace options, along with their attendant benefits, can prove even more significant to attracting and retaining talent.

When developing and positioning your flexible work initiatives as part of a diversity and inclusion initiative — especially to senior leaders — it is important to include relevant external data as part of the business case. That data must take into account the fact that every segment of the population will desire flexibility in their job at some point in their career.

> **D&I Connect**
> In a survey of work-life, 32 percent of respondents reported that diversity and inclusion has been connected with flexible work for only three to five years.
> *Source: Working Mother Research Institute, 2010*

Multigenerational Workforce

Results from a 2009 survey by the Sloan Center on Aging & Work at Boston College demonstrate how strongly today's multigenerational labor force feels about the contribution of flexible work benefits to their quality of life (Table 1)[1].

Table 1: In all of the age groups below, more than 70 percent indicate that flexibility contributes moderately or strongly to their quality of life.

Table 1: Flexibility Contributing to Quality of Life by Generation

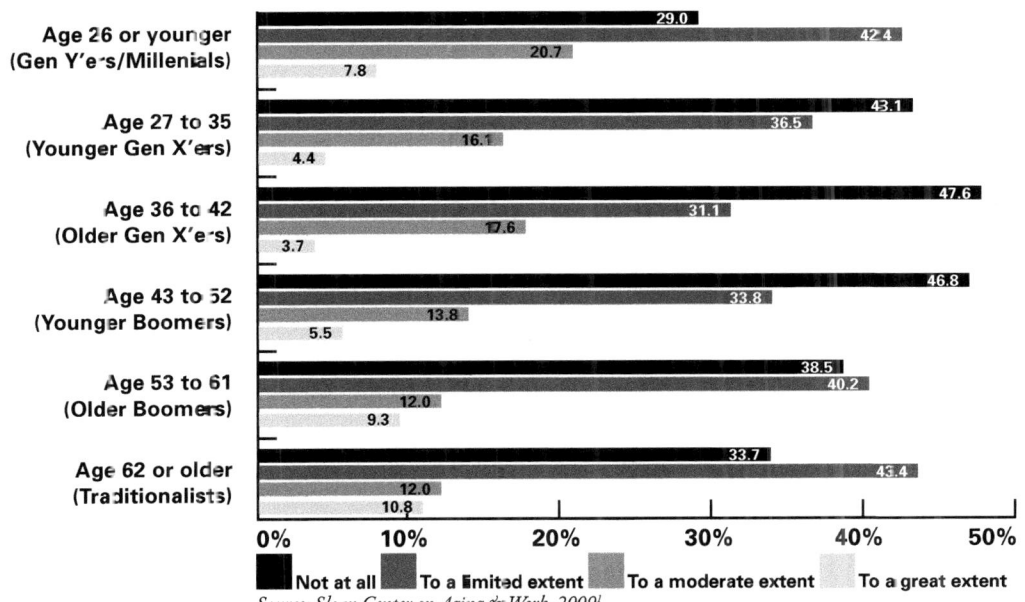

Source: Sloan Center on Aging & Work, 2009[1]

Dual Focus Workers

"Dual focus workers" is a term coined by Dr. Sandy Burud in her book, *Leveraging the New Human Capital*.[2] In it, she describes a new workforce focused on both work and personal life. Similarly, a 2002 study conducted by the Families and Work Institute (FWI) used the term "dual-centric workers" to describe the 32 percent of business executives (both female and male) who were placing equal priority on their work and personal lives. Regardless of what you call it, it is apparent that today's employees must manage both their work and personal lives effectively in order to survive and thrive. In a 2008 FWI study, dual-centric mothers and fathers were shown to be experiencing an increasing amount of conflict as they tried to manage work and family responsibilities. Clearly, the ability to allocate time differently — or to actually work differently — could go a long way toward helping workers feel more competent at both. There are still only 24 hours in a day, and only seven days in a week, so it is increasingly important that employers provide opportunities to leverage flexible work in ways that help the diverse population of dual focus workers succeed.

Working Parents

Michael Aitken, SHRM's director of government affairs, said in a 2010 SHRM panel discussion that flexible work is an issue for all workers; it should not be seen as solely an issue for women or individuals with young children.

However, the need for flexible work options is a major concern of working parents as they struggle to find affordable quality child care for very young children, manage school-age children's activities, and try to keep track of older children — not to mention dealing with the unique needs of special-needs children. Without flexibility in how, when and where they work, working parents experience undue stress and anxiety, which can be very costly for their employers. For example, research shows that flexible work hours that allow employees to pick up their children from school can alleviate employee stress, particularly in relation to their children's after-school activities. An estimated one-third of the workforce experiences such stress, leading to decreased productivity and increased absenteeism that can cost anywhere from $469 to $1,984 per employee per year.[3]

According to The Institute for Women's Policy Research, a significant number of women and men (76 percent) endorse laws to provide paid leave for family care and childbirth — 71 percent of men and 81 percent of women. Similar patterns are seen in support for laws to improve the quality and affordability of childcare and after-school care, where 79 percent of women and 75 percent of men agree with the need for these policies. Similarly, the right to refuse to work overtime is supported by 59 percent of registered voters. The right to refuse overtime shows only minimal differences by gender and parent status.[4]

Baby Boomers

In 2009, the Hidden Brain Drain Task Force, a group of 50 multinational companies committed to global talent innovation, embarked on two large-scale, nationally representative surveys addressing the importance of flexible work options to the Baby Boomer population. It found that people, especially Boomers, are looking for what is called a "remixed" set of rewards: flexible work arrangements and the opportunity to give back to society. That was true before the economic downturn, and continues to be an important driver for older workers.[5] Patricia Kempthorne, president and CEO of the TWIGA Foundation, says she thinks it's important to remember that older workers may need flexibility for a variety of reasons, including caring for a parent or spouse; or they may want to volunteer or participate in community activities while continuing to work.

Women

While the need for flexibility is not solely a women's issue, the benefits of flexible work for women have been clear for decades, and continue to be reinforced by research. In 2006, *The Harvard Business Review* noted that nearly half a million professional high-earning women leave the workforce and don't return — not because they don't want to, but because they can't find an employer that is flexible enough to not penalize them (financially or otherwise) for taking a career break. A 2009 Catalyst study entitled, "Women Leaving and Re-entering the Work Force," found that the common assumption that women find it easy to leave their jobs to stay home with their children is not true. Through exit interviews and assessment projects, Catalyst found that most women are conflicted about leaving their jobs. When they do leave, it is often because employers are not offering ways for them to effectively combine work with family responsibilities. As long as women — who represent at least 50 percent of the current workforce and are projected to be an even larger percentage in coming years, given their high rate of participation in almost every area of professional academic study — continue to be the primary caregivers, access to flexible work options will be one of their top demands from employers.

Men Want Flex, Too

It is becoming increasingly clear that men also need flexible work options. A 2008 study found that for employees age 50 years and older, for example, a higher percentage of men reported using flexible work than women in every age group. The study also found that 31.2 percent of men aged 45 to 54 use flexible schedules in contrast to 26.8 percent of women; 28.8 percent of men aged 55 to 64 use flexible schedules in comparison to 23.5 percent of women; and 36.7 percent of the men aged 65-plus use flexible schedules in comparison to 22 percent of women.[6]

This study focuses on the decrease in quality of health reported by employees from 2002 to 2008 in the *National Study of the Changing Workforce*. Further, in a 2008 AARP survey, 31 percent of men and 36 percent of women ranked the ability to work from home as an essential part of their ideal job.[7]

People with Disabilities

A review of data from the American Community Survey, presented at the Annual Disability Statistics Compendium 2010, shows that the percentage of people with disabilities who are employed (35.3 percent) is less than half of the percentage of people without disabilities who are employed (74.3 percent). Similarly, unemployment numbers released by the Bureau of Labor Statistics for September 2010 reveal the difficulty jobseekers with disabilities face today. The unemployment rate for people with disabilities stands at 14.8 percent, which is staggering even when compared to the current 9.0% percent unemployment rate for people without disabilities.

According to a survey by the RAND Corporation, 63 percent of people with disabilities who are not working would prefer to be working. According to the U.S. Department of Health and Human Services, 12 percent of this group said they would require special work arrangements such as flexible work or reduced work hours in order to take a job. Clearly, people with disabilities remain a relatively untapped segment of the population, a group that could put their abilities and talents to work if they were offered more flexibility in terms of where, when and how they worked.

To assist in this effort, the Department of Labor's Office of Disability Employment Policy and Women's Bureau entered into a memorandum of agreement in 2010 to cooperate in their efforts to expand and promote the understanding and use of workplace flexibility strategies for employees with complex needs, including people with disabilities. In addition to planning a one-day workplace flexibility roundtable forum focused on flexibility for people with disabilities, the two agencies are creating a roadmap of actions to expand the understanding of, and access to, best practices in workplace flexibility.[8]

> **D&I Connect**
> Nearly 70 percent of diversity leaders surveyed indicated that in order to attract talent the organization's support of flexible work is extremely important.
> *Source: Working Mother Research Institute, 2010*

Next Generation

In the 2008 study, "Engaging a Changing Workforce: A Study of Four Generations," conducted by The Learning Café, a firm specializing in workforce and leadership development, Gen Xers, who are the likely demographic to be knee-deep in childcare, placed "healthy work-life balance" and "flexibility" on their list of top four motivators to accepting a job. Further, in response to a survey conducted in 2008 by Radcliffe Public Policy Center, men in their 20s and 30s stated that a flexible work schedule that afforded time with family was the most important job characteristic. This group is also most comfortable working anytime, anywhere and they want to be able to do it their own way — whether it's taking time to climb a mountain, run a marathon, or just hang out. These results clearly indicate a growing trend among the youngest segment of today's workforce toward making flexible work a priority when considering whether to take a job.

The Benefits of Flex as a Component of Diversity and Inclusion

Diversity and inclusion is in the position of approaching flexibility as a culture change initiative as opposed to a program or a policy. Flexible work is highly desired across all demographics and creating a more flexible work environment requires a focus on different work styles. This means diversity and inclusion must be a driving force in designing and positioning the flex initiative and in making sure it addresses the important business issues related to finding and keeping diverse talent.

Recent research highlights the effectiveness of flexible work as it relates to diversity and inclusion as follows:
- It enables organizations to attract a more diverse talent pool
- It helps women and people of diverse backgrounds — including people with disabilities — more effectively manage their career and personal needs
- It allows organizations to retain talent they may otherwise lose
- It addresses the needs of different generations in the workplace

The need to have more control over how, when and where work is being done is fundamentally a diversity and inclusion issue because it is unique to each individual. It benefits both genders, cuts across generations, and is job neutral. Being able to make use of occasional or more formal flexible work arrangements as work and life needs change is highly valued by all segments of the workforce.

Understanding the Challenges

When we add flexibility to the list of things diversity and inclusion leaders need to consider in order to attract, retain and engage diverse talent, a number of challenges emerge. Most organizations resist change and tend to do things the way they have always been done, even when the tried and true is clearly not achieving the desired result. Attracting and managing a flexible workforce requires new skills and behaviors. It requires culture change on the part of the organization, as well as changing manager and employee perceptions about flexible workers. The old notion that there is only one way for work to be done is based on a manufacturing model that required synchronized, standardized approaches to work, and there was little diversity in the workforce. But things are more complex in today's customized, individualized environment.

Diversity and Inclusion

Hiring employees that all have the same skills and expecting the same output is not, as many employers have realized, a competitive advantage.

Your organization may be choosing employees for development and/or advancement for reasons that are no longer valid. For the new breed of worker — the committed and ambitious person who nevertheless requires flexibility — the old ways of identifying good performance and future leaders no longer apply.

WORKSHEET
Flexible Work and Diversity and Inclusion

The following questions can serve as discussion points for your diversity and inclusion group:

1. How is a high-potential employee identified? If you consider drive and commitment important, how are those measured? (For example, by output or by how many hours the person is willing to work, never missing work, always available?) Do you measure whether their job is done well and on time? Does your organization look for a person who is compliant or someone who pushes the envelope?

2. Do you look outside the ranks of full-time employees for potential leaders?

3. What does a star performer look like? Can someone with a life outside of work — to whom work isn't their entire life — be a star?

4. What behavior is rewarded, directly or indirectly? Is never taking a vacation or frequently working through the night viewed positively or negatively?

5. Have you considered how attendance polices might need to change in light of changes in households, including the growth of dual-career households and single-parent households? (Whereas once absenteeism reflected a lack of responsibility, today some of the best workers can have instances of tardiness or absenteeism.)

6. Does the workload, the resource availability, staffing and way the work is organized, make it possible for people to work in a healthy and productive way? Or is there chronic overwork, lack of predictability, and/or frenzy?

If these questions give you pause, take it as a sign that flexibility can open up new opportunities for your company. By expanding the role of flexibility in your talent management processes, you can find and develop new talent and expand your internal talent pool and become more efficient and successful at your talent management tasks.

Diversity and Inclusion

Hidden Bias Regarding Flexible Workers

Does your organization value those who work traditional hours over those who work flexible hours? Consider the *Seinfeld* episode when George Costanza's car breaks down in the stadium parking lot and is there for days. His co-workers praise George for how hard he's working because they see his car there morning, noon and night. Soon George decides to go on vacation and let his car do the work. Sometimes perception is not reality.

Diversity and inclusion leaders need to pay attention to the hidden, and in some cases, overt bias toward employees who request flexibility. When a company recognizes and promotes employees who only fit a certain model (for example, those who can work long hours uninterrupted by family concerns or those who can travel at a moment's notice) many employees will automatically be eliminated from consideration. Flexible work clearly provides the diversity professional a new and innovative tool to counteract this trend and ensure that hidden barriers limiting employee potential are removed from the organization's talent acquisition and talent management processes. Further, creating models of success that include on and off ramping, dialing up and dialing down, and, as one executive at Deloitte puts it, "swapping the career ladder for a career lattice," offers a variety of pathways to achieve success that are aligned with employees' career and personal goals.

> **D&I Connect**
> Some 91 percent of diversity and inclusion leaders surveyed cite better communication and improved manager training as important for increasing the effectiveness of flexible work.
> *Source: Working Mother Research Institute, 2010*

Hidden bias, according to Freada Klein, founder of Level Playing Field Institute, an organization that promotes innovative approaches to fairness in the workplace, creeps into all of our decisions about flexibility. Judgments about flex workers include asking, What's a legitimate purpose for a flexible schedule? Who deserves or has earned a flexible schedule? Is this employee serious about her/his career?

Neuroscientists agree that we are wired to be biased, and this needs to be addressed. Mark Effron, president of Talent Strategy Group, a consultancy that works with companies to develop talent, sees senior executives who struggle with trying to decide whether to relocate in order to advance. He considers this part of this dilemma of bias — one that assumes there is only one model or way to be successful in organizations.

Leveraging Diversity and Inclusion to Make Flex Real

Diversity and inclusion leaders are well positioned to create a culture in which flexible work is valued and policies are implemented because they benefit diverse talent. According to Dr. Shirley Davis, Global Diversity & Inclusion Officer at SHRM, one of the main challenges diversity and inclusion leaders face in terms of leveraging the value of flexibility is engaging middle managers in the process. Even in companies that offer flexibility, some employees may be afraid that using flex will negatively impact their career development. Therefore, they won't take advantage of it, even if doing so meant they could remain in their job. The Corporate Voices for Working Families' 2011 report, "The Business Case for Flexibility: An Imperative for Expansion," which summarizes internal business data from 28 major U.S. companies, showed that effective flexibility programs increase productivity through commitment and retention, and have a direct impact on financial performance. These findings were documented for lower wage hourly as well as for higher wage salaried workers.[9]

Making the Necessary Changes

As awareness of the needs of a diverse workforce have increased, support for flexible work among managers has also grown. In a 2008 FWI study, a majority of employers (71 percent) reported that supervisors at their companies are encouraged to assess employees' performance by their accomplishments rather than how much time they spend in the office. Further, 60 percent said supervisors were encouraged to be supportive of employees with family needs and find mutually beneficial solutions. However, room for improvement remains. Just 20 percent of those surveyed responded "very true" to statements asking whether management rewarded those within the organization who support flexible work arrangements, and only 21 percent said their organization made a real and ongoing effort to inform employees of the availability of work-life assistance.[10]

> **D&I Connect**
> More than 80 percent of diversity and inclusion leaders surveyed say they support flexible work in order to "impact the company culture."
> Source: Working Mother Research Institute, 2010

These results indicate that although incorporating flexible work practices into an organization's diversity and inclusion efforts can enhance the recruitment, retention and engagement of diverse talent, it is not enough to provide flexible programs, guidelines and policies. There must be a more concerted effort to implement flexibility into the cultural DNA of the organization, including removing barriers that punish employees who desire flexibility.

Margaret Regan of The Future Work Institute, has some concerns that senior leaders — based on their own life experiences — have much to learn when it comes to recognizing the connection between the diverse needs of employees and the positive influence of flexibility on the workplace. The stigma of flexible work continues to exist, but must be removed, in order for organizations—and employees—to gain the full benefits of flexible work practices.

Diversity and Inclusion

What Can Diversity and Inclusion Leaders Do?

Diversity and inclusion leaders have a lot of influence in this area. Companies can create a plan for educating managers and employees about the importance of using flexible work options, and how to manage diverse, dispersed teams.

Diversity and inclusion stakeholders require access to the research, assessments and resources that would allow them to integrate flexible work practices into a day-to-day workload. For example, when preparing a diversity and inclusion presentation to management, relevant statistics about the role flexible work can play in attracting and advancing diverse talent should be included. In addition, examining current systems and processes and identifying ways to integrate flexible work practices across all aspects of talent attraction, retention and engagement can provide more consistent leadership messages and practices related to flexible work, as well as better outcomes.

Jacqueline Akerblom, national managing partner for Women's Initiatives and Programs at Grant Thornton LLP, points out that to create successful culture change, real and transparent flexibility must be encouraged. "It's not the way we used to do it. It's one of the benefits of having a really robust women's initiative. We had existing flex work arrangements, but not a lot of sunshine around them. We found that a lack of flexibility was far and away one of the biggest reasons we were losing female employees. Leadership got around this, and committed to being the kind of employer we want to be."

She commended the firm's leadership for walking the walk. "A lot of our male partners would sneak out to coach their son's little league teams — we highly encouraged them to let employees know that that's what they were doing. As long as our employees act professionally and settle client requirements, they can work flexibly."

Diversity and Inclusion

BEST FLEX PRACTICES
Hand-On Tips for Integrating Flex and Diversity[11]

Kodak

Eastman Kodak has gone from a photographic giant to a modest, yet still formidable, 20,250-person imaging company. Throughout the company's major transformation, which included reducing its workforce, scaling back on recruiting and focusing on the retention and development of existing employees, flexibility has been key to retaining a diverse range of talent and remaining competitive.

"We must have people, so whatever impacts their work and life is important," says David Kassnoff, director, community affairs at Kodak. As part of the Rochester, N.Y.-based company's flexibility initiatives, which fall under the umbrella of diversity and inclusion, the company offers a 52-page guidebook, downloadable from the Kodak Intranet, for corporate leaders. At Kodak, flex serves as both a recruitment and retention tool. Mary Ann Detmer, Kodak's director of workplace equity & compliance, says the company monitors changes in the careers of its employees and asks them how they are faring in an effort to help them progress professionally.

While Kodak offers flexible work options, executing and managing these initiatives is not without its challenges. The three greatest hurdles for the company are providing quantitative data about the effectiveness of flex programs, raising awareness about the importance of flexibility and the options available, and assuaging managers' wariness about the impact of flex on employee performance.

Kodak offers the following advice to diversity practitioners looking to incorporate flexibility into their work:
- Don't miss the boat—use flex as a huge selling point in your efforts to attract new employees, especially new entrants into the workforce.

- Focus on flexible work as a retention strategy—doing so will help sustain diversity at your organization.

- Promote flexible work internally and externally—make flex a "value add" for senior leaders who are highly vocal and visible.

Royal Dutch Shell

In the 1990s, Shell was one of the first energy companies to offer alternative work schedules. Since that time, flexibility has been woven into various aspects of company culture, an approach that aids in removing barriers within the organization, says John Sequeira, D&I consultant, global diversity & inclusion practice for Shell, which has global headquarters in The Hague, The

Netherlands. One of the company's core values is "Respect for People," which includes respect for the need for individual work arrangements. In addition, Shell's general business principals serve as the pillars that encourage employee involvement in planning and directing their work, while the company's people standards state that it's the individual's responsibility to manage their work and personal demands.

At Shell, flex is a function of the human resources department; however, Sequeira says the company's Diversity & Inclusion practice partners with HR colleagues to help reinforce the importance of flexibility in the workplace. For companies looking to successfully engage flexibility within diversity and inclusion, Sequeira suggests the following:
- Establish accountability measures using data to show how flex is working in different parts of the organization.
- Use flex as a competitive differentiator.
- Tie flexible work to your core business values and use those values when you get push back.
- Leverage the connections between the strategic intent of having an inclusive work environment and meeting the flex needs of an ever-growing diversity in our workforce.
- Explore win/win solutions for the individual and the organization.

Pitney Bowes

At Pitney Bowes, diversity includes the whole person, which in addition to typical characteristics such as age, race and gender, includes how one works and one's work-life experience, says T. Hudson Jordan, the company's director of global diversity and talent strategies. The Stamford, CT-based customer communications technology company encourages its employees to choose the work environment that best suits their job requirements and personal workplace preferences.

The 90-year-old company is so committed to this philosophy that in 2009 it introduced "Agile Workforce," a pilot program run in the Fairfield County, CT, offices designed to empower employees to take advantage of flexible work options. Through the program, workers were able to make arrangements with their managers to leverage mobile technology, Pitney Bowes' office buildings and their home workspaces to manage work tasks throughout the week.

As a result, the company experienced improved employee engagement (90 percent of participants reported feeling more positive about Pitney Bowes because of the program), increased productivity (80 percent of participants said they felt more productive) and better work-life effectiveness (98 percent of participants felt they had improved work-life balance) from the pilot participants. Agile Workforce was so successful that the program is now being introduced to other parts of the organization.

"Pitney Bowes is committed to providing employees with the tools and resources to more effectively manage their work and life, along with a supportive environment to do so," says Jordan. "We encourage our employees to utilize the benefits that help them accomplish this

Diversity and Inclusion

while meeting the business needs of the organization. This flexible work environment has been a distinctive way Pitney Bowes engages and retains its employees."

Yet, despite having a formal flex initiative, the company has faced some management resistance and skepticism, control issues, and culture change barriers. Jordan says the company tackles these challenges by equipping managers with the ability to measure results, rather than face time. Also, training is required of all managers and employees who participated in the pilot program. More comprehensive training is being developed as the program expands to other parts of the company. Pitney Bowes employees also engage the following strategies, which can benefit all companies looking to leverage flex to bolster their diversity and inclusion efforts:

- Set goals and objectives with telecommuters so performance is based on output rather than face time.
- Provide routine and timely feedback to avoid surprises and allow for timely changes and modifications.
- Set realistic, mutually agreed upon deadlines.
- Delegate assignments equitably between telecommuters and non-telecommuters.
- Recognize and acknowledge results in meaningful ways.

PepsiCo

At PepsiCo, flexibility is viewed as a productivity tool that can drive performance. Official responsibility for the management and execution of flexibility lies within the organization's human resources department; however, Rachel Cheeks, PepsiCo's senior manager of global diversity & inclusion, understands the benefits of flexibility firsthand. A 17-year veteran of the company, Cheeks once held an old-school view about how employees should work.

She was a firm believer that everyone should be in the office, but her perspective changed when she recently needed to spend time in the hospital with a sick child. After several days away from the office, Cheeks leveraged the ability to connect to her office using wireless access at the hospital. Doing so allowed her to manage her work responsibilities while tending to her ailing child.

Since that experience, Cheeks has become a staunch supporter of using technology to make flexibility work. She tries to take advantage of the host of technology — telepresence, webcams, etc. — available at the company. In fact, the last two global human resources diversity and inclusion meetings at the Purchase, N.Y.-based soft drink and snack maker were conducted virtually.

At an organization-wide level, PepsiCo has instituted "One Single Thing," an initiative designed to encourage employees to identify a facet of work they could change to help them better manage their professional and personal needs. The program allows employees to request scheduling changes and develop an individualized description of flexibility.

"It's important to define flex as 'what's right for me' and, as one's career and life changes, you need to adapt and do things differently," says Cheeks. "I've learned to work smarter, delegate more and be clear about saying 'No, I can't' when necessary."

Diversity and Inclusion

McKesson Corporation

"Flex is the glue that helps foster a culture of inclusion," says Daina Chiu. As a working mother practicing law with a remote team, flex options were critical for Chiu's professional success. Now, as the corporate diversity officer at McKesson Corporation, Chiu is making flex a focus. With four generations in the workplace with differing views of how and where work is done, Chiu says the healthcare services company, headquartered in San Francisco, Calif., views flexibility as an important emerging opportunity to aid in expanding the business and engaging and retaining employees.

"It is important to adapt and align company goals and activities in an evolving business environment," says Chiu. "At McKesson, our goal with diversity and inclusion initiatives is to make sure that we harness all of our capabilities and talent to innovate and develop the best solutions for our customers. Flex allows people to bring their best to work."

Chiu offers the following insights for building flex into a company's business strategy:
- Don't do flex for flex's sake. It must reflect the enterprise perspective and help achieve business objectives; otherwise, why would a company want to do it?
- Make the business case. For McKesson, it's an emerging opportunity.
- Understand the obstacles and barriers you may face. Anticipate the "face time" question and concerns about employee productivity and be prepared to redirect the discussion to performance and outcomes.
- Recognize that one size doesn't fit all when it comes to flexibility. It's fundamentally a diversity issue: what works for one person or a specific role may not work for everyone or for all jobs.

The Timken Company

"Timken is young in this journey and we're still defining our approach," says Traci Dunn, director, global inclusion and talent acquisition at the friction management and power transmission products and services company headquartered in Canton, Ohio. "We have policies and tools, but no formal definition for flex, which is informally, but not explicitly, considered part of diversity."

Timken views flex as a critical component in attracting diverse talent and differentiating the company in the marketplace. Dunn says the challenge resides with mid-level managers who need to see what's in it for them and to understand why it is important.

Dunn provides these suggestions for incorporating flex into the workplace:

- You don't have to own flex to make it effective and to drive it and align strategies.
- Build the business case. In an engineering environment, like the one at Timken, numbers count.

- Use existing data to make the case. Use culture or engagement survey questions and exit interviews and track the number of job offers presented against the number of candidates placed to support the case for flex.
- As the employment landscape improves, the war for talent will be back. How you treat employees in difficult times will determine whether you can keep and attract the talent you need.

Procter & Gamble

For Cincinnati, Ohio-based Procter & Gamble, flexibility is not only a part of the company's diversity and inclusion strategy, but rather an overarching element of all human resource efforts. A multi-disciplinary HR approach means flex practices are approved for human resources account managers who then work with the global human resources division to ensure that the programs are embedded in the organization's DNA. "The goal is to have every line leader own flex and lead policy," says Helen Tucker, Procter & Gamble's director of global diversity and inclusion.

While the company has focused on talent management practices and processes and a culture of inclusion, Tucker says providing a flexible environment remains an exciting area on which the company can capitalize. Procter & Gamble's focus on flexibility is strongly supported at the senior level. Company CEO Bob McDonald showcases his commitment to flexible work benefits on a recently launched Intranet page. "The CEO believes that P&G's goal is to touch and improve the lives of customers and he wants to reflect the same philosophy with employees," says Tucker.

Tucker notes that "integrating all the energy and direction in diversity and inclusion where everyone feels empowered and has a sense of ownership can sometimes be challenging." However, she goes on to say, "there is a great deal of energy and interest and we are making real progress by more effectively communicating our flexible work practices across the enterprise."

Walmart

Walmart's executive vice president and general counsel Jeff Gearhart recently updated the company's outside counsel guidelines to reflect the best practice recommendations of the PAR Diversity & Flexibility Connection. The Diversity & Flexibility Connection is an ongoing discussion between prominent general counsels and law firm chairs on the retention of diverse attorneys through the inclusion of an effective work-life program. Walmart has taken a leadership position by including the following in its outside counsel guidelines:
- Non-stigmatized flexible work: all external firms are to implement flex-time policies, or obtain a waiver, by February 1, 2011, to promote retention, prevent loss of institutional knowledge, and create a more balanced and inclusive work environment.
- Referring work to reduced-hours attorneys: firms will be including at least one partner working a flextime schedule as a candidate for Walmart relationship partner.

- Origination credit: firms will annually certify that the Walmart relationship partners have received origination credit. This guideline is also a best practice recommendation of the PAR/MCCA study on partner compensation.

The Diversity & Flexibility Connection was designed to facilitate a conversation about how in-house and outside counsel could work together more effectively to support balanced hours programs, with the ultimate goal of making the legal profession more inclusive. As the biggest company in the world, Walmart's guidelines will likely lead to positive changes in many law firms, where more women will hopefully be able to take advantage of non-stigmatized flexible work as a viable career option.[12]

Conclusion

It's all about the talent. Mary Jones, VP of global HR at John Deere, describes a growing trend for organizations to recognize flexible work as a key business enabler that can attract and retain talent around the world. The fact that diversity and inclusion initiatives must address the needs of global teams adds to the significance of expanding diversity leaders' perception of the role flexibility plays.

Whether an organization is initiating, enhancing or advancing a flexible work initiative, the connection between flexible work and diversity and inclusion should be clearly defined, articulated and leveraged. Nora Spinks, president and founder of Work-Life Harmony Enterprises, points out that flexible work is essential to develop a diverse group of leaders in the workforce of the future. Offering more control over where, when and how work is done can increase the ability to attract, retain and engage a diverse talent pool. Flexibility is being requested by these diverse employee segments to increase the effectiveness of their work and personal lives. Diversity and inclusion leaders must according to Margaret Regan, acknowledge the role they can play in changing the way work is done.

Flexible work is an effective tool for removing barriers that impact the productivity and career advancement opportunities for many employees, especially those with diverse or special needs. And it's a powerful tool businesses can use to achieve a competitive advantage by hiring and keeping the best, most diverse talent. In the end, it is about organizational survival. As John Daniels, executive VP and chief diversity officer of First Tennessee Bank, notes, the diversity of skills required for today's demanding work means it is essential to include flexibility into the mix to attract the right talent.

Diversity and inclusion leaders must take the initiative to create solid business practices that attract and retain a more flexible workforce and promote a more flexible work environment. When diversity and inclusion leaders connect the organizational dots and provide resources that will support and encourage managers and employees to use flexible work practices as an effective tool to achieve business and personal goals, everyone benefits.

TIP SHEET
Attracting, Engaging and Managing Diverse Talent

Connect the dots: Align diversity and inclusion policies and practices to include the needs of a flexible workforce and a flexible workplace,

- ❏ Partner with leaders in recruitment, learning and development, performance management and organizational development to identify opportunities to attract, advance and engage a more diverse, flexible workforce.
- ❏ Ensure that when people need to work flexibly — either on an ongoing basis or occasionally — they are not at risk of being marginalized.
- ❏ Employees who work flexibly should not be penalized by receiving less challenging assignments or growth opportunities. Neither should they be removed from the core group or be less involved in strategy sessions.
- ❏ Examine performance review systems to assure that employees who work flexibly — either on an ongoing basis or occasionally — advance at the same rate as others. For those who work less than full-time, create a system that prorates their time.
- ❏ Do not expect those who work part-time to do more work than can reasonably be accomplished given their reduced schedule. In addition, they should earn the same rate of pay as those doing the same job on a full-time basis.
- ❏ Examine work processes to ensure they include flexible workers; for example, are meetings planned at times when they can participate?
- ❏ Choose and develop leaders from among a pool that includes flexible workers and encourage them to serve as role models.
- ❏ Create opportunities for flexible careers that include off/on ramping, working a reduced schedule, taking sabbaticals or unpaid leave to demonstrate what's possible.
- ❏ Be sure to include flexible workers in mentoring and coaching programs. Ensure that they are specifically coached on career flexibility, building relationships and developing skills required to work flexibly.
- ❏ Ensure that flexible workers receive equal attention and resources for professional development as those who are not working flexibly.

REFERENCES: CHAPTER 2

1. (2009), Marcie Pitt-Catsouphes, Christina Matz-Costa, and Elyssa Besen, Sloan Center on Aging & Work at Boston College.
2. (2004) Sandy Burud, Mary Tumolo, Leveraging the New Human Capital: Adaptive Strategies, Results Achieved, and Stories of Transformation, Davies-Black.
3. (2010) Jean Flatley McGuire, Kaitlyn Kenny, and Phillis Brashler, "Flexible Work Arrangements: The Fact Sheet." Workplace Flexibility 2010, Georgetown University Law Center.
4. (2010) http://www.iwpr.org/initiatives/the-status-of-women-and-girls Majority of Workers Support Workplace Flexibility, Job Quality, and Family Support Policies
5. (2009) Center for Work Life Policy.
6. (2008) Flexible Work Options: Flexible Schedules, The Center on Aging and Work at Boston College.
7. (2008) Groeneman, S., Staying ahead of the curve 2007: The AARP work and career study. Washington, D.C. AARP.
8. (2010) The Institute for Women's Policy Research (IWPR).
9. (2010) Shaffert, R. Huffington Post.
10. (2011) BUSINESS IMPACTS OF FLEXIBILITY: AN IMPERATIVE FOR EXPANSION, Corporate Voices for Working Families
11. (2010) Rose, K., Flexible Work: A Critical Component of a Diversity and Inclusion Strategy, Diversity Best Practices, FlexPaths.
12. (2010) "Wal-Mart Implements Diversity & Flexibility Connection Best Practices," posted by Project for Attorney Retention.

Chapter 3 | Flexible Work and Technology

Technology

We have seen the incredible impact technology and social media can have on entire countries such as Egypt. It is therefore no surprise that technology and social media are also dramatically impacting the workforce and the work environment. Technology has become the catalyst for the development of the agile workforce and workplace of today and tomorrow.

Technology enables work to be done anywhere, any time. For many employees, that translates into working everywhere, all the time. According to an article in the February 2011 issue of *Carolina Parent* magazine, there is now a new term to define a parent's sense of being constantly on call for work and family: "weisure," the combination of work and leisure. Coined by sociologist Dalton Conley in 2009, the term is often used in the context of how technology requires us to be constantly on high alert.

While organizations are constantly looking to maximize the use of technology to increase productivity, there are a lot of challenges embedded in the never-ending search for increasing connectivity using smaller, more mobile devices. Add to that the impact of social media, which allows and enhances collaboration in ways that can accelerate the rate of innovation. These two areas of technological advancement — the tools themselves and social media — are shaping and accelerating changes in the way we work and live. They also represent some of the greatest challenges for today's employers and employees.

Technological advances have changed the very nature of what we consider a workplace. They have forced organizations to reconsider where work is done, how work is structured, how workspace is designed, as well as their reliance on face time as a measure of productivity. Technology has also forced organizations to reexamine how their information is protected and how people are managed. In

Technology

effect, technology has touched every nerve ending in the world of HR and other internal stakeholders. When you add the new influence of social media, which allows instantaneous sharing of ideas and opinions, and the range of resources for remote meetings and telepresence, you have what Margaret Regan, president and CEO of The Future Work Institute, calls a convergence of events powerful enough to change the way we define going to work.

In Chapter 3, we will explore the following questions:

✔ What are the benefits of connecting technology for remote work?

✔ What are the challenges for technology and flexible work?

✔ How does technology impact where work is done?

✔ How does technology impact the way work is done?

✔ What is technology's impact on workplace design?

✔ How can technology be leveraged to work more flexibly?

✔ What is technology's impact on the future of work?

✔ How can technology be used to attract and retain diverse talent?

The Benefits of Leveraging Technology for Remote Work

According to Suite101.com[1], a number of recent studies confirm that flexible work arrangements promoting healthy work-life balance are a significant benefit that employees look for when they are searching for a new job. A March 2010 poll conducted by Harris/Decima for TELUS, polled more than 1,000 respondents, including managers and employees, and found that 89 percent of employees said that offering a flexible work program makes a company more attractive. "With the economy gaining strength, people will be increasingly selective about the companies they look to work for," says Jeff Lowe, VP of TELUS. "Organizations that leverage technology to allow their staff to work anywhere — in the office, on the road or at home — will have a measurable advantage in the competition to attract top talent. At the same time, they'll increase their ability to retain the best and the brightest, inspiring the kind of productivity and loyalty that only the strongest companies in the world successfully generate amongst their teams."[2]

Similarly, a Workplace Options' survey released in May 2010 reveals that in the United States flexible work arrangements, including homeworking and teleworking, are a highly valued benefit. Of 997 working Americans surveyed in April 2010, 69 percent said they would have more loyalty to their employers if they were offered greater flexibility in managing time and schedules.[3]

On the list of benefits desired by employees is the ability to telecommute in order to work from home when needed. "With continuous advancements in technology, it may soon be possible for more and more organizations to allow workers the opportunity to work remotely, as opposed to physically being at the office," says Alan King, president and COO of Workplace Options, a Raleigh, NC-based provider of work-life benefits.

In addition, there are numerous other benefits that result from leveraging technology to support anywhere, anytime flexible work, including:

A reduction in overhead costs. Businesses can trim office space and facilities and utilities costs by promoting telework, flexible schedules and remote work.
- For every 100 employees who work full-time from home or virtually, a typical business saves more than $500,000 in space costs.[4]
- IBM saves more than $1 billion per year in facilities costs through its mobile work initiatives.[5]
- AT&T saves $25 million per year in facilities costs (and $65 million in improved productivity and $15 million in retention) due to its flexibility policies. At AT&T, 25 percent of managers telework at least twice a week and have no reserved office space; 10 percent are totally virtual. Half of all employees telework some of the time.[6]
- Sun decreased office space by 30 percent and saved $69 million in facilities costs in 2005.[7]
- Unisys cut office space by 90 percent.[8]

Technology

A reduction in energy consumption. Through expanded telework initiatives (not including reductions in commuting through flexible work schedules, such as compressed work weeks) the following energy savings occur:

- A company gains an estimated 2,400 pounds of carbon offset credits for every 100 employees not traveling to work.[9]
- People commuting to work in personal vehicles consume 44 billion gallons of gasoline a year. Increasing the number of full-time equivalent teleworkers by 10 percent would reduce consumption by 4.4 billion gallons per year. The EPA reports that 40 percent of job are suited for telework, but only 14 percent of those jobs are actually teleworked.[10]
- AT&T teleworkers drove 110 million fewer miles in 2001 and avoided the consumption of 5 million gallons of gasoline.[11]
- Staff who work from home use less energy than those in commercial buildings — a difference of 3,000 to 4,400 kWh per year.[12]

A reduction in harmful emissions.

- Commuters in private vehicles release 424 million tons of carbon dioxide into the atmosphere a year, 23 million tons of carbon monoxide, 1.8 million tons of volatile organic carbons and 1.5 million tons of oxides of nitrogen.[13]
- At AT&T, teleworkers avoided commuting 100 million miles, which reduced carbon dioxide emissions by 45,000 tons, or 1.8 tons per teleworker.[14]
- An estimated 3.5 billion square feet of unused commercial space would save 35 million metric tons of greenhouse gases. Elimination of these buildings would save another 36.4 million metric tons of greenhouse pollution.[15]

Findings by The World Wildlife Fund estimate that an increase in telecommuting and virtual meetings "could, without any dramatic measures, help to save more than 3 billion metric tons of carbon dioxide emissions in a few decades; this is the equivalent to approximately half the current U.S. carbon dioxide emissions."[16]

In the United States, reduced commuting accounts for 75 percent of the potential savings, with the other 25 percent coming from reduced air travel. Savings on this level are possible when telework is embraced at scale — when 30 percent to 45 percent of workers are teleworking two to four days a week and one-third to two-thirds of business trips are replaced with virtual meetings.

Understanding the Challenges

Despite these benefits, the number of employees regularly working outside the office remains relatively low. Microsoft recently sponsored a study by the World Wildlife Fund, which found that 17.5 percent of U.S. employees work outside the office at least once a month, with the average doing so 2.7 days per month. While this is a small percentage of the employee population, it is still higher than in Europe, where just 8 percent work outside the office at least once a month, with an average of one day a month.

Given the level of connectivity possible and the proven benefits of telework in terms of productivity, loyalty, engagement and reduced costs, it is surprising that a larger percentage of employees are not working remotely. As technology continues to expand into every area of our work and personal lives, employers are learning to use it to create more efficient, productive work environments and workforces. Along with the growth of technology, however, comes questions about how organizations and employees actually utilize these resources, and whether they can be used even more effectively to meet business and personal needs.

In the 2008 study "Flexible Work: Rhetoric and Reality," a survey was conducted of Citrix's 750 knowledge workers. It examined their work patterns, use of technology, and their likes and dislikes about the IT tools they depend upon. Surprisingly, even though modern technology offers increased flexibility as to where employees can work, more than 75 percent of the managers and almost half of the individual contributors who responded to the survey say they still spend the vast majority of their time inside corporate facilities in their assigned offices or cubicles.[17]

This finding suggests that although more advanced technologies have made remote work more accessible to more workers, there remains a significant gap between the possibilities technology offers for more flexible work arrangements and its actual use.[18]

The gap between the availability of technology resources and their use to promote and support increased flexibility can be addressed with more marketing communication, awareness building, and active demonstrations of the benefits provided by collaborative technologies.[19]

Maryella Gockel, flexibility strategy leader at Ernst & Young, described the Firm's initiative, Making It Real, as a recent attempt to leverage social media to support the firm's long-standing focus on flexibility. Making It Real encourages team members to post success stories describing how they are using flexibility to change the way their work is done. In addition, the use of social media is providing a lot of opportunities for sharing and learning about what works. (Adapted from Making It Real, Ernst & Young, 2010)

> **Tech Connect**
> A survey of corporate work-life practitioners nationwide found that although 25 percent of survey respondents said technology has been connected with flexible work at their organization for 15 years or more, nearly 54 percent said that it was still important to clarify practical issues such as remote set-ups, communication systems and data recovery.
> *Source: Working Mother Research Institute, 2010*

Technology's Impact on WHERE Work is Done

It's time to redefine the twin notions of what an office is and what going to work means. Today, most employees have the ability to work wherever they want to, driven in large part by the available technological tools and the complexity of their work and personal lives. A major challenge is to identify the types of jobs that can be done remotely all or some of the time and make sure the technology support required to work in this way is in place. This process requires coordination among IT and HR departments, as well as managers and employees. According

Technology

to Kerrie Peraino, VP of human resources and chief diversity officer for American Express, HR cannot be successful without partnering with IT, among other departments. In its Blue Work initiative, American Express mentioned IT and real estate as two departments that are critical to work with when implementing a flexible work program.

Gail Henderson, manager of global work life management at Deere & Company agrees that IT is critical in creating a more flexible workplace and workforce — basically, it's technology that drives the program.

Maryella Gockel of Ernst & Young notes that the future is all about the type of jobs that can be done remotely: "Where, when and how work will be done is overlayed with what technology will become and how it impacts the way we work," she says.

The concept of a "living" workspace, one that is created in the moment, is a direct byproduct of the need for more flexibility in where, when and how work is done. The evolution of the living workspace is continuing to develop, as revealed in a 2010 survey commissioned by Skype that involved 1,000 technology-enabled professionals in the United States, including 500 business end users and 500 technology decision makers across small-, medium- and large-sized businesses.

Among the most interesting takeaways of the living workplace survey were:
- Flexible and remote work environments have become commonly accepted and are important for hiring and productivity, with 62 percent of surveyed firms employing remote workers.
- Remote workers are spending, on average, 40 percent of their time away from their offices.
- Flexible working benefits the employer with increased collaboration.
- Flexible working benefits employees with a better work-life balance.

Technology is bringing together a dispersed workforce, ultimately empowering businesses to grow faster, scale and save on costs. That in itself can give businesses an edge in a hypercompetitive global business environment.[20]

Technology's Impact on the WAY Work is Done

As working remotely becomes more popular, and line-of-sight management is no longer necessary, new technologies are being developed to allow employers to monitor when work is done. This is not only important in terms of managing performance, but for legal issues stemming from overtime and worker's compensation issues. In addition, the increased use of smartphones and affordable laptops has brought an end to the concept of dead time, sparing many workers the need to head back to the office to follow-up with correspondence after being on the road.

Technology

Similarly, in only a few short years, the virtual office has benefited from the easy access to and reduced costs of high-speed internet connections. This has significantly reduced the expense of setting up work-from-home programs, and with Virtual Private Networks in place, it is becoming simpler and safer to grant workers remote access to company networks.

Some organizations concerned about potential employee abuse when working remotely are adopting messaging tools and presence indicators that make it easier to evaluate remote workers' activity and productivity while helping them to stay motivated through regular contact with colleagues.

On-line scheduling and flex working

> **Tech Connect**
> Nearly 70 percent of survey respondents at U.S. corporations said that technology eases the implementation of flexible work.
>
> Source: Working Mother Research Institute, 2010

Technology forces organizations to consider using virtual time management and timekeeping services. Recent studies have found that online scheduling costs between $1.25 and $5 per month per employee[21], but despite this added cost, technology offers a way for employees to document when and where they are working — and for managers to observe work being done. Such scheduling resources can help organizations plan and manage workload more effectively.

To that end, here are some real-life ways companies use online scheduling to improve both flexibility and productivity.

Alpine Access, a customer service call center for a national financial institution that employs 1,200 people, has an on-line site that allows employees to specify what hours they want to work, and what hours they normally would not work, but could in an emergency. This service allows the company to ask employees to schedule the number of hours they are interested in working and gives employees more control over their schedule so they can more effectively manage their work and personal needs.

Marriott's Global Reservation Sales and Customer Care Center, a 24/7 call center with 200 sales agents in Salt Lake City, created a web-based system that handles its broad array of flexible work options, which can be accessed through an on-site Web station. "Without the technology, it would be a nightmare to manage," said one manager.

JCPenney's On-Line Schedule Changes and Availability Requests, or OSCAR, enables associates to customize their work hours, add or drop shifts, or make last-minute schedule changes to meet their family obligations or other needs.

At **PNC Financial Services Group**, a bank with 2,500 branches and 59,000 employees, one department posts its schedule online. Staff then finds their individual work-life solutions by shift swapping, working half-shifts on two days instead of one, or considering other workers' needs when scheduling vacation.[22]

L&E Research in Raleigh has created a custom-designed software system providing employees greater flexibility in their work — which entails recruiting and facility services for market research companies — much of which can be done by phone at home at various times of the day. The new software enables recruiters and project managers to stay connected through a secure online database.

Expedite Group, a Cary, N.C.-based company, is also providing flexible work options through its virtual work environment. Employees are connected to the office through conference calls, e-mail and the occasional onsite meeting, and even fulltime employees are able to arrange flexible schedules within their own teams, as long as all the hours in the day are covered.[23]

Technology's Impact on Workplace Design

We are beginning to see the traditional, industrial model of the workplace evolve into something that more effectively and efficiently supports knowledge-based and conceptual work. Driving the speed of change is the integration of human resources, information technology and real estate working together to achieve cost-reduction strategic imperatives. Whether new facility designs enable a company to reduce real estate costs, optimize limited space and/or meet "green" initiatives, technology is a strategic asset and internal partner to help achieve such goals.

In many ways, workplace design is shifting in line with changing workforce attitudes. This transformation is from a work environment that has been based on hierarchy, boundaries and individual entitlement to one that is more open, requires less physical space and increasingly involves virtual team meetings and collaboration. For example, Danielle Hartmann, director of corporate partnerships at the Boston College Center for Work & Family, sees more companies recognizing that flexible work, and in particular full- or part-time remote work, is a tool that can be used to innovate as organizations think about work location.

Even closer to the bottom line, however, is the cost savings that the technology and flexible work partnership can bring. Nancy Didia of Boehringer Ingelheim USA, for one, says she believes technology minimizes capital expenditures for brick and mortar and real estate leases, noting that fewer individual workspaces and offices will be needed and that there will be much more sharing of common space.

WORKSHEET

FLEXIBLE WORK AND TECHNOLOGY

Consider these questions when beginning to incorporate technology into your flexible work planning.

1. Is there a way for IT and HR to partner on planning for the needs of flexible workers and their managers?

2. How does IT know what employees' current and potential future technology needs are?

3. How will IT allocate internal resources and equipment? Will employees have to supply their own equipment when working remotely?

4. What are the different needs of employees who work remotely all the time vs. those who only occasionally work from another location?

5. Have you assessed the cost of the various IT options required and determined who will pay for them – the company, the department, the manager and/or the employee?

6. As more employees work anytime, anywhere, how will you protect the company's information?

7. What kind of tech support will be provided for employees who work remotely?

8. Have you explored technology options that support the global, virtual work environment, that facilitate virtual meetings or that help with scheduling and tracking flexible work arrangements?

Leveraging Technology to Work Flexibly

The flexible worker of today has access to virtually all of the technological tools they use at the office — no matter where they are. The following technology tools were cited as particularly important for a successful telework program (based on a survey of 18 organizations from Microsoft Corporation):[24]

- Pervasive broadband, both fixed and mobile, that enables employees to connect seamlessly from anywhere through secure networks.
- Unified communication that integrates all communication into a single, easy-to-use interface.

Tech Connect

When asked how technology could help increase the effectiveness of flexible work, almost half of the respondents indicated that providing a bigger budget was important to expanding technology's role in support of increased flexible work.

Source: Working Mother Research Institute, 2010

- Presence status, which shows the real-time availability based upon status on the network (free, busy, in a meeting, in a call, offline) and ensures employees can be reached instantly by the most appropriate means.
- Instant messaging.
- Secure mobile email and calendaring.
- Voice over IP.
- Hardware devices.
- Laptops and/or smartphones that allow employees to remain connected from any location.
- USB headsets that plug into laptops and replace traditional desk phones.
- USB webcams for video conferencing.

While these technology tools are necessary to promote flexible work, their use alone does not make a policy work. Mary Jones, VP of global HR at Deere & Company, notes, for instance, that it is also critical to have flexibility tools in place — such as websites that provide information assessments and checklists — to support the conversation between managers and employees. Additionally, Nora Spinks, president and founder of Work-Life Harmony Enterprises, argues that companies need to create standards for when and where technology tools will be used to promote remote work and support both the employer's and employees' needs.[25]

Technology's Impact on the Future of Work

Writing in Personnel Today, Peter Thomson, director of the Future Work Forum at Henley Management School, anticipates that within the next 20 years, the office will evolve into a central rendezvous, based around meeting rooms and casual meeting space. "Work is a thing you do, not a place you go," adds Alex Reeve, director of the mobile business group at Microsoft UK. The software giant has recently been collaborating with the consultancy, The Future Laboratory, to produce the report, "Work and Mobile Cities." The report identifies a new generation of workers, labeled "flexibods," who work in third spaces such as trains, hotels and parks.

Margaret Regan, president and CEO of The Future Work Institute, says the increasing use of cloud computing will accelerate the speed with which companies move toward a more mobile workforce. According to Regan, technology is creating a population of nomad knowledge workers who will insist on "my job, my way" and that, combined with advances in technology, demographic changes in the employee population — more women, people with disabilities, working parents — and the constant pressure on organizations to cut costs while improving productivity, will create even more dramatic changes in where, when and how work is done in the future.

At the software company Adobe, Debbie Jones, UK marketing manager for Acrobat and E-learning, predicts that the technology needed for flexible work in the next decade will be built on opportunities to use such innovative products as Webcams, which allow e-learning and e-meetings to take place. "The next 10 years will be about getting as much interactivity as possible," she says. As more resources that support and promote the virtual work environment become available, it will be easier for organizations and individuals to gain confidence in working more flexibly.

The British law firm, Keystone Law, is a good example of this trend. The firm runs its office virtually and flexibly. Its 70 lawyers work from satellite offices, which are often located in their own homes, supported by a small London office where eight employees handle administration and meeting facilities.

Keystone's systems are hosted on a third-party server and all lawyers are given a BlackBerry and laptop computer, providing them with online data back-up, call forwarding, email reporting and archiving, as well as VoIP (Voice over Internet Protocol) applications such as Skype. They all have access to Keystone's intranet, which helps with calendar management and case management. Managing director James Knight points out that technology allows the firm to cut out waste, commuting and high rent bills, all of which results in lower fees for their clients. The company's remuneration system allows solicitors to work as many hours as they choose, and billing targets have been removed to relieve the pressure on them.[26]

Capital One is another organization that has maximized the use of technology tools to provide employees with everything they need to work anytime, anywhere. Its Flexible Work Solutions (FWS) initiative was created to enhance organizational performance and real estate asset utilization while supporting better work-life integration for its thousands of associates. The initiative, which began as a result of associate feedback, supports working when and where it is most effective by enabling mobility through technology and providing supportive and unique workplace atmospheres to reinforce flexibility. As a result, the company has increased associate productivity and satisfaction by offering flexible work arrangements, lowered real estate costs by requiring less overall space, and even generated environmental benefits through reduced commuting.[27]

Technology's Role in Attracting and Retaining Diverse Talent

Technology plays an important role in creating a more flexible work environment that can attract and retain a diverse workforce. It can serve as an equalizer for people with disabilities, health issues and family obligations by removing workplace barriers and increasing opportunities for employment. Today, employers can look for skilled employees in new and creative ways. Rolando Balli, Connected Workplace program manager at Dell, says the organization has embraced the use of technology to promote flexible work because there is renewed awareness of the cost savings and its ability to attract and keep the best talent.

In fact, companies that "fail to offer flexible work are missing out on some of the best talent available and will be at a distinct recruiting disadvantage within the next five years," says Kyra Cavanaugh, founder of Life Meets Work, a Park Ridge, IL-based consultancy dedicated to fostering the flexible work movement.

For people with disabilities, technology has been able to reduce barriers by promoting workplace flexibility and assistive technology for communication. While there is still a high degree of unemployment among people with disabilities (over 60 percent), a trend has been seen

Technology

in the rising number of people with disabilities graduating from major universities and training programs and entering the job market.

In addition, AARP reports that 69 percent of employees over the age of 45 plan to continue working past 65. By creating flexibility initiatives that are targeted to people of retirement age, such as part-time work, flexible schedules and tailored benefits, employers can retain and attract knowledgeable workers. More flexible scheduling, including telecommuting, job sharing or part-time hours, will help companies tap into the boomer work force.

Technology

FLEX IN-DEPTH: Cisco

Creating a Global 'Pay for Performance' Culture Through Flex

Submitted by: Anne Formalarie, senior manager, and James Brooks, director

CHALLENGE/SITUATION:

In October 2009, Cisco formally launched its flexible work practices initiative. To address the needs of our 67,000 global employees, Cisco HR deployed options including part-time, job share, remote work, and a career break called Off/On Ramp. These programs have seen consistent growth since the launch.

This initiative was designed to increase employee engagement and productivity, increase adoption of Cisco's own technology, and improve the employee experience to enable career development and work-life integration opportunities. By formalizing Cisco's flexible work practices, with systems and processes behind them, there's a framework to evaluate job characteristics and the employee's professional and personal goals in the context of Cisco's results-oriented culture.

At Cisco, the convergence of HR policy, innovative workspace design, and collaborative technology changes the way people work, inside and outside the company sites. A one-size-fits-all employment model would not support Cisco's growth, productivity goals or culture. Flexibility enables employees to mix and match how, when and where work gets done and how careers are developed.

WHO WAS INVOLVED:

The Employee Engagement team drove the global Flexible Work Practice (FWP) initiative, which was sanctioned at the senior executive level. Cisco wanted to introduce the FWP program in not just one, but many countries during the first year of implementation, to reflect the company's international footprint (40 percent of employees are outside the U.S.) and growth. An extended team was formed, including experts from the Benefits, Legal, Inclusion & Diversity, Compensation, Staffing, and Communication teams and local HR leaders in more than 20 countries. This team determined the final FWP options and developed the launch plan, which was phased to enable a successful introduction with executive and management support.

PROCESS:

Once the launch plan was developed, an extensive communications and change management effort was created, including training for both managers and employees. The training was delivered both in live and in video on demand (VoD) formats, so future employees could utilize it as well. Additionally, a comprehensive website was developed. The website contains executive level messaging, guidelines, policies, forms, examples, videos and best practices.

Technology

SOLUTION:
The following design principles were foundational to the Flexible Work Practices (FWP) initiative:
- Encouraging a results-focused, "Pay for Performance" culture, where results produced are of primary importance — not location or work hours.
- Work can be designed to maximize employee productivity while enabling employees to provide input on how they integrate their work and personal needs.
- FWP should support our culture, including a focus on collaboration between employees and managers.
- Business needs and responsibilities of the job are a significant consideration factor in determining whether flexibility is appropriate in a given situation, and what types of flexible practices can be included.
- Not every job is appropriate for a flexible work option, but many, if not most, jobs can be done in a variety of different ways and locations.
- Managers are responsible for making final decisions on employee work practices and options. However, managers are expected to approach employee requests with an open mind and meaningfully consider employee input and preferences about how they work.

Our approach developed from multiple internal pilots, employee and manager input, plus extensive benchmarking with other multinational companies. Cisco developed a three-pronged deployment methodology:
- Process/policy — options and guidelines that support current and future work practices
- Technology — leverage collaboration and Web 2.0 infrastructure and tools
- Culture — provide training, communication and reinforcement that foster culture change, while driving productivity and accountability

The implementation team completed a business needs assessment, which led to a phased release by country or region. The team targeted countries with the larger employee populations and introduced the program to nearly 90 percent of Cisco's workforce in 12 months.

The FWP options were developed to include both formal and informal options, and account for nearly all types of flexibility that employees could utilize. Telecommuting and flex time are informal options that most employees are likely to use (either daily or occasionally) with support of their manager. Telecommuters work away from a Cisco office, and flex time is a variation in a regular work schedule. Both are very popular, with 89 percent of our employees reporting that they use these options.

Formal flexible work practices require management approval and are tracked in our HRMS system. These include part-time, job share, full-time remote work (usually at the employee's home), and an extended leave program called Off/On Ramp. This career break allows employees to step away from their work while still being connected to Cisco. With each option, we emphasize the importance of work impact, productivity, and accountability to employees. Eligibility is based on performance, readiness and suitability. Local laws and regulations apply.

These options were introduced in 24 countries in a 12-month timeframe.

Technology

RESULTS:
Employee engagement indicators show that our flexible workers are significantly more likely to stay at Cisco, more likely to recommend Cisco as a great place to work, and have higher productivity levels. Employees tell us that flexibility is a key differentiator making Cisco a great place to work, helping them integrate their work and lives and helping Cisco deliver on its vision to "change the way the world works, learns and plays."

Additionally, flexible workers are leaders in adopting Cisco's technology, drive network usage, and utilize collaboration technology at a high rate. Cisco employees model the workforce and the workplace of the future.
- 94 percent say Cisco technology allows them to work effectively with distributed colleagues.
- 93 percent say Cisco technology enables them to work from anywhere.
- 83 percent say that the ability to communicate and collaborate with coworkers is the same or better when working at home.

Flexibility saves time and money by reducing commute time, energy consumption and facilities costs:
- Incremental productivity gained by aligning with employee work preferences.
- Incremental productivity increased using collaboration technology to avoid travel time.
- Of the time saved by avoiding a commute, employees report that they reinvest 60 percent of that to work.

MEASUREMENT/METRICS:
We evaluated the effectiveness of the program based on participation and employee satisfaction. Since the formal rollout:
- Mobile workers have increased 21 percent.
- Full time remote workers have increased almost 20 percent.
- Part time workers are up 31 percent.
- Participation in the new Off/On Ramp leave is relatively low, but interest is growing and adoption dramatically exceeded our expectations.
- Performance ratings are tracking high and trending upward for mobile and remote workers.
- 96 percent report a desire to work from home.
- 83 percent say Cisco is a great place to work.
- 73 percent would turn down a comparable offer from another company.
- 74 percent say that timeliness of their work output improves when working at home.
- 67 percent say their quality of work improves when working at home.

MODIFICATIONS:
Flexible Work Practices are formally available in 24 countries. The countries with smaller offices manage employee requests on an ad-hoc basis. We continue to assess whether to introduce formal FWP programs in those countries with lower employee populations.

Interest in more part-time opportunities in our multi-generational workforce is growing. The program office continues research and development in this area and is looking at how the FWP options can fit with the needs of any employee, at any life and career stage.

Technology

> Technology, especially Cisco's hardware and software, continues to fuel our ability to work anywhere and any time. HR and IT are working closer than ever to increase productivity and collaboration through pilots, training, best practice sharing and policy.

Conclusion

Technology is changing everything about where, when and how work is done. According to Dell's Connected Workplace Program manager Rolando Balli, leveraging technology to support virtual work is a business imperative and a critical component in terms of getting and keeping the best talent. Indeed, the technology train has left the station. Employees are already using technology to do their work from everywhere, all the time. Organizations are, in many cases, playing catch up in order to maximize the opportunity to use technology most effectively to achieve business objectives.

Technology leaders play a significant role in anticipating and addressing the needs of the flexible workforce. It is mission-critical that IT be involved in planning and implementing flexibility in the organization. Today's work cannot be done successfully without the support and expertise that IT brings to the table. IT leaders need to examine the current and future technology needs of the workforce and workplace. They must align with other departments such as recruiting, facilities, diversity/inclusion and HR to create the most appropriate technology support. They must come to the table with the vision and guidance necessary to assure that employees are equipped with the necessary tools to get work done anywhere, anytime, while staying connected to the workplace. There's no turning back. The key is to embrace the new freedom and opportunities technology and social media offer in order to be a great place to work and gain a competitive advantage.

TIP SHEET
FLEXIBLE WORK AND TECHNOLOGY

Connect the dots: Create a cross functional team that includes IT and other interested stakeholders like facilities and HR, in order to:

❏ Identify common needs of key stakeholders regarding technology and flexible work.

❏ Coordinate communication and training across stakeholder groups.

❏ Audit existing technology tools and resources in terms of the fit with remote work.

❏ Clarify costs and responsibilities regarding technology equipment: determine whether these costs are paid by HQ, charged to the department or manager, or provided by employees themselves.

❏ Determine how telework technology troubleshooting will be handled.

❏ Develop a process that incorporates appropriate telework technology resources with employee requests for telework.

❏ Differentiate between technology resources for occasional work from another location vs. full-time remote work.

❏ Evaluate the effectiveness of current technology support for remote work.

❏ Experiment with new ways to assess technology needs.

❏ Involve managers and employees in the decision-making process regarding what they need to support their work.

❏ Have a process to collect or update technology tools as there are changes: for example, an employee no longer works remotely or leaves the company.

REFERENCES: CHAPTER 3

1. (2010) Suite 101.com, Flexible Working Arrangements, Telus, S. Smolkin,
2. (2010) New Harris/Decima survey reveals 89 per cent of Canadians attracted to companies that offer flexible work, Telus Corporation
3. (2010) U.S. Workplace Options Survey
4. (2005) Calculation assumes 30 square feet per employee at $168 per square foot — the national cost average according to a study by Old Dominion University Center for Real Estate and Economic Development, 2005 Market Survey.
5. (2003) Brad Allenby and Joseph Roitz, "Implementing the Knowledge Economy: The Theory and Practice of Telework," Batten Institute Working Paper.
6. (2007) Allenby and Roitz, p. 44–45, 26.
7. (2007) Arnold, in Fuhr and Pociask, Broadband Services: Economic and Environmental Benefits, 2007, p. 19–20.
8. (2007) Balaker, p. 24, in Fuhr and Pociask, p. 20.
9. (2007) Calculation from www.home2office.com.
10. (2007) Assumes fuel efficiency of 21 miles per gallon, EPA in Fuhr & Pociask, 2007, p. 24.
11. According to a survey conducted by Rockbridge the potential for telecommuting could reach 25 percent participation. Cited in Fuhr and Pociask, 2007, p. 24.
12. (2008) CDW-G, Telework Report, 2008.
13. (2009) Brad Allenby and Joseph Roitz , p.51.
14. (2007) Romm, p. 35. Cited in Fuhr and Pociask, 2007, p. 21.
15. (2007) Environmental Protection Agency, cited in Fuhr & Pociask, p. 24.
16. (2009) From Workplace to Anyplace: Assessing the Opportunities to Reduce Greenhouse Gas Emissions with Virtual Meetings and Telecommuting, The World Wildlife Fund.
17. (2008) Flexible Work: Rhetoric and Reality, Citrix
18. (2009) "FDIC uses tech to make remote work easier", Fierce Government.com
19. (2008) Flexible Work: Rhetoric and Reality A White Paper Prepared for Citrix by the Work Design Collaborative
20. (2010) "The Home Office, Starbucks and Flexible Work: It's A Reality," Small Business Technology
21. (2011) "Improving Work-Life Fit in Hourly Jobs," the UC Hastings College of Law
22. (2011) "Improving Work-Life Fit in Hourly Jobs," UC Hastings College of Law
23. (2009) Microsoft Corporation
24. (2007) Expedite Group named one of the Best Places to Work in the Triangle, Morrisville, North Carolina
25. (2007 N. Spinks and C. Moore, "Special Focus on the Nursing Workforce," The Changing Workforce
26. (2008) "Flexible Working: Bouncing Back," Personnel Today
27. (2010) Flexible Work Solutions (FWS), Capital One, D&I Practices

Chapter 4

Flexible Work: Business Continuity and Disaster Planning

Business Continuity

Companies are discovering that preparing employees and managers to work from multiple locations can be a very effective approach to business continuity and sustainability. While it's impossible to predict what kind of business interruption any one company may experience, the fact is that every company is at risk for some kind of emergency situation. And, when it does occur, the companies that have given employees the tools to work from other locations will be ahead of the game. When those responsible for the organization's disaster plans work in partnership with HR and IT to support a variety of flexible work options, they can create an environment where workflow proceeds uninterrupted or can resume quickly during a crisis.

In Chapter 4, we will answer the following questions:

✔ Why should an organization connect flexible work and business continuity?

✔ What are the benefits of mobility preparedness?

✔ What are some of the challenges?

✔ What are some ways to include flexible work in business continuity plans?

Why Connect Flex and Business Continuity?

It is becomingly increasingly clear that more attention must be paid to business continuity and disaster planning in light of the natural and man-made disasters businesses continually face.

One in five U.S. businesses suffer a disaster that causes it to cease operations for a period of time. Further, 43 percent of companies that go through a disaster never open their doors again, while another 29 percent fail within the following two years, according to federal statistics.[1] These percentages do not even take into account lesser problems that can occur like flooding, snow storms or loss of electrical power, which may not put a company out of business but certainly can significantly minimize its level of productivity.

Many companies have some form of disaster plan, but too many of these plans tend to focus only on securing and preparing for alternate space to protect data and information. Imagine minimizing these extra costs simply by encouraging and supporting employees to work flexibly. Not only would the need to rent an alternate space be reduced, but so too would any downtime in employee productivity, since they would already be accustomed and equipped to work in alternate spaces.

> **Continuity Connect**
> Almost half of respondents to a recent Working Mother poll said that business continuity promotes flexible work.
> *Source: Working Mother Research Institute, 2010*

Fortunately, Capitol Hill is one place that is waking up to the importance of flexible work for business continuity, as well as the cost savings that go along with it. In September 2010, the Senate passed the Telework Improvements Act of 2010 (H.R. 1722), which provides agencies with 180 days to determine the eligibility of all employees to telework as well as to establish policies for eligible employees. After employees are deemed eligible, they must enter into a written telework arrangement with the agency. The bill also orders the Office of Personnel Management to expand telework training opportunities for employees and managers so that they are prepared to telework at least 20 percent of the hours they work each two-week period. H.R. 1722 also requires agencies to incorporate telework into their continuity-of-operations plans, allowing them to head off the effects of events such as the blizzards that struck the Washington, D.C., area in 2010.

The Benefits of Mobility Preparedness

Just as business continuity is driving the need for flexible work, mainstream mobility demand is also rising within organizations. Eighty-four percent of recently surveyed IT decision makers believe the need for mobility in their organization increased in 2010, with telework the leading driver.[2] In the next three years, public-sector IT decision makers expect telework to increase by 65 percent, while private-sector IT leaders forecast a 33-percent rise. "It is no longer a question of if, but when organizations will need to utilize their business continuity plans," says Nigel Ballard, director of federal marketing for Intel. "The reality is that IT has a false positive on plans and falls short on implementation. Organizations must assess current inventory and address shortfalls, before operations grind to a halt."

Cindy Auten, general manager of Telework Exchange, agrees. "The benefits of mobility are clear. Not preparing for a business continuity situation can hinder organizational performance," she says. "Plans must be in place, but organizations need to also focus on engaging management and ensuring employees are well-equipped to work remotely. The writing is on the wall. Failing to act would be reckless."

This level of urgency is perhaps best supported by the results of the recent 2009 Telework Exchange study, "Mobilizing Against Pandemic."[3] Based on a survey of 301 public- and private-sector IT decision makers, it found that 81 percent of government and business IT decision makers have written business continuity plans. However, the study also found a sense of inflated confidence, since IT professionals from both the public and private sectors report implementation challenges and the lack of assurance that employees could work remotely during an emergency.

With each fall season come new warnings about the serious threat posed by the H1N1 ("swine flu") virus. It is more than likely that employers can count on plenty of workers calling in sick when the flu begins to make the rounds.[4] One strategy in planning for this possibility is looking at alternative work options to ensure continuity in the event of an outbreak. Having employees work remotely makes much more sense than risking the rampant spread of a virus that could quickly level an office. With this in mind, it is quite possible that organizations that have been slow to embrace — or have outright resisted — flexible work arrangements in the past may find themselves, by necessity, finally taking the leap.

There seems to be marked evolution and constant movement where workforce flexibility is concerned, which is one of the reasons i4cp, a consultancy focusing on workplace productivity, has tracked the issue closely. For a long time, flexible work options were viewed as a softer work-life balance issue. In some areas, there has been an emphasis on flexibility as an employee perk and not necessarily as a management tool to get work done efficiently under a variety of circumstances brought on by external events. But as each new emergency or disaster occurs, more companies recognize that they can address at least some of these challenges.

While pandemics can be far-reaching and result in lost productivity, it is not the only emergency that companies must prepare for. Incidents both large and small can force work to halt, and the consequences are wide-ranging:[5]
- In 2008, the Federal Emergency Management Agency reported 75 major declared disasters, not counting many smaller incidents that caused a halt to a vast variety of business operations.
- One in five U.S. businesses suffered a disaster that caused operations to cease for a period of time.
- Even when companies survive a disaster, they must still deal with losses in productivity and earnings, as well as damaged customer relationships.

The solution? Create experienced flexible teams to minimize lost productivity. When a business team is knowledgeable, equipped at working virtually and has managers that can supervise from a distance, it can continue operations, often with very little interruption. For example, according to a study by CDW-G, Telework Report, 2008, 71 percent of employees in companies with flexible work initiatives were able to continue working even when the office was closed due to a storm or disaster, versus 17 percent in companies where employees were not working flexibly.[6]

Daniel Pink, author of *Drive: the Surprising Truth About What Motivates Us*, says that today's home office typically has as much computing capability as whole companies had just 30 years ago. In fact, the concept of "home office" no longer refers to "headquarters", but rather, individual employees are working out of their homes. This capability is critical to organizations' ability to sustain business operations when the traditional home office is not accessible.

> **Continuity Connect**
> When Working Mother survey respondents were asked to rate the business reasons why Business Continuity supports flexible work, the highest response rate (39 percent) indicated that it "improves the business case."
>
> *Source: Working Mother Research Institute, 2010*

Understanding the Challenges

Although many businesses report they were negatively impacted by network disruptions in 2010, most still remain ill-equipped to handle future emergencies. According to a recent poll of 200 information technology decision makers at medium and large U.S. businesses by technology products provider CDW, 92 percent of respondents admitted that network disruptions had detrimental effects on their businesses in the past year. Of those disruptions, power loss ranked as the top cause of business disruptions, while hardware failures caused 29 percent of network outages, and a loss of telecom services to facilities had the third largest impact, at 21 percent.

The survey also looked at remote access plans for employees and found 53 percent of respondents said employees are instructed or given the option to work from home when a foreseeable network disruption approaches, such as a weather event. However, only one-third of businesses activate standby communications and network systems to support increased remote access when warned of such an event. Among the organizations polled by CDW, 44 percent of the workforce normally has telework options, on average, but only 39 percent of employees said they were actually able to telework during their most recent network outage.

Regardless of the cause of disruption, more than one-half of businesses, 57 percent, reported productivity losses as the top negative effect of their network disruptions, primarily due to reduced access to the network itself or to applications, data and communications systems, including:
- Problems connecting to their IT networks from other locations (51 percent)
- Problems connecting from inside their business locations (50 percent)
- Employees who could not access the necessary company resources to do their jobs (46 percent)

- Employees who had problems communicating with each other via internal phone systems and/or e-mail (29 percent)
- Networks that were slower than expected and could not support the increased traffic from remote locations (28 percent)

These disruptions did not occur without lessons learned, according to the report. Nearly 34 percent of the organizations polled said these events prompted them to improve disaster recovery capabilities by updating their business continuity/disaster recovery plans. However, one in five businesses (20 percent) said they still have no plans for immediate change.

> ### Continuity Connect
> When work-life practitioners were asked which items would support business continuity to increase the effectiveness of flexible work, the highest response (almost 30 percent) was "better communication."
>
> *Source: Working Mother Research Institute, 2010*

Making It Real

While flexible work clearly needs to be positioned as part of an effective preparedness plan for organizational sustainability, organizational silos can still present a challenge. Those working on disaster plans may not typically consider the role employees play in preparedness, instead choosing to focus on protecting data and business processes. However, there is a new opportunity to improve financial performance and shareholder value through stronger business continuity plans; flexible work is key to fulfilling this promise. Dell, for one, has developed a business model which shows that for every 1,000 employees that telecommute, the company saves $4.2 million in replacement costs, healthcare costs and facilities costs, and leads to an additional $11 million in savings from productivity gains, reduced sick leave and enhanced business continuity programs.

Clearly, businesses can leave themselves exposed and vulnerable to business interruptions if they don't integrate flexible work into their disaster and business continuity plans. The ways in which businesses can avoid these losses are many, including: Leverage flexible work options to avoid disruptions; provide the technology for employees to work anywhere, any time; educate managers and employees to be prepared for the unexpected; and make business continuity a priority objective for your flexible work policies and practices.

At Cisco, Marilyn Nagel, chief diversity officer, and James Brooks, director of human resources, employee engagement, believe that while ideas for many business continuity programs may originate from human resources, other parts of the organization, including other business units, IT and facilities are instrumental in creating a truly flexible workplace — one that is critical to the success of a global organization and its ability to respond to the unexpected. That's because these teams roll out the technology that supports telecommuting and the collaboration of virtual teams. They also push for the transitions in the physical workplace environment, implementing designs (with shared work spaces and hot spots) that lead to more choice around where, how and when employees work.

Indeed, workplace flexibility is the sum total of a flexible leadership philosophy and all of the resulting policies, practices and behavior that enable an organization to adjust fluidly to whatever obstacles and opportunities are encountered. This makes flexible work a powerful tool that can be used in times of crisis, as well as in day-to-day operations. That's why telework initiatives that allow employees to work productively from home or other locations can serve as a key part of any business continuity plan.

A recent study by WorldatWork, a non-profit focused on human resources issues, and the Work Design Collaborative, a small "think and do" tank co-founded by Dr. Charles Grantham and headquartered in Prescott, Arizona, found that a much higher proportion of employers than expected already allow non-exempt workers to telework despite limitations like work-hour and safety requirements.[7] The caveat is that 44 percent of the 135 organizations polled had no formal processes in place for telework. And they are not alone; there are a large number of companies that have no plan specifically focused on flexible work options, particularly telework, as part of their business continuity plan for a broad range of employees, including hourly workers.

Creating an organization-wide committee that is responsible for developing these strategies and addressing these challenges can positively impact business continuity.

Competition, regulation and other predictable challenges make business tough enough. But what can really bring an organization to its knees are the unpredictable and highly selective floods, fires, terrorist attacks and the like that have the potential to cripple one business while leaving its competitors unscathed. The real issue is not simply an increasingly threatening external environment. Rather it is the combination of external threats and the potential fragility of some modern business systems. Both efficiency and customer focus — essentials in modern business — are highly dependent on the uninterrupted availability of computing and communications systems.

So what can be done? The obvious answer is to be prepared. Think about what can go wrong and how to implement flexible work options that can be incorporated into your response. As Gartner, a U.S. based firm that provides security consultation to businesses, observed in the October 2007 report on The Top 10 Risk and Security Audit Findings to Avoid by Paul E. Proctor, "Every enterprise should have a minimal plan in place to protect business operations in the event of reasonably anticipated threats." Maybe less obvious, but just as crucial, you will also need to adopt flexible work practices. This is not just because employees increasingly expect them, but because they make your business much more resilient to disruptive events, large and small. The key concept here is flexibility. As any wrestler will tell you, if you tense your muscles and lock your joints, you're much easier to push over than if you adopt a more flexible posture. It is the same in business: If your business systems require people to be in specific places to do specific things, then they won't be able to function when those places are unavailable or inaccessible. The good news is that, just as information and communications technology is often credited with the death of distance, so too can it end the primacy of place — the crucial impediment to flexible work.

The toolkit of flexible work technologies includes three basic components: secure remote access to company systems so that staff can access files; access to office phone lines, so that staff can continue to receive calls; and conferencing, so that people can continue to meet and stay connected.

Necessary Changes

It is important to note that, contrary to popular myth, accessing corporate networks from outside the office doesn't necessarily mean an increased threat to key systems and data.[8] According to Bharat Thakrar, head of business continuity, BT Global Services, as long as users are properly authenticated and encryption is used to prevent eavesdropping, security can remain strong. Well-established networking protocols with the ability to address both requirements are readily available, and can turn a host of locations — homes, hotels, temporary offices — into secure work places.

But the IT systems and the networks that connect these locations must themselves be resilient. If the applications and databases employees need exist only on computers in buildings affected by the same problems that have forced employees to seek other places to work, the option to connect remotely will be very limited. "To counteract this," says Thakrar, "businesses need to consider outsourcing the operation of networks and data centers, which could also serve to build in much greater levels of resilience."

A similar strategy applies to maintaining access to phone services, with IP telephony the most flexible and resilient solution. The big difference between IP telephony and regular land-line telephone service is that with IP services telephone conversations are bundled into packets and shipped across the internet much like packets of data. The bundling is done by a computer equipped with a microphone, speakers and the necessary software, or by IP phones, which carry the same functions in a handset resembling a conventional phone.

The significance of IP telephony for flexible work is that it eliminates the fixed relationship between a line and a phone number, thus enabling users to make any phone their own simply by logging in, which can be done from any location that offers an IP connection to the corporate network. If, for example, a fire closes a head office, IP telephony can allow a company to stay in business by having teleworking employees make and receive calls as if they were at their desks in the office.

It is also important that firms ensure they have addressed both the technical and human factors involved in security, since some flexible workers may carry valuable corporate data with them. This data needs to be protected against theft or loss, and to that end, staffers must be taught to understand what they need to do to protect their business and its assets, including power-up password checking, encryption measures, and the ability to remotely de-activate lost devices when necessary. Flexible working is not just good for business as usual, but also an excellent form of disaster insurance.

Conclusion

It is no longer sufficient for organizations to just focus on data and information security in case of a business interruption. While most companies realize that the unexpected might happen, not all are aware that ensuring that employees can continue to function successfully during a crisis is mission-critical to the success of the enterprise. When employees and their managers are prepared to work and manage work remotely, they are prepared for the unexpected. The fact that telework works for employees and the organization in terms of productivity as well as a number of other measures has been well documented. Traditionally, flexible work has been seen as an HR initiative. What's needed now is for other stakeholders — IT and business continuity in particular — to recognize the value of telework and other flexible work options as a significant resource in getting their job done. By partnering with HR and others, business continuity leaders can create effective plans to deal with a broad range of unexpected events in ways that meet business, as well as employee, needs.

WORKSHEET
Business Continuity Strategy

WorldatWork suggests the following steps when planning a business continuity strategy in *Exploring Telework as a Business Continuity Strategy: A Guide to Getting Started.*[9]

Lay the groundwork. Establish goals for a cross-functional business continuity planning team.

Analyze risks. Investigate risk factors and identify how telework can help your organization mitigate risk. Remember that loss of employee access to the workplace is a major risk for most businesses.

Identify key resources. Review your work-life support services, HR policy, employee assistance programs and childcare support. All work-life systems and services should be updated and communicated as part of the safety net available to employees. When it comes to HR policies, it is imperative to check in to see how well your company is positioned. You might think about more lenient sick leave and time-off policies; or about increasing the threshold of absent days, or pool sick, vacation and personal days into a PTO program. You will also need to consider whether absence over a PTO allowance is covered by short-term disability or salary continuation benefits.

Other important issues to consider include:

1. How and under what circumstances will employees be paid during an office shutdown?

2. What about employees who have children sent home from schools that close?

3. Will PTO be required for those who choose to not work because of personal comfort or safety reasons, or those who are unable to work due to self or family illness?

4. Do you have any employees not currently on direct deposit who still receive a paper paycheck? What will you do with them during a flu epidemic? (If nobody's allowed to come to an office for a period of time, you might not want people touching pieces of paper. If you have a perfect attendance award incentive program, this might be the time to revise and communicate what your goals are.)

5. Are your health insurance policies sufficient? Will policies stay in place during periods of no or reduced salary payment? (Remember that a self-funded short-term disability plan can be amended.)

6. Do you need to revisit some or all of your disciplinary processes and consider using flexible work arrangements proactively for employees considered vulnerable? (In the case of a flu outbreak, for example, that might include pregnant women, people with particular kinds of illnesses and older employees.)

7. What about your travel policies?

Consider the cost of implementing telework. Be quick to point out that while the initial cost of setting up teleworkers might be high, it will save the company money over time.

Develop procedures that show how you'll use telework in your business continuity program. Encourage people to make a personal emergency backup plan including a home office backup kit.

Sell the plan to leadership and staff. Consider revising your current policies (with the support of executive leadership).

Test and maintain plans and procedures. Don't leave things to chance. Conduct practice drills to test plan components and update plans to stay current.

REFERENCES: CHAPTER 4

1. (2009) FEMA, retrieved from http://www.fema.gov/news/disaster_totals_annual.fema
2. (2009) M. Cox, "Middle Managers Primary Obstacle to Greater Workforce Mobility", http://www.echannelline.com/usa/story.cfm?item=25259
3. (2009) "Mobilizing Against Pandemic," Telework Exchange.
4. (2009) L. Lykins, "Trendwatcher: Fighting the Flu (and Other Challenges) Flexibly", *HR World* magazine.
5. (2009) "Federal Assistance From Seven Disaster Declarations Tops $180 Million", FEMA.
6. (2009) S. Burid, "Flexible Work: In Whose Best Interest? A Business Case Analysis", FlexPaths.
7. (2009) "Business Continuity Planning: A Guide for Total Rewards and HR Professionals", World at Work.
8. (2005) "Exploring Telework as a Business Continuity Strategy: A Guide to Getting Started", ITAC.
9. (2009) B. Thakrar, "Flexible Working and Business Continuity", Continuity Central.

Chapter 5: Flexible Work and Facilities Planning

Facilities

There was a time when facilities managers in organizations were mainly charged with finding new space to expand operations. Today, that role is being reversed as facilities managers are often asked to find ways to reduce or eliminate office space in an effort to save costs. In some cases, space is eliminated and employees are told they must work from home, whether or not they want to — or are prepared to. In such situations, companies frequently find that what they save on real estate costs they lose on productivity and retention. This is due to the fact that employees have not been given the support they need to work effectively from a remote location, while managers are not given the help they need to successfully manage a virtual team.

Many companies now realize that only by combining facility objectives and good people management with a systematic approach to flexible work can they create the greatest savings for the organization. In a time when work is often conducted from homes, park benches, café couches and beachfront lounges, the role of the facilities manager has changed. The 24/7/365 work environment enabled by smartphones, laptops and computer tablets creates enormous challenges for facility and real estate managers. How they accommodate the need to reduce office space to save money along with the need for employees to be most productive will significantly impact their organizations, as well as employees and managers.

In Chapter 5, we will explore the following questions:

✔ Why has flexible work become part of facilities planning?

✔ What are some of the challenges of connecting flexible work options with facilities planning?

✔ What are the benefits of connecting facilities planning with flexible work?

✔ What are some ways organizations are connecting facilities planning and flexible work?

The Connection Between Flexible Work and Facilities Planning

Given recent economic challenges, the movement to reduce office space has increased dramatically, resulting in a renewed interest in flexible work options, including telework (working from home or a remote location all or some of the time) and hoteling (featuring common space in an office that is shared by a number of employees).

Based upon the latest American Community Survey, just over 2 percent of the U.S. employee workforce (2.8 million people, not including the self-employed or unpaid volunteers) considers home their primary place of work.[1] This shift is not simply about more people working from home, however. Today many, if not most, jobs can be done from anywhere at any time. Still, while the U.S. Environmental Protection Agency reports that 40 percent of jobs can be done virtually, only 5 percent are. This represents a huge opportunity for businesses to reduce current and future office space costs by creating a more flexible work environment that encourages and supports flextime, telework and other initiatives that impact the amount of time employees spend in the office. According to Daniel Pink, author of *Drive: The Surprising Truth about What Motivates Us*, the changes in office space design can actually be leveraged to facilitate more collaborative work because they provide more opportunities for employees to interact when they are actually in the office.[2]

> ### *Facilities Connect*
> Nearly one third of work-life professionals surveyed indicated that their facilities department impacts the implementation of flexible work initiatives and helps promote flexible work initiatives.
>
> *Source: Working Mother Research Institute, 2010*

> ### *Facilities Connect*
> The biggest share of respondents (25 percent) reported that the facilities department and flexible work have only been connected for three to five years at their organizations.
>
> *Source: Working Mother Research Institute, 2010*

Challenges of Connecting Flexible Work and Facilities Planning

While it is true that most large companies have had flexible work policies in place for nearly a decade, the truth is that many employees are often reluctant to use them for fear of being viewed as less committed or potentially dispensable, due to an "out of sight, out of mind" mentality. In light of today's greater awareness of the potential savings of telework and other flexible work options, flexibility is starting to be seen as less of an accommodation for an individual and more of a compelling business driver that can result in significant immediate and longer-term cost savings.

Facilities

John Anderson, president and CEO of PeopleCube, a global leader in integrated workspace and energy management solutions, says that when it comes to implementing flexible work initiatives, Facilities must serve many masters, including HR, Finance, IT and Procurement. Given that personnel is the No. 1 cost to most organizations, followed closely by real estate and energy, it is vital that the cost benefit of efficient asset utilization is highlighted when building the case internally for a flexible work initiative. By implementing tools that can not only help manage the utilization of space and energy when the mobile worker is in the office but can also measure the performance of the initiative based on productivity and collaboration levels, facilities and other stakeholders will have the ability to accurately represent the ROI of the flexibility initiative and the systems in place to support it.

As facilities managers tackle the challenge of reducing office space, they can move flexibility to the top of an organization's agenda by presenting it as a business imperative and, by doing so, can potentially change the way employees are managed, how virtual teams operate, and the way work is done. This is not the typical role for facilities and real estate leaders. But simply reducing physical space will not be sufficient to meet the organization's business goals; the "people" part of the equation needs to be taken into consideration.

Telework has been particularly difficult for many managers and executives to accept because many still equate face time with productivity. When managers can't see employees, they assume they're not working at all. With a focus on the reduction of office space, managers and executives are becoming more accepting of flexible work options.

These changes require a new partnership between facilities managers and those in the organization focused on talent and performance management. There is also an increased need to help managers and employees figure out how to effectively work in this new normal. Facilities managers must carefully analyze the way employees work and what their needs are in terms of where the work is done. Billie Williamson, partner and Americas Inclusiveness Officer at Ernst & Young, finds, for example, that for a professional services firm where many associates spend all or some of their time at clients' offices, the calculation for space requirements can be a challenge. Similarly, some organizations report that taking a simple walk-through to see when offices and cubbies are occupied shows that as many as 30 percent are empty at any given time. The trick is to make sure the redesigned space accommodates those who need to be there 100 percent of the time, while ensuring that less-frequent workers have access to workspace and technology support, as well as the privacy they need to do their jobs most effectively. The General Services Administration estimates a company could save an average of $5,000 per remote worker per year (2009, Star Workforce Solutions).

> **Facilities Connect**
> Nearly four out of 10 respondents indicated that facilities supports flexible work by easing its implementation and improving its business case within their organizations.
> *Source: Working Mother Research Institute, 2010*

The challenge for the business enterprise lies in creating the appropriate infrastructure — technology, security, policies, behavioral protocols, performance management — to best support the distributed workforce in how, where and when they perform their jobs. It may seem a daunting task, but it is well worth the effort. With a strong business framework for virtual work, a company can benefit from both cost savings and the maximum level of employee productivity.[3]

The Stegmeier Consulting Group, a globally recognized leader in workplace change management, has explored the resistance to workplace change initiatives that can contribute to a disappointing return on investment in the new workplace solution. This research was originally initiated in 1996 after the organization witnessed numerous employers' struggles to drive behavioral change through physical workplace transformation. In learning about the frustration of senior business leaders who were attempting to overcome workforce resistance, Stegmeier decided to learn what barriers existed that were not being addressed by the enterprise. Its study eventually involved 140 organizations in 24 diverse industries over the course of 10 years, many of whom had intended to create environments that would improve productivity, enable flexibility, foster teamwork, inspire collaboration and produce more innovative outcomes. Every one of them expected better business results.

A key result of the research was the discovery of 15 interdependent tangible and intangible factors that impact behavior in the workplace, enable or hinder the success of the workplace strategy and, ultimately, steer the achievement of overall corporate goals no matter what the size of the company. These factors include:

1. vision and mission
2. core values
3. culture
4. image
5. leadership behavior
6. compensation
7. rewards and consequences
8. technology
9. knowledge management
10. organizational structure
11. autonomy and authority
12. business processes
13. communications
14. performance management
15. physical and virtual workplace

The data was specifically compiled on best practices in leading workplace change gathered from a broad range of enterprises throughout North America and Western Europe, with particular attention on winners of *Fortune* Magazine's "Best Companies to Work for in America" and the Great Places to Work® Institute's "Best Small and Best Medium Companies to Work for in America." By applying new knowledge of these factors when implementing workplace strategies, facilities managers can contribute to the attainment of the organization's desired results in behavioral change as well as ROI in the physical work environment.

One of the first steps in strengthening the business case for virtual work is anticipating the case the organization may have against workforce mobility and developing a plan for the enterprise to overcome the issues and concerns of six stakeholder groups:
1. organizational leaders
2. managers and supervisors
3. IT professionals
4. facilities professionals
5. individual contributors eligible to work remotely
6. individual contributors not eligible for remote work initiatives

Debbie Phillips, VP of client relations at WFD Consulting, for one, finds that the biggest cost opportunity is found through bringing in other stakeholders such as those focused on IT and HR to help support and manage the changes that take place when employees work from another location.

Benefits of Connecting Facilities and Flexible Work

The Future of Work Initiative, a research program focused on enhancing both individual and organizational productivity while reducing the cost of workforce support, provides information to senior HR, IT, and Facilities/Real Estate leaders and other professionals who seek new solutions to the challenges of attracting, retaining, and leveraging knowledge workers. At major progressive companies like HP, Agilent and Accenture, facilities managers encourage significant numbers of employees to become mobile workers, thereby allowing companies to redesign space to increase its versatility. Following the organization's decade-long research program focused on new workplaces, it has found extraordinary growth in the use of "third places" by knowledge workers. (A third place is defined as a place other than a central corporate facility or an individual home office).[4]

Recent studies by the International Facilities Management Association (IFMA) show that the cost of providing a workspace to an employee ranges from $8,000 to $14,000 per year. If the average utilization for each space is 50 percent, then a company wastes $4,000 to $7,000 per year for each workspace. If you multiply that total by the number of workspaces, potential savings reach millions or tens of millions of dollars just by implementing an effective remote work initiative and effectively eliminating or reducing the need for some office space.[5]

A senior real estate executive for the Government Services Administration, which manages 350 million square feet throughout the United States, noted that federal agencies have little money in their budgets to spend on real estate; funds are currently being diverted to serving the mission of each agency. With no money to house additional people, agencies must leverage flexible work options and talent management planning in order to serve their mission. It's a solution currently

Facilities

being considered in the commercial sector as well, where the need for real estate stewardship has reached the executive level in many organizations.[6]

Businesses that provide flexible work options also benefit from a reduced carbon footprint as well as improved performance. Danielle Hartmann, director of corporate partnerships, Boston College Center for Work & Family, points out, for example, that companies are realizing that they can use flexible work options not only to minimize their footprint, but also to meet employee needs — thus, creating a significant win/win opportunity. They can use hoteling and collaborative huddle space to support employees who have more autonomy over where they work. And Nora Spinks, president and founder, Work-Life Harmony, a consultancy that helps individuals achieve balance in their home and work lives, points out that the benefits of real estate reduction go beyond savings of square footage. The cost of utilities can also be reduced when more flexible workspace is being designed.

Here are some specific examples of how space reductions have helped companies shrink costs while enhancing productivity.[7]:
- At IBM, 40 percent of its global workforce does not keep a dedicated office. IBM, which started its mobile workforce program in the mid-1990s, saves an estimated $100 million a year in facilities costs alone.
- Sun Microsystems reduced its excess facilities capacity after realizing that at any given time 40 percent of its employees were not at their desks. By redesigning office space, Sun increased its agility and customer satisfaction while saving $69 million in 2005. In addition, it has been able to decrease IT expenditures by $24 million annually.
- Ernst & Young used a policy of encouraging virtual work to eliminate 1 million of its total 7 million square feet in rent nationwide, offering a dedicated desk only to employees who were in the office more than half of the working day.
- Accenture maintains a hotel policy for all consultants, resulting in a savings of $3,400 per year per participant. By saving 25,000 seats, it has now attained a 4:1 ratio of workers to workplaces.
- Best Buy introduced Results-Only Work Environment (ROWE) in 2003, which eliminated any requirement to be physically in the office, as well as doing away with a set number of work hours. Employee performance was instead based upon output. This program resulted in a productivity increase of 35 percent for those participating in ROWE. By the end of 2007, all 4,000 staffers were on ROWE.

At Citi, Karyn Likerman, head of Employee Networks and Flexwork, notes that the company's real estate initiative started as a work-life opportunity that was designed to address employee needs to work from other locations some or all of the time. The goal was to maximize various space options like hoteling without impinging on employees needs, but the company also found that the creation of more flexible space uses also allowed the workforce to grow without requiring it to acquire more space.

American Express has also taken an aggressive approach to reducing real estate, in part to align with the changing nature of work and the workforce. The company implemented an innovative approach called BlueWork that identifies various ways employees can work — Home, Roam, Hub, Club — and provides all the online tools and IT resources to support the various choices. This process, says Kerrie Peraino, VP of HR and chief diversity officer, required a cultural shift in terms of mindset to make sure that real estate, technology and HR were in lockstep, but also required that employees understand that the choice was about how best to get the job done.

FLEX IN-DEPTH: British Telecom
Making Next-Generation Flexibility Work

Flexible working is clearly increasing since the British government gave all parents with children ages 16 and under the right to request it. The principles of flexible work are now so much a part of commonly drawn-on ideas that British Telecom is no longer interested in operating under the term's banner since, to them, flexible work is first-generation thinking. BT has moved on to the next generation of management thinking, which it calls agile working.

BT's agile working initiative is based on the idea that the old concept of the office no longer exists; globalization and the inflation of consumer demands have done away with it. Now stands agility, which is based on the premise that you will get the best out of people by freeing them, and that they will achieve most when they feel most in control of their work.

BT launched this new corporate culture with a massive data-collection exercise as an attempt to map the work activity of people working across 8,000 properties in 66 countries. Using the e-census system, which integrates data from IT and security systems, BT was able to plot property utilization against cost centers to create time-series information. On the foundation of this modeling work BT is revolutionizing its working practices. Currently, 80 percent of its workforce is already working agilely, and in the next six years the telecom behemoth is aiming to increase its people per workstation ratio from 1.1 to 1.6, a move that would see 23,000 workstations eliminated in the United Kingdom.

As a result, some workers have shown a 30 percent increase in productivity after they transitioned to flexible work methods. This is in part due to the fact that, on average, homeworkers devote 60 percent of the time they save commuting to and from work on work. They are also more likely to do out-of-hours work because it's that much easier to fit around other things.

But agile working isn't just about more work, it's also about better work. BT has used it as a "catalyst for change" by declaring war on hierarchy and territoriality. Staff work in large team zones (like property and HR) and each of these zones has desks made available for visitors from other teams. There are also spaces (the World Zone) in which anyone can book space.

Further, the firm has reduced its carbon footprint by 60 percent between 1996 and 2006, and it has set itself a target of 80 percent by 2015. Already, remote conferencing has helped BT to reduce its carbon footprint by 97,000 tons. The firm is also striving to curb the amount of waste that it puts into landfills. A waste segregation scheme has already been rolled out to 16 major office sites, and the business is aiming to reduce its waste output by 6 percent this year. Estimates suggest that if just 10 percent of EU workers adopted flexible work practices, the annual saving in carbon emissions would be 22.17 million tons.[8]

Facilities

Blue Cross Blue Shield of Massachusetts (BCBSMA) is another example of a company that has created a systematic approach to combining facility planning with flexible work options. The company's e-Working program allows associates to work seamlessly from home, electronically, full-time, five days a week, when it meets both the needs of the business and the needs of the associate. The program includes a step-by-step application process with the appropriate equipment needs (including hardware, software and peripheral equipment, as necessary) for each e-Working arrangement on a case-by-case basis, BCBSMA has established equipment standards for associates who are eligible for and work in a formal e-Working arrangement that include the following:

- One standard laptop with department software template
- One docking station to be installed in either the home office or the business site
- One monitor to be installed in either the home office or the business site
- Standard Virtual Private Network (VPN) set-up
- Access to the Internet is required through an internet service provider (cable/broadband)
- Cable lock
- Keyboard
- Mouse
- Printer/Shredder (designated by business)

Cardinal Health created hoteling space for a group of employees as part of its effort to vacate a building. Employees use a web portal to submit requests for participation in telework initiatives. By entering the requested information, the employee can determine if he or she can work from home and how frequently they need hoteling space.

Essentially, the benefits of flexible work successfully reduce costs, while also enhancing performance. Here are some of the potential benefits realized from flexible work initiatives:

Reduce Costs[9]

$ Operate more productively with fewer resources.
$ Analyze workspace utilization and refine workplace strategy based on actual usage.
$ Establish business continuity strategy.
$ Offer low-cost employee perks to offset reduction in company-paid healthcare coverage.
$ Reduce energy consumption through corporate-wide green initiative.
$ Enhance security and control to prevent costly compromise of data.
$ Implement productivity-enhancing technology and provide 24/7 support without increasing IT staff.
$ Eliminate upfront costs of purchasing hardware and installing software by adopting browser-based solutions.

Improve Performance

↗ Increase productivity through teamwork and collaboration despite the location.
↗ Improve employee morale.
↗ Provide staff more choices and control to manage work-life issues.
↗ Create a workplace to attract, inspire and retain talent.
↗ Accommodate the needs of a multigenerational workforce.

↗ Enhance employee access to company information where and when they need it.
↗ Challenge managers and supervisors to focus on results, as opposed to the tasks of their direct reports.
↗ Reinforce the corporate values of trust, teamwork and customer centricity.

Critical Facility and Flexible Working Success Factors

Even though facilities managers may be the catalyst to implementing flexible work, successful integration and implementation requires a combination of players — facilities, HR, and corporate leaders — working together to provide the critical technology, communications equipment, tech support and training for dispersed workers to function without constant intervention from a manager. But the importance of consolidating space, creating more flexible shared space, and developing space that works for stable, mobile and super-mobile employees should not be underestimated.

Each company and employee's functional requirements are different, and the decision for an organization to formalize a flexible work program that supports its facility goals is not necessarily an easy one. For many business leaders, the most difficult question is whether to grant employees the autonomy to control where and when they do their work. The true complexity surrounds gaining consensus on often-conflicting objectives, developing the appropriate policies, determining the best-in-class technologies, establishing a screening process to select teleworkers and ensuring performance management systems will support the mobile workforce.

> **Facilities Connect**
> The majority of respondents said that they believe that adding to the facilities budget, more than any other item, would have the biggest impact on the effectiveness of flexible work within their organizations.
>
> *Source: Working Mother Research Institute, 2010*

One major consideration in reducing office space and creating remote workers is determining where the work will take place. If employees don't have a home environment that is conducive to their work — that is appropriately professional and private — this must be addressed proactively. Sending employees home to work without first determining their work environment and providing some form of safety assessment can cause difficulties down the road. The following is a sample checklist for employees working from home:

SAMPLE: Home Office Safety Self-Assessment Checklist

Employee _____ Date _____

OPTIONAL STATEMENT TO BE APPROVED BY COMPANY'S LEGAL GROUP:
Each employee working in a telecommuting arrangement from his/her home under the provisions of the (Your Organization here) *Guide to Workplace Flexibility* must perform an initial and annual review of the home office work environment. Note: It is the sole responsibility of that employee to provide and maintain the safety of the work environment.

Please promptly return the completed form to your manager.

Please Mark 'X' If Corrective Actions Are Needed, And Then Assure That Corrections Are Made

ERGONOMICS EVALUATION

Computer Workstation:
- ❏ Workspace Sufficient
- ❏ Monitor at Eye Height
- ❏ Monitor Alignment Straight
- ❏ Document Holder Used
- ❏ Screen Glare Minimized
- ❏ Keyboard Level & Straight
- ❏ Wrist in Neutral Position
- ❏ Arm Reach <16 inches
- ❏ Neutral Arm Position

Seating:
- ❏ Chair at Comfortable Height
- ❏ Feet on Floor or Footrest
- ❏ Seat Pan Size Comfortable
- ❏ Lumbar Back Supported

Life Safety:
- ❏ Exit Access Unrestricted
- ❏ ABC Fire Extinguisher

Electrical:
- ❏ Circuit Breakers or Fuses
- ❏ Grounded Receptacles
- ❏ Surge Protectors for Computer
- ❏ Wires Safely Secured

Housekeeping:
- ❏ No Trip & Fall Hazards
- ❏ Materials Safely Stored

Notes:

_____

_____

Real estate and facilities managers need to be aware of how flexible teams can be successfully supervised. If done well, shifting to a flexible way of working can force teams to develop better advance planning initiatives, set clearer expectations, and communicate more deliberately. Managers will therefore require retraining, incentives and models to change their methods; this can effectively be done by providing employees, managers and teams with appropriate on- and offline resources to help them work flexibly. They will also need to maximize online capabilities to complement real time and in-person connections (high-tech and high-touch), as well as streamline and create efficiencies, while retaining critical human relationships.

Further, it is important for management to establish new, objective ways to evaluate how well employees and teams are performing. This approach will reduce objections from managers who express concern about whether employees are actually working. This change can be accomplished by shifting the focus of decision-making from line supervisors and managers to employees/teams. By charging the teams with figuring out how to reconfigure their work, and evaluating which work is unproductive and ways to streamline it, employees will gain more control over how best to do their jobs.

Conclusion

The physical environment needs to be planned in such a way that it aligns with the way work is done today. As part of that process, the need for some space will be eliminated or significantly modified. However, these are just the physical changes. There are cultural changes that need to take place as well for the new physical plans to be most successful. At its heart, flexible work reflects the shift from the standardized, synchronized, centralized way of managing production — where things are done at the same time, in the same place and in the same way — to a more modern, organic approach. In organic environments, uniqueness and self-regulation, rather than control and sameness, are the goal. Physical environments become more open, fluid and creative. To be successful, facility and real estate managers need to be willing to experiment with these new environments, which will drive employee creativity and engagement. It is also important that managers focus on a more dispersed, and employee driven, collaborative work environment.[10]

By broadening the conversation, employees and managers can be brought into the discussion, enabling them to work together to determine innovative ways to convey essential information across dispersed teams and how to sustain the critical knowledge sharing that occurs when people are in the same room. By rethinking outdated assumptions about work space and face time, and by considering which types of spaces work best for what types of work, managers can make the best determination of how to hold employees responsible to meet goals.

As the versatility of flexible workplaces continues to emerge, facility managers now have a unique opportunity to expand their professional contribution beyond simply managing facility space. By partnering with HR and others directly involved in establishing policy and supporting flexible work practices, they can advise their companies on how to create a more productive, environmentally responsible and successful work environment.

TIP SHEET
Flexible Work and Facilities Planning

- ❏ Use a variety of approaches to determine the actual space utilization and needs of the organization, including documenting when offices/desks are actually used.
- ❏ When making the business case to reduce physical space, be sure to include a solid list of why employees can increase their effectiveness when working remotely.
- ❏ When a telework program is implemented, use the opportunity to determine if the company can reduce the size of its individual workspaces and reallocate real estate to increase the number of meeting rooms and collaborative team spaces.
- ❏ Anticipate what would happen if all of the teleworkers showed up at the office on a given day.
- ❏ Allow for some "hoteling" space where employees can occasionally check in to an office or workspace.
- ❏ Create a reservation system for hoteling.
- ❏ Partner with HR to determine the guidelines for teleworking.
- ❏ Create a checklist that specifies what type of furniture and equipment is best suited for a home office.
- ❏ Work with IT to decide how much and what kind of technology the company will provide a teleworker (computer, phone line, high-speed Internet service). Stipulate what employees must supply themselves.
- ❏ Set up a system for employees to obtain the appropriate technology and equipment based on their job and telework arrangement.
- ❏ Consider how the organization will sustain its corporate culture as people spend more and more time outside of the physical office.
- ❏ As business and/or personal needs change, make sure the facility design is flexible and can adapt accordingly.
- ❏ Develop a people plan that parallels the facility redesign so that people involved (managers, flex workers, traditional workers, etc.) are all prepared to be successful working in the new environment.
- ❏ Use technology systems to educate stakeholders across the enterprise about how to make the transition to a more flexible work environment and as a just-in-time learning platform so they can continually improve their skills.

REFERENCES: CHAPTER 5

1. (2010) K. Lister, Telework Research Network.
2. (2009) D. Pink, *Drive: The Surprising Truth about What Motivates Us*, Riverhead Books.
3. (2010) "The Business Case for Web Commuting: How to Reduce Workplace Costs and Increase Workforce Performance," a white paper by Stegmeier Consulting Group.
4. (2010) "The Future of Work Workforce Survey," The Work Design Collaborative.
5. (2010) IFMA, www.ifma.org/worldfmday/index.cfm
6. (2008) "Network of Space" and "Make Your Workplace as Agile as Your Workforce," AgilQuest Corporation
7. (2010) S. Burud, Ph.D., "Working Away from the Office: Implications for the Facilities Manager," *Facilities Management Journal*.
8. (2010) A. McNestrie, "British Telecom moves one step beyond Flexible Working — to Agile Working Test of Agility."
9. Stegneier Consulting Group.
10. S. Burud & M. Tumolo, *Leveraging the New Human Capital* (Davies-Black Publishers), 2004

Chapter 6: The Connection Between Employee Wellness and Flexible Work

Health and Wellness

When it comes to employees' health and wellness, common sense is not always common practice. On a personal level, we know that when we have more control over our work and our life, both benefit. And, as a result, we feel better, less stressed, more rested and focused. It is what we call work-life effectiveness. There is no such thing as balance. Both work and life circumstances are constantly changing due to internal and external influences, and, therefore, it is imperative that employees have the flexibility they need to manage these changes most effectively. The ability to have control over how, when, where and how much work is done has been shown to positively impact employee health outcomes. The challenge is for health/wellness professionals to recognize that fact and to create ways to leverage flexible work options for the good of employees, as well as the organization.

In Chapter 6, we will explore the following questions:

✔ What does research say about the connection between health/wellness and access to flexible work?

✔ Why is it critical to address wellness issues at this time?

✔ What are the health/wellness benefits of flexible work?

✔ What is the role of health/wellness professionals?

✔ What are some companies doing to connect flexible work with their health/wellness initiatives?

Why Connect Flex and Health/Wellness?

When employees have flexibility in how, when and where they work, they ultimately manage their professional and personal responsibilities more effectively. The bonus: their health improves as well. When work schedules align with their energy levels and personal needs, employees' stress is minimized. Until recently, however, there has been very little research to back up this theory.

We now know that employees with high levels of conflict between their work and personal lives are likely to be less committed and engaged at work, have higher levels of job stress and strain, absenteeism, drug use, depression and burnout, and report greater use of health care resources[1]. In contrast, employees with supportive managers experience higher job satisfaction and greater commitment to the organization, lower levels of overload and job stress, fatigue, depression, poor health, and absenteeism, and greater intent to remain with the organization.

> **Health Connect**
> Almost two-thirds of respondents to a survey of work-life practitioners indicated that improving employee health was "very" or "extremely" important to their company's support of flexible work.
> *Source: Working Mother Research Institute, 2010*

Experiencing a supportive and flexible workplace may even add years to an employee's life. A nationwide study found that employers' work-life policies directly impact workers' risk of cardiovascular disease, the amount of sleep they have each night, their families' well-being, and their personal job satisfaction. For example, workers are twice as likely to develop cardiovascular disease if they have a boss who shows little willingness to accommodate their family needs[2]. When employees can modify their work schedules and/or work location, research shows that they tend to exercise more, sleep more, and spend more time with friends and family — all of which results in better health. According to Joe Grzywacz, associate professor at Wake Forest University School of Medicine, flexibility directly enables and complements health/wellness activities in terms of 1) reducing exposure to stress from work-life conflict and 2) encouraging positive lifestyle benefits.

> **Health Connect**
> More than 50 percent of respondents indicated that their health & wellness initiative promotes the use of flexible work.
> *Source: Working Mother Research Institute, 2010*

Among Grzywacz's findings:
- Enabling flexible work reduces illness-related absenteeism and increases job commitment and performance.[3]
- Employees whose employers offer more flexibility have lower work-related stress outcomes.

- Psychosocial factors such as stress and life/job satisfaction have an equal or greater impact on presenteeism (lost productivity that occurs when employees come to work but perform below par) than physical health factors.
- The best health outcomes result from specific types of flexible work options, which include remote work and part-time schedules.[4]

The Benefits of Flex as a Component of Health/Wellness

An article entitled "Implications of Worklife Balance and Mental Health" (from Canadian-based news service CNW), documented responses to a survey clearly showing that Canadian workers desire a more holistic approach to work-life effectiveness. Most organizations recognize the importance of protecting their assets, including employees, which are among an employer's most crucial assets. Providing more options for flexible work is certainly one way to support and protect this important asset.

In the 2006 Canadian survey, "Under Pressure: Implications of Worklife Balance and Job Stress (Human Solutions)," employers across the country were asked: In the past 12 months, has your location/organization experienced an increase in difficulties in any of the following areas: recruitment, engagement, absenteeism, safety, morale, workload and work-life balance? The majority of the 600 employers surveyed rated workload and work-life as major workforce challenges. When asked to rate their supervisors on a number of criteria, a majority of employees gave supervisors the lowest rating for work-life support.

Specifically, 76 percent of respondents considered their supervisor or manager ineffective, or moderately effective, in helping employees achieve work-life balance. Indeed, workload awareness; creative, flexible or customized scheduling; and clear and supportive communications are all key components of creating a culture that encourages work-life balance. "The ability to create a workplace where good work-life balance is fostered is important to the long-term success of the organization," says Judith Plotkin, national director of business development at Human Solutions. "Our survey found that workers who agreed that they have a good balance between their work and personal or family life experience less stress than workers who lack this balance, regardless of the other factors in their lives or the type of work performed."

When rating changes in work-life, 62 percent of participating employees blamed their work for creating the imbalance, while just 27 percent said family or personal life made the balance harder to achieve.[5] A recent Families & Work Institute study, Overwork in America: When the Way We Work Becomes Too Much, found that overworked employees are more likely:[6]
- To have higher levels of stress. (Only 6 percent who experience low overwork levels are highly stressed compared with 36 percent of those who are highly overworked.)
- To have more symptoms of clinical depression. (Only 8 percent of those with low overwork levels have high levels of depressive symptoms compared with 21 percent of those who are highly overworked.)

Health and Wellness

- To report that their health is poor. (52 percent of employees experiencing high overwork levels report that their health is good versus 65 percent of those experiencing low overwork levels.)
- To neglect caring for themselves. (Only 41 percent of employees who experience high overwork levels say they are very successful in taking good care of themselves versus 68 percent of those experiencing low overwork levels.)

Why Wellness, Why Now?

For too long, according to Wake Forest's Joe Grzywacz, flexible work has been seen as a tool used by only one area of the organization, most often Human Resources. Instead, it needs to be viewed as a tool that supports overall management practices and is used consistently across different organizational functions in a way that highlights possible synergies.

> **Health Connect**
> Close to 60 percent of respondents said that flexible work's effect on health and wellness "impacts the company culture," and 41 percent indicated that it "improves the business case for flexible work."
> *Source: Working Mother Research Institute, 2010*

The important point is that flexible work is beneficial for workers and for workers' health. For instance, the World Health Organization has even identified night shifts as carcinogenic because of the impact these schedules have on employees' health. As a result of these and related factors, there is growing and substantial interest in the potential health implications of workplace flexibility from a variety of public and private organizations. The Employee Wellness Network, for example, cited the White House Forum on Workplace Flexibility's commitment to explore ways Americans can meet the demands of their jobs without sacrificing the needs of their families as one of the top 10 developments in employee wellness in 2010.

Ways to Help Employees Use Flex to Improve Their Health

Physical

- Think about what time of day employees are likely to exercise and adjust work schedules to allow for a regular workout schedule.
- Suggest ways employees can work fitness into their day. Encourage them to break up the work day with short walks. Just taking the stairs a few times during the day can make a difference.
- Consider offering yoga, meditation or other stress-reducing activities.
- What energizes one employee may stress out another; make individual plans.
- Pay attention to circadian rhythms. Some people work best late at night; others early in the morning.
- Does your employee's commute cause stress? Would adjusting employees' work hours to allow commuting during non-rush hour traffic help? Even working at home or a remote location a day or two a week can go a long way toward relieving stress.

- Overwork can cause stress. Make adjustments to the way work is organized and partner with team members to eliminate low-value work.
- Coordinate workload and flow with colleagues so that it is shared more equitably.
- Employees often complain that workplace interruptions create an inability to concentrate. Offer the option of working from home a few days a week, or when the need to concentrate on a particular assignment is crucial.
- Allow employees to compress work into fewer, longer days so that they have one weekday off to help them better focus on work while they are at work.
- Plan ahead with work projects so employees know what to expect. That alone will help them feel less stressed.
- Encourage employees to speak up for what they can handle in terms of overtime; ask them to be realistic in their assessment of how much work they can handle.
- Help employees eliminate unnecessary activities from work and personal life and prioritize; they cannot do everything.

Prevention
- Encourage employees to take time for regular medical check-ups and preventive care.
- Offer occasional flexibility so employees can take time off for doctor appointments for themselves and family members.
- Make sure employees take time to interact with friends and family, participate in community activities, relax, and rest.
- Encourage employees to take vacation time, and once on vacation, allow them to disconnect.

Understanding the Challenges

Advocates suggest that workplace flexibility contributes to better health in part because it helps workers better manage their work and family lives.[7] One of the biggest challenges to improving employees' health is the ability to connect 24/7. In the past, work was confined to the workplace. When employees left that place, they stopped working. This boundary no longer exists. Our management practices need to catch up with the dramatic changes technology has created for anywhere, anytime work, as well as address the issue of overwork, if we're going to truly impact employee health.

"We're killing ourselves with the way we're working today," says Kathie Lingle, executive director for the Alliance for Work Life Progress (AWLP). "For the sake of improved health outcomes, companies need to encourage — and perhaps, for the sake of employees' health, even impose — limits." While work may be 24/7, make sure it's not the same employees working 24/7, "which as we've seen, results in burnout and increased health problems."

Research has shown that flexibility clearly enables workers to maintain healthier lifestyles[8] in ways that represent a tremendous opportunity for organizations. By expanding employee access to flexibility, employers will experience a concrete approach to improving employee health. In 2009, The New America Foundation's Workforce and Family Program teamed up with the Congressional Mental Health Caucus, the American Psychological Association and Workplace

Health and Wellness

Flexibility 2010 to look at the interaction between work and health outcomes. The event, "Supporting a Healthier American Workplace: Workplace Flexibility and Mental Health and Wellness," explored the benefits of giving employees more control over when, where, and how long they work. Over time, the group found that employees with flexible work arrangements were less likely to experience a decline in their physical or mental health.[9] This is even more important to consider as the workforce ages and requires more time to attend to medical needs. AARP, for one, recommends flexible work as a key solution for both older workers and those who care for them (who tend to be working women).[10]

A review of recent global flexibility research by Durham University in England has also lent support to the importance of control over work and its positive impact on employee health. The review found that people who have some control over their work schedules may enjoy better physical and mental well-being than those in less flexible jobs. Further, and perhaps not surprising, in all of the studies included in the review, researchers found no evidence for negative effects of more flexible work schedules. "Given the absence of ill health effects associated with employee-controlled flexibility and the evidence of some positive improvements in some health outcomes," states researcher Clare Bambra, "more flexibility in work schedules has the potential to promote healthier workplaces and improve work practices."[11]

The review's authors sought to measure the effects on health of "flexible work" — particularly measures that provide employees with increased autonomy. They also evaluated other types of interventions, such as involuntary part-time employment and mandatory overtime, which may help employers meet business needs but can be a detriment to employee health. The Durham University study examined the health of employees in various ways. For example, one Finnish study found that both average systolic blood pressure levels and pulse rates dropped in airline maintenance workers who had more flexibility with shift work. Additionally, another Finnish study linked more flexibility over shifts of hospital midwives to lower mental strain and stress.

In the United States, a separate study that looked at whether men who were employed "inadequately" (i.e., they had involuntary part-time jobs) found that they were more depressed than were fully employed men, which speaks to the importance of employees being in control and satisfied with how much they work. Yet another U.S. study looked at flex time at a Midwest company where workers were allowed to set their own schedules as long as they were at work between 1:30 p.m. and 3:30 p.m.[12] Researchers could not find any negative effect on the physical or mental stress among the workers who were given this option. Ron Goetzel, director of Emory University's Institute for Health and Productivity Studies states that while there is relatively little research into flexible work schedules, the research that has occurred does suggest that "the more you feel in control over your work, over the schedule and the demands and timetable and so forth, the healthier you'll be."

Improving Employee Well-being

The key to improving employee wellness is giving workers access to the flexibility they need to most effectively manage their work and personal life. It is that simple. The challenge is also to change employee — and manager — perceptions about the impact working flexibly will have on their performance review and, ultimately, on their career prospects. In too many organizations employees are reluctant to request a flexible arrangement for fear they will be perceived as less than committed to the job. In addition, in a recent poll conducted by ComPsych Corporation, an employee assistance program provider, 77 percent of respondents reported going to work when they were sick for the following reasons: 33 percent "because my workload makes it too difficult to take off"; 26 percent "because it feels risky to take off in the current work environment"; and 18 percent "because I have to save my sick days for when my kids need me." [13]

While a number of organizations do have a long history of health/wellness initiatives — including GlaxoSmithKline, Johnson & Johnson and IBM — in many cases the focus continues to be to encourage employees to change their behaviors through a combination of carrots and sticks, including health-risk assessments, incentives to lose weight or eat healthier, smoking cessation classes, yoga and napping rooms. Yet healthcare costs, stress and obesity rates continue to rise. Flexible work options can help to reverse these trends.

By placing greater emphasis on making changes to the entire organization, rather than focusing only on the individual, health outcomes tend to improve. As recently reported, when organizations re-examine how, where and when work is done, and support employees in managing their complex lives by providing flexible work options, healthier behaviors can develop. These behaviors include longer hours of sleep, increased physical activity, stronger personal resilience, and participation in health education. It is not surprising, therefore, to find a connection between how people work and how they feel. As organizations change how they approach their human capital, and provide flexibility to help their employees manage their work and personal lives, they will experience the health/wellness benefits.

WORKSHEET
Flexible Work and Health and Wellness Strategy

The following questions can serve as discussion points for your health/wellness group:

1. Do we understand what working flexibly is all about in terms of its relationship to employee health and wellness? Do we understand that it is a way of managing that considers how each person works best and allows managers to treat people as individuals?

2. In what ways do we recognize that enabling people to work in the way they work best enhances their performance so they are more rested, less distracted and have fewer work interruptions?

3. How do we help managers and employees think outside the flexible work arrangement box so they use a variety of flexible work options to support employee empowerment and engagement?

4. In what ways do we disseminate the message that greater use of flexible work options increases positive health outcomes and encourages employees to find a solution that fits their personal needs while also meeting business needs?

5. Are we open to new ways of working? Are we willing to experiment to find the right flex option for each employee and the team?

6. Do we encourage managers to try new ways of organizing and streamlining work to get overwork under control? Do we ask employees for their suggestions so they can help eliminate unnecessary tasks?

7. In what ways do we help leaders and others examine subtle and not so subtle 24/7 work accessibility expectations and messages that set expectations for working all the time, from everywhere?

8. How can we help share stories of success so employees are encouraged to use flexibility to meet their health/wellness needs?

9. How can we help leaders reconsider the need for face time that requires everyone to be in the same place at the same time?

10. How can we work with learning and development and others in HR to set measurable performance objectives based on output instead of relying on proxies for performance like time spent in the office?

11. What messages will help assure that we give employees authority and responsibility to determine where and when their work is best done?

Health and Wellness

12. How can we make sure that managers:
    - Hold themselves accountable for creating a climate that recognizes and respects employees' work styles and responsibilities outside work?
    - Establish an adult-adult working relationship that is based on trust rather than suspicion?
    - Understand that the organizational climate that managers create actually makes flexible work successful, and therefore they need to pay attention to subtle messages and behaviors that signal acceptance of flexible work?
    - Plan ahead and minimize unrealistic deadlines?
    - Shift their mindset to thinking of flexible work as an opportunity to improve performance and create a healthier work environment at the same time?
    - Consider their own biases about where and when work is best done?
    - Be a role model for using a flexible work style to reduce their own stress (e.g., schedule personal time on their calendar for everyone to see; tell employees that they are taking time to be with their child, or blocking out a regular exercise schedule)?
    - Recognize and reward team members who plan and execute their work and avoid excessive work hours and/or last-minute time pressure?

FLEX IN-DEPTH: Cardinal Health

Building in Work-life to Competitive Advantage

Perspective

Competitiveness was the primary driver for Cardinal Health instituting flexible work options. Each year, the drug development company benchmarks its core benefits against the Fortune 500, 100, and its custom comparator group. Cardinal Health is always competitive when compared with its peers. However, in the area of work-life, each of its competitors listed various options related to flex that Cardinal Health did not offer as a formal program, including telecommuting, job sharing and phased return from maternity leave.

These types of programs have become even more critical over the years. In order to compete, to meet customer needs in a 24/7 environment, and to attract and retain top talent, Cardinal Health knew it was critical to offer these programs. As a healthcare company, the health and well-being of its employees is a top priority: Flex and work-life are an important component of its Healthy Lifestyles program.

Key Players

At Cardinal Health, the CFO is the executive sponsor for Work-life Effectiveness. This team reports to the Diversity and Inclusion Steering Committee, which is led by the CEO; membership includes the chief HR officer and the presidents of each division. The activities of the Diversity & Inclusion Steering Committee are led by the VP of Diversity. There is also strong integration with WIN (Women's Initiate Network), which is led by the president of one of Cardinal Health's divisions. Healthy Lifestyles, which includes flex and work-life effectiveness, is led by the Director of Healthy Lifestyles. It is a newly created position that emphasizes healthy lifestyles and is charged with creating a companywide culture of health.

Solution

Since Cardinal Health did not have internal expertise in this area, it partnered with FlexPaths, a provider of web-based and advisory flexibility solutions, and leveraged that organization's tools and resources. Cardinal started with a couple of focused pilot programs, educating and training employees and managers on flex. It complemented those tools with its own established forms of internal communications.

Cardinal Health identified employees and managers across the company willing to explore flex options, including telework, phased return from maternity and informal flex. It implemented a pilot as follows:
1. Conducted pre-assessment survey.
2. Rolled out pilot over six months
    a. Implementation of FlexPaths' Educate website
    b. Web training/Educate demo for managers, employees and HR
    c. Regular meetings to touch base with each group
    d. Reminder links directing participants to the enrollment portal

3. Conducted post-assessment survey.
4. Analyzed results.
5. Communicated results.
6. Identified next steps.

Measurement and Metrics

To determine the impact on productivity, Cardinal Health asked:

Q How productive are your employees when they are able to effectively manage work and personal situations?

A 57 percent of managers reported a "strong positive impact" on productivity, up from 26 percent previously (119 percent improvement).

Q What do employees say is the impact on productivity when they have the flexibility to manage work and life?

A 71 percent of employees reported a "strong positive impact" on productivity, up from 47 percent (51 percent improvement).

To judge effectiveness, Cardinal Health asked:

Q What do managers say is the impact on effectiveness when employees have the flexibility they need to manage work and life?

A 57 percent of managers report a "strong positive impact" in employee effectiveness, up from 39 percent previously (46 percent improvement).

Q What do employees say is the impact on effectiveness when they have the flexibility to manage work and life?

A 67 percent of employees reported a "strong impact" on their own effectiveness, up from 47 percent previously (43 percent improvement).

To determine ability to focus on work, Cardinal Health asked:

Q What do managers say is the impact on employees' ability to focus when they have the flexibility to manage work and life?

A 57 percent of managers report a "strong positive impact" in employee ability to focus, up from 39 percent previously (46 percent improvement).

Q What do employees say is the impact on their ability to focus when they have the flexibility to manage work and life?

A 78 percent of employees report a "strong positive impact" in their own ability to focus, up from 54 percent previously (44 percent improvement).

Going forward, Cardinal Health's use of FlexPaths' Educate website will be made available to more employee/manager groups, and tools to help managers and employees plan for maternity leave will be created. In addition, the pilot results will be presented to various groups to help them understand the ROI for flex.

FLEX IN-DEPTH: GlaxoSmithKline

Attracting a Performance-Focused Workforce Through Health, Diversity and Worklife Solutions

A dual focus on customer and employee health is central to GlaxoSmithKline's (GSK) mission to improve the quality of human life by enabling people to do more, feel better, and live longer. "To be fully engaged, employees need to be healthy, energetic and resilient," says Kay Campbell, U.S. Manager, Employee Health Support & Resilience.

According to GSK, resilience is the set of skills and behaviors necessary to be successful, both personally and professionally, in the midst of a high-pressured, fast-paced, and continuously changing work environment. Early on, the company adopted a strategy of creating a resilient workforce. The concept, dubbed "Team Resilience Program," resonates with senior leadership as a positive and powerful concept.

Campbell notes that "attracting, developing and retaining a performance-focused workforce that's adaptable and flexible requires a commitment to health, diversity and innovative worklife solutions." Integration between GSK's employee health management, human resources, and environment, health and safety functions assures that global programs and processes keep healthy people healthy, help to manage the effects of ill health, and leverage the culture of the company to influence well-being.

GSK's resilience strategy helps to communicate the case for workplace health and well-being to managers and staff and encourages them to pay close attention to pressure in the work environment. It also promotes balance between work and life responsibilities.

Actions

More than 400 teams and 5,000 employees worldwide have participated in GSK's Team Resilience Program, which is aimed at stress prevention and intervention. Components of this program include: personal resilience training; a Team Resilience website offering tools and resources, such as an online resilience assessment; and team action planning workshops to help teams practice new behaviors and experiment with alternative ways of working.

The Team Resilience Program uses behavioral signs and symptoms to determine what level of pressure a team is under and what type of intervention is required. Assessing where teams are on the Pressure Curve helps them move from stages of "dysfunction" and "strain" to "stretch" and "comfort." Teams that have participated in this program work together more effectively to get the job done and specifically report: a better ability to clarify and focus on critical tasks, more support and trust among team members, and increased time for activities outside of work.

Health and Wellness

Future Goals
Pulse surveys and health risk assessments reveal that GSK employees' dedication to getting their work done is not always matched by a rigorous commitment to their health. GSK's main goal is to further promote the value of health and well-being by "continuing to integrate resilience into the fabric of the way people work at our company," says Campbell.

GSK is also working toward compiling metrics that demonstrate the impact of the company's health and well-being efforts in order to attach value to their effect on optimal human performance, the direct and indirect costs of ill health, as well as corporate image and reputation.

Health and Wellness

FLEX IN-DEPTH: Prudential

Helping With Everyday Challenges To Achieve Optimal Health

Perspective

Prudential Financial incorporates work-life programs with health and wellness offerings to help employees and their dependents face head-on the challenges to achieving and maintaining optimal health.

For example, balancing everyday family needs through services such as child and adult care can help employees keep scheduled medical appointments. Additionally, utilizing flexible work arrangements enables employees to better manage their work and personal lives so they can accommodate activities such as exercise. According to Gary Giannone, VP for health and wellness, "the best-designed programs become ineffective if employees can't use them because life is getting in the way."

The company's partnership mindset creates opportunities to pull various services together for total solutions. "An integrated approach that connects Diversity, Work-Life, Health and Wellness, Employee Assistance, and Behavioral Health helps us look at employees more completely," says Giannone.

One example is Prudential's Life Coaching, which takes advantage of an employee's ability and desire to achieve a certain goal. Through integration, the company can match employees with programs such as Miavita's Healthy Living Program, an online diet, nutrition and fitness resource.

Actions

"Whenever you have an opportunity to motivate someone to advocate for them, encourage or support them, both the employee and the company benefits," says Giannone. Prudential provides some health and wellness information through Prudential Life Solutions, its work-life resource and referral program. This program encourages employees to become better consumers of healthcare by providing answers to their questions and prompting them to schedule health screenings and medical exams. The company also targets information to specific employee groups, such as Generation X and Y employees, by providing relevant content on topics such as self and career development, wellness, and healthy relationships

Future Goals

Prudential's overall goal is to empower employees to manage their work and personal lives effectively and encourage them to take responsibility for their own healthcare. By having access to a resource like Medstat, a healthcare data warehouse, Prudential gains critical information about the cost and quality impact of its healthcare benefit programs. This information helps the company better understand where to direct future efforts in order to achieve the most significant results.

Health and Wellness

Prudential is currently developing health and wellness programs for the company's international populations. An exciting prospect, this effort is also quite challenging due to the cultural differences and laws that govern each of Prudential's three global regions: European Union, Asia-Pacific Rim, and South America. "As our employees continue to serve millions of individual and institutional clients in the United States and abroad, our work-life efforts will further expand in response to our global presence," says Giannone.

Health and Wellness

FLEX IN-DEPTH: Wells Fargo

Helping Employees Find Time to Exercise, Eat Right and Reduce Stress

Perspective

"People as a Competitive Advantage" is one of Wells Fargo's 10 Strategic Initiatives, which recognize that team members are valued. "Focusing on employees' overall health and well-being is an investment worth pursuing and helps ensure personal and professional success, which in turn promotes our company's success," notes Susan Pon-Gee, manager for corporate wellness.

Five years ago, Wells Fargo conducted a team member survey focusing on life-event management needs and work-life factors that impact retention, wellness, absenteeism, productivity and other business indicators. The results revealed that more than 53 percent of individuals who responded indicated the desire to make health and wellness a top priority.

"Our team members want time to exercise, to learn about good nutrition and to learn how to reduce stress," reports Pon-Gee. The survey results were shared with senior business human resource leaders with recommendations to increase wellness services to meet team member needs.

Actions

Wells Fargo takes a whole-person approach to well-being and encourages balance between work and home life. Recognizing the multifaceted nature of health, the company offers services that incorporate the physical, mental, social and spiritual components of total well-being. Such services include online tools to promote exercise and good nutrition, a walking program, timely wellness newsletters, behavioral health assistance and a wellness incentive program.

"Our external partners, including our health plan carriers and wellness and work-life vendors, further enhance our healthy lifestyle and well-being environment through disease management programs, health and wellness fairs, health screening events, flu shot clinics and onsite wellness workshops," says Pon-Gee. Additionally, Wells Fargo integrates efforts with internal partners, such as Health and Employee Assistance Consulting (the company's internal EAP), in promoting wellness.

Future Goals

The company's main goal is to have a healthy and dynamic workforce. Wells Fargo realizes that healthy team members bring more energy and productivity to work and their lives while reducing health care expenses for themselves and the company. Wells Fargo actively seeks opportunities to further ingrain health promotion in its corporate philosophy and instill the value of wellness in its team members.

Flex Fits All

"Every workplace, small or large, can undertake efforts to treat employees with respect, give them some autonomy over how they do their jobs, help supervisors support employees to succeed on their jobs..."
National Study of the Changing Workforce, Families and Work Institute, 2008

No matter the size of a company, it can use flexible work to promote employee well-being.

Small employers are creating innovative systems to connect well-being and flex. For example, Fenwick & West LLP, a law firm in San Francisco, Calif., with 245 employees, created "workflow coordinators" and "balanced-hours advisors" who review attorney hours regularly to ensure that those on reduced schedules are not subject to "schedule creep" or overlooked for good assignments.

Humantech's workplace experts design industrial and office environments. To provide healthy situations for their own employees, the company gives its staff generous private workspaces, a relaxed environment and access to laptops, pocket PCs, smartphones, wireless broadband and an extensive music library. Because it considers work flexibility intrinsic to a healthy work environment, the Detroit firm also gives its employees a great degree of control over the hours they work. Project-scheduling teams ensure that consultants aren't overworked; extended travel stretches are managed; and attention is paid to supporting a healthy work-life fit.[14]

Large companies are also creating innovative programs, conducting internal research and rebranding their messaging to link flex and health. KPMG, the global professional services firm, for one, uses "wellness scorecards" to determine if someone is working too much overtime or skipping vacation. Supervisors are encouraged to use these scorecards to monitor their people's progress in taking better care of themselves.

MITRE structurally integrates flex and health/wellness under its "Embrace Your Health" initiative, with three areas of health and well-being: 1) work-life balance; 2) exercise; and 3) nutrition. MITRE recognizes that the ability to flex one's time is directly connected to eating right and exercising. The company analyzes health insurance claims data alongside the use of flexible work to measure the link between flex and health/wellness.

Conclusion

It is clear that improving access to flexible work options can have a positive impact on health outcomes. The role for organizations' health/wellness professionals is to assure that the connection is made both strategically and programmatically. "We need to create a culture that redefines how business gets done and how it creates a new ecosystem that eliminates barriers to increased use of flexible work options," says Wake Forest's Joe Grzywacz. A useful exercise, he says, would be to define the places and ways that flexible work relates to the various functions in an organization, emphasizing the points of connection and disconnection. Doing so would ultimately create a roadmap that would illustrate how flexibility works in all areas.

Health and Wellness

Health and wellness professionals can seize the opportunity to make a significant difference in employee and organizational health by integrating into their "wellness portfolios" flexibility in how, when and where work is done. This can be accomplished by supporting flex stakeholders as they connect with colleagues focused on wellness. It is truly not possible to discuss employee well-being without considering it within the context of employees' daily lives — lives that include commitments to family, work, communities and themselves. When organizational flexible work initiatives and employee well-being activities and plans are leveraged simultaneously, it is possible to maximize the synergies so they can become mutually reinforcing, and thus obtain the most positive health outcomes.

Health and Wellness

TIP SHEET
Connecting Health, Wellness & Flexibility

Here are some ways your organization can connect health and wellness and flexible work to create a more effective and healthier work environment.

Measurable Results
- When conducting engagement or satisfaction surveys, include items that ask about health/wellness and access to flexibility. For example, if you ask about employees' level of stress, analyze the responses by how much flex they have access to. Use this information to help shape flex and wellness efforts going forward.
- Note if there are changes in employee satisfaction, engagement, and/or commitment scores over time and whether they are related to shifts in the number of employees working flexibly.
- Look for indicators of employee stress as it relates to absenteeism.
- If your company has an Employee Assistance Program, discuss collective findings regarding stress, overwork and anxiety as these relate to flexible work situations.
- Look at the information and data collected by health/wellness initiatives. If you offer stress reduction activities like yoga, fitness or self-help courses, document use and where appropriate raise the issue of rest and downtime. Keep tabs on the findings.
- Some employee surveys ask employees if they feel they spend enough time with family, friends and in their community. If you collect this information, be sure to examine it in the light of your flexible work initiatives. For example, determine whether people have the necessary access to flex required to make this time possible.
- Include questions in surveys, focus groups and/or interviews to determine if employees feel they have time to exercise regularly, are taking their full vacations and are not working during their time off, all of which can be indicators of stress.

Activities
- Encourage your health/wellness staff to talk about flexible work as part of an overall wellness plan. When exercise is recommended, your staff should talk with the employee about when the optimal time is. Then, they can help the employee work out a schedule to present to his/her manager.
- Make sure health/wellness and flex staff share information and coordinate initiatives so that information on flexible work options are presented in health care fairs or EAP activities. Discuss the importance of creating a personal approach to when, where and how work is done that reduces stress and gives more time for health.
- Include messaging and information about flexible work in training for managers to help them consider flexible work to address employee health/wellness issues.
- Communicate the use of occasional flex as a way to meet personal needs such as doctor appointments, care for sick child/parent, attendance at personal activities that can reduce employees' stress related to scheduling these activities.

Health and Wellness

Communication/Messaging
- ❏ Provide senior management with the language to connect health/wellness and flex in their messaging/communication.
- ❏ Make sure key internal stakeholders — leaders, managers and employees — understand the business case for the connection of flex and health/wellness and know about any resources to help them incorporate flex in their health/wellness plans.
- ❏ Examine on- and off-line wellness communication material for opportunities to reinforce the message that flexible work options can support well-being and positive health outcomes.
- ❏ Share best practices about wellness and flexible work with leaders and managers and look for examples in your organization that you can highlight.

REFERENCES: CHAPTER 6

1. (2007) Higgins, C.A., Duxbury, L.E. & Lyons, S. Coping with Overload and Stress: Men and Women in ... Advances in Developing Human Resources
2. (2009) ABCNews.go.com
3. (2008) Casey, P.R.; Grzywacz J.G. "Employee Health and Well-being: The Role of Flexibility and Work-Family Balance", The Psychologist-Manager Journal
4. (2007) Wayne, J. H., Grzywacz, J. G., Carlson, D. S. and Kacmar, M., (2007), "Work–family facilitation: A theoretical explanation and model of primary antecedents and consequences", Human Resource Management Review
5. (2006) "Rethinking Work", EKOS Research Associates & Graham Lowe Group National worker survey, The Graham Lowe Group Inc.
6. (2005) "Overwork in America: When the Way We Work becomes too Much", Families and Work Institute
7. (2005) Corporate Voices for Working Families & WFD Consulting
8. (2008) G. Grzywacza*, Dawn S. Carlson, and Sandee Shulkinc, "Schedule Flexibility and Stress: Linking Formal Flexible Arrangements and Perceived Flexibility to Employee Health", Community Work and Family
9. (2009) "Quality: Workplace Wellness Linked to Flexible Work Arrangements", The New Health Dialogue Blog
10. (2009) "Making Work More Flexible", AARP Public Policy Institute
11. (2010) A. Norton, "Flexible Work Tied To Some Health Benefits", Reuters Health
12. (2010) Joyce K, et al. "Flexible Working Conditions and Their Effects on Employee Health and Well-being", Cochrane Database of Systematic Reviews
13. (2004) ComPsych Corporation
14. (2008) E. Galin "When Work Works, 2008 Guide to Bold New Ideas"

Chapter 7: Flexible Work and Legal/Compliance Issues

Legal/Compliance

Flexible work is the future of work – a continual evolution that characterizes the "new normal" of a global working culture. The legal implications of this transformation in how, when, and where work is done are substantial. The rapid growth of flexible work makes it essential that employers understand and mitigate legal exposure associated with how it is executed.

In the next few years, organizations will begin placing much greater emphasis on the operational and legal issues associated with shifting to the new paradigm of flexible work practices. While many employees have had flexible work policies in place for years, their practices often began as individual deals between a few highly valued employees and their managers. Far from transparent, these initial policies were not meant to expand flexible work, but rather to limit the number of such deals. These ad hoc arrangements were deliberately invisible, inconsistent and even discriminatory, often relying on a single manager's attitude, knowledge and comfort level, as well as how the employee presented his/her case. Because of that legacy, flexible work is still inconsistently offered at many companies, promoted only to certain demographic groups (women, for example) and not integrated into business processes or the organization's culture. Employees may hesitate to take advantage of the opportunity to have a more flexible work arrangement, fearing a subtle, or not-so-subtle, penalty. Managers, the lynchpin to the success of flexible work, remain ambivalent, apprehensive and ill-equipped to change the way they manage their employees and get work done.

For many organizations the transitional stage — moving from discreet flexible work policies for what are considered non-traditional work arrangements to a systemic and pervasive change in how work is done and performance is measured — is the most challenging. This stage is complex, impacting organizational systems, attitudes and behaviors, and is not accomplished without careful scrutiny and planning.

It is not enough to have flexible work policies in place. Changing how work is done and how people are managed calls for particular attention to the legal implications employers should be aware of in implementing and managing flexible work.

In Chapter 7, we will explore the following questions:

✔ What are the legal issues in the U.S. that relate to flexible work?

✔ What are some of the issues that have been raised when organizations don't manage flexible work well?

✔ How can companies make sure their flexible work initiative is legally compliant?

Legal Issues

There are many inconsistencies in the way flexible work is implemented and managed in U.S. companies. These inconsistencies can cause discrimination and potential risks for the organization that internal legal stakeholders need to be aware of.

Consider the following statistics from Workplace Flexibility 2010, a national campaign to support the development of a comprehensive national policy on workplace flexibility:

- 32 percent of employers do not allow any workers to change their starting and quitting times, and 67 percent do not allow all or most employees to do so.
- 61 percent of employers do not allow any workers to control what shifts they work.
- 47 percent of employers do not allow any employees to move from full-time to part-time and back again while remaining in the same position
- 79 percent of employers do not allow most or all employees to move from full-time to part-time and back again while remaining in the same position
- 54 percent of employers do not allow workers to share jobs; 66 percent do not allow any employees to work part of the work week at home on either an occasional or a regular basis; and
- 61 percent of employers do not allow workers to work a compressed work week.

Even when flexible work is part of official company policies, managerial commitment to the benefit and discretion in its approval significantly impact actual use. Public and private studies indicate that the following are needed to protect the organization and to improve adoption of flexible arrangements across job settings: leadership at the highest levels; written policies and broad dissemination to workers; implementation training for decisional managers; and review and enforcement mechanisms including employee surveys, utilization data collection and review, and managerial performance assessments. Available literature suggests that some of the most successful flexible work initiatives are those that are developed jointly by employees and company management.

> **Compliance Connect**
> More than 50 percent of work-life practitioners surveyed reported that their company's Legal/Compliance department has been "extremely supportive" of flexible work at their organization.
>
> *Source: Working Mother Research Institute, 2010*

Corporate lawyers are realizing that they have a role to play in how flexible work efforts are shaped and managed and that the organization's focus on flexible work must take into account current and future legal issues. Some legal issues to consider in terms of flexible work arrangements include: equal employment opportunity compliance and equal employment opportunity laws mandating non-discrimination in wages, hours and other terms and conditions of employment. Accordingly, employers should take steps to ensure that flexibility is offered and implemented without discrimination on any prohibited basis. As with all other employment practices, clear policies, consistent decision-making and careful documentation are needed to be in compliance and to fend off possible discrimination charges.[1]

Separating Myth from Reality

Employers are often concerned about two kinds of risks regarding flexibility policies and practices: practical risks and legal risks. What could go wrong in implementing flexibility? Will I be sued? To protect against risk, it is imperative that risk managers and legal personnel understand a new area of the law directly related to flexibility. Some employers remain concerned about the risk that occurs when they offer flexibility. They worry, for example, about backlash from employees who do not have access to flexibility or about the risks related to security or injury from employees working remotely. But there's a disconnect between what employers worry about and what actually happens. In reality, the risk comes less from offering flexibility than from implementing it in inappropriate ways.

Since flexibility has been successfully utilized by employers for more than a decade, it is possible to learn from experience how to minimize the risk involved. Some of the issues to be aware of include the following:

Wage and hour compliance

Flexible work arrangements traditionally have been the domain of exempt, salaried employees, but now more companies are using them for nonexempt hourly workers. According to a recent study by WorldatWork and Work Design Collaborative[2], 45 percent of survey respondents report that they include nonexempt employees in their flexible work arrangements. That number exceeded the expectation of researchers, who thought they would get an affirmative response from just 15 percent of the 135 employers surveyed.

Offering nonexempt workers flexible work arrangements may require some changes to the Fair Labor Standards Act (FLSA), which, among other things, regulates how employers keep track of overtime for nonexempt workers. Tracking overtime can be complicated if an employee is working a flexible work schedule or teleworking. FLSA requires that nonexempt employees who work more than 40 hours a week get paid overtime. This is problematic for nonexempt employees who occasionally want to work compressed workweeks and more than 40 hours a week on other weeks.

In May 2009, Workplace Flexibility 2010, which is based at Georgetown University Law Center in Washington, D.C., held a public policy platform on flexible work arrangements. The group called for the Department of Labor to provide written guidance, technical assistance and training on how the majority of flexible scheduling arrangements comply with the requirements of the FLSA. The group suggested that such guidance should provide examples of flexible work arrangements that comply with the FLSA, examples of those that do not, and an explanation of the underlying analysis.

While workplace flexibility advocates argue that more employers will embrace these arrangements for nonexempt workers because they will cut costs and improve engagement and productivity, some are doubtful that this issue is high on companies' agendas. "Until you see this issue triggered by collective actions under FLSA or we see a number of overtime claims under FLSA, it's unlikely that employers will want to have this addressed," says Drew Matzkin, a partner at law firm Mintz Levin.[3]

Employers must be mindful of both federal and state wage and hour laws when implementing flextime. For example, if nonexempt employees are allowed flextime, it is especially important to track their actual work hours to ensure compliance with the Fair Labor Standards Act.

State wage and hour laws may pose challenges to the use of compressed work schedules if these schedules require daily overtime, for instance, if payment of overtime is required for work that exceeds a certain number of hours in a 24-hour period. (FLSA requires overtime only for hours in excess of 40 in a week.) Telecommuting, where employees are working from home or another location raises even more issues, including:
- Identifying compensable working time.
- Controlling unauthorized off-the-clock work.
- Controlling unauthorized reported work.

Family Responsibilities Discrimination

The definition of sex discrimination now includes employment actions based on assumptions about how workers may act based on their family care-giving responsibilities. Now termed Family Responsibilities Discrimination (FRD), it is established in case law with courts ruling that taking negative employment action because of a worker's family responsibilities is unlawful.

Some case examples include:
- Assuming that a woman who requests to work on a reduced schedule (following childbirth or to care for an aging parent, for example) will be or is doing lower quality work.
- Applying stricter workplace rules and performance standards to men or women who use flexible (including part-time) schedules while applying more lenient standards to others.
- Requiring employees using flexibility to prove their competence in ways that other employees are not required to.
- Judging employees on flexible schedules (including part-time) strictly on their accomplishments, while judging others in part on their potential.

In comparing treatment of employees in these FRD cases, the proper comparison is not how female vs. male employees are treated, but rather how an employee with family responsibilities is treated as compared with an employee without family responsibilities.[4] Practices that, at first look, may seem gender neutral may garner scrutiny because they disparately impact caregivers — predominantly women — and therefore constitute sex discrimination. The Center for Work-Life Law recommends that employers should take the following steps, in order to avoid legal action from employees and applicants who assert that because of caregiving responsibilities they have been rejected for employment, subjected to a hostile work environment, denied promotion, or terminated:

- Rewrite your existing antidiscrimination policies to add FRD to your company's list of unlawful policies. (Alternatively, you can create a new stand-alone policy.)
- Notify employees of the change to existing policies and to any changes in the employee handbook.
- Hold antidiscrimination and anti-harassment training for employees and managers that includes family discrimination.

EEOC Guidelines on Employee Caregivers

Flexibility is often provided by employers for employees with caregiving responsibilities, including those with children, aging relatives or family members with disabilities. It's important to know about the new EEOC guidelines that outline the legal issues for these employees. The EEOC guidelines state that although federal laws do not prohibit discrimination against caregivers per se, there are "circumstances in which discrimination against caregivers might constitute unlawful disparate treatment." Caregivers are not mentioned specifically in these guidelines, but employers should evaluate whether a particular employment decision affecting a caregiver might unlawfully discriminate on the basis of prohibited characteristics under Title VII of the Civil Rights Act of 1964 or the Americans with Disabilities Act of 1990.

Real Life Lessons from Recent Cases

Request for Flexible Work Leads to Demotion and Dismissal

A customer service representative was an excellent employee and received several promotions, ending up with a managerial position. She became pregnant and, fearing miscarriage, asked for a compressed workweek or a job-sharing arrangement. Her employer told her she would be demoted from her managerial position and would lose her salaried status. In fact, she would receive a decrease in her pay such that she would make less per hour than she had made as a full-time employee. Her employer made several comments alluding to the belief that she would no longer be able to do her job well once she became a mother. The employer and employee exchanged angry words; the employer ordered the employee to leave. The employee believed she had been terminated, and the court agreed that the employer's actions would lead one to so believe. She sued for pregnancy discrimination and constructive discharge. The court denied the employer's motion for summary judgment and set the case for trial. The case later settled out of court.

Case: Patrick v. Jansson Corp., 392 F. Supp. 2d 49 (D. Mass. 2005).

Lesson for Employers: The court's ruling relied in large part on the fact that the employer had planned to demote the employee and pay her a lesser wage, which the court believed supported the idea that the employee was constructively discharged. The employer here let discriminatory stereotypes about mothers get in the way of retaining a valuable employee. The far better course would have been to have let the employee continue to work after she became a mother and to address any performance issues as they arose, much in the same way that any performance issues would be addressed with any employee.

Legitimate Business Reason Saves the Day for Employer

A customer service representative had been working part-time but was moved to full-time status when the number of accounts handled by her office grew. The rep soon found out she was pregnant and informed her employer. Several months later, her employer told her she was being reverted back to part-time status due to the decline in the number of accounts. After she gave birth, the rep was uncertain when she would be able to return to work and was terminated. She sued for pregnancy discrimination because she was returned to part-time status while pregnant. The court held that moving the employee back to part-time was not pregnancy discrimination because the employer had evidence of legitimate business reason.

Case: Schlett v. Avco Financial Services, 950 F. Supp. 823 (N.D. Ohio 2006).
Lesson for Employers: The employee's return to part-time status was based on express standards for staffing determined by the number of cases being handled by the office. Basing personnel decisions on articulable, legitimate business reasons almost always prevents liability for discrimination.

Disparate Pay for Part-Time Employees

A female chemist who worked 30 hours per week was paid at a lower wage rate than men who performed the same job but worked 40 hours per week. In other words, she worked three-quarter time but received less than three-quarters of the pay that full-time employees, doing the same job, were paid. The employer defended its actions based on the fact that part-time workers were not similarly situated to full-time workers. The court rejected the absolute nature of this reasoning, explaining that "where the plaintiff's actual tasks, duties and responsibilities are essentially similar to those of the putative comparator," the question of whether a part-time employee could be compared to a full-time employee was one of fact for the jury to resolve. The court further opined that in determining whether two employees are comparable for purposes of the Equal Pay Act, the jury should focus on whether the full-time employee performs any additional tasks or job duties, rather than focusing on the number of hours worked. After a jury found that the female chemist did indeed perform the same job functions as the full-time male chemist, it awarded her more than $400,000.

Case: Lovell v. BBNT Solutions, LLC, 295 F. Supp. 2d 611 (E.D. Va. 2003).
Note: Several other courts have decided differently on such cases, most of which pre-date this case. The court that decided Lovell is in a circuit generally thought to be pro-employer, so this case may prove to be influential in other cases.
Lesson for Employers In setting pay for employees who are working non-standard schedules, the safest course is to focus on business-related criteria such as skills, responsibilities and experience rather than on the number of hours worked.[5]

Legal Issues Associated with Telecommuting

A number of legal issues should be addressed before an organization allows an employee to work from a home office:[6]

- **Workers' Compensation.** If a telecommuter is injured while working at home, is the injury covered by workers' compensation? Many workers' compensation laws do not distinguish between home-based and central-office-based workers. Injuries to home-based employees can be particularly problematic because of the employer's inability to control the physical working conditions, as well as the potential for fraud.
- **Occupational Safety and Health.** On February 25, 2000, the Occupational Safety and Health Administration (OSHA) issued a policy on "home offices" (defined as "office work activities in a home-based work site"), indicating the agency "will not conduct

inspections of the employee's home offices, will not hold employers liable for employees' home offices" and "does not expect employers to inspect home offices of the employees."
- **Disability Accommodation.** Telecommuting is sometimes requested as a reasonable accommodation under the Americans with Disabilities Act. Employers are not obligated to agree to such an accommodation in all cases, but they are required to engage in the standard give-and-take with respect to a requested accommodation.
- **Privacy and Confidentiality.** Such concerns are particularly difficult to address in a telecommuting environment. As telecommuting becomes more common, employers must address the unique issues that arise from use of e-mail and the Internet by the home-based worker.
- **Independent Contractor Status.** Sometimes employers attempt to avoid legal issues by classifying all off-site workers as independent contractors. If the individuals are not truly independent contractors, however, the employer may create more problems than it solves by taking that approach.

Flexible Work and Accommodation
The ADA requires employers with 15 or more employees to provide reasonable accommodation for qualified applicants and employees with disabilities. Flexible work, including flexible work locations, may constitute an appropriate accommodation, but employers must take into account that not all persons with disabilities need, or want, to work flexibly. Further, if flexible work would impose an undue burden, or if the essential functions of the job cannot be performed remotely, flexible work is not mandatory under the ADA.

Assigning Flexible Work
The assignment or denial of flexible work on the basis of disability, gender, race, age or caregiver status constitutes unlawful discrimination under federal law.

Workplace Attitudes and Promotion
The attitudes of managers and other employees regarding those who take advantage of flexible work opportunities can create as much exposure to liability as the policies under which flexible work is offered. For example, in a recent class action alleging gender discrimination, one class member quoted her supervisor as indicating he did not like to hire young women, explaining, "First comes love, then comes marriage, then comes flex time and a baby carriage." Though the company maintained flexible work policies for the benefit of all of its employees, and offered them in an otherwise nondiscriminatory manner, the attitudes of its supervisors and non-flex time employees toward employees who work flexibly were sufficiently discriminatory to result in a substantial judgment against the employer for gender bias. The proliferation of such perspectives could also result in a finding of unlawful hostile work environment harassment on the basis of gender or association with an individual with a disability.

Flexible Employment Relationships
Employers face unique legal concerns when dealing with workers who are engaged in flexible employment relationships. There are many different types of workers who fall into the flexible employment relationship category, and some are employees while others are not. For example, freelance workers are workers who are self-employed and typically hired on an as-needed basis. Similarly, project-based workers are hired to do specific projects or assignments, and may be

employees or independent contractors. Independent contractors are workers who contract to do work according to their own processes and methods and they are not subject to another's control except for what is specified in an agreement for a specific job. There is a stringent test for determining whether a worker is an independent contractor or an employee, and that determination has a number of implications as to how a worker is paid, the benefits that worker is entitled to, and the federal and state tax withholdings an employer is obligated to pay. Independent contractor misclassification is a hot button issue, with many states recently enacting misclassification legislation and plaintiffs procuring large class action settlements pertaining to misclassification.

Policy Considerations and Implications

The direction of proposed and newly enacted legislation also sheds light on trends and what may lie ahead in terms of policy related to flexible work. It is definitely the case that the transformation to the virtual, flexible workplace as both an economic reality and business necessity has brought the issue of flexible work to the attention of policymakers in Washington and state capitals across the country. The White House, in fact, has chosen to give it special focus by, among other things, hosting a Forum on Workplace Flexibility in March 2010. At that meeting, President Obama stated:

"Workplace flexibility isn't just a women's issue. It's an issue that affects the well-being of our families and the success of our businesses. It affects the strength of our economy — whether we'll create the workplaces and jobs of the future that we need to compete in today's global economy."

During the 111th Congress in 2010, numerous bills were introduced to expand federal family leave requirements. Among the proposals garnering the most attention was the Healthy Families Act. The bill, which was reintroduced in the Senate by the late Senator Ted Kennedy (D-MA) and in the House of Representatives by Representative Rosa DeLauro (D-CT), would require employers with more than 15 employees to adopt paid sick leave policies. Specifically, the Healthy Families Act would require employers to provide up to seven days of paid leave to care for themselves or sick family members as well as for needs stemming from domestic violence. So far, the Healthy Families Act and other mandated leave legislation have failed to advance in Congress, due to concerns about the increased cost and regulatory burden of a federal mandate. Concerns were also raised that federal mandates such as those imposed by the Healthy Families Act would inhibit rather than promote flexible work policies by limiting flexible work options.

Additionally, several bills introduced in the 111th Congress are designed to facilitate flexible retirement, by which employees can reduce their work hours to less than full time prior to retirement. The Older Worker Opportunity Act of 2009 (S502) includes tax credits for businesses with employees over the age of 62 who participate in a "flexible work program" of part-time and flexible work that includes full pension and health care benefits.[7]

Other bills focus on the federal government's role as a catalyst to promote flexible work. HR1007 proposes that federal contractors are allowed to have employees telecommute,[8] while others concern the federal government as an employer and focus on supplementing existing policies that endorse flexible work and telework for federal employees. Already adopted is the Federal Employees Flexible and Compressed Work Schedules Act, which permits (but does not require) agencies to establish "flexible work schedule" programs and/or "compressed work schedule" programs for their employees.[9]

Federal legislators are making efforts to expand the use of telework arrangements in the federal government. The Telework Enhancement Act of 2010 was signed by President Obama on Dec. 9, 2010, to make federal employees presumptively eligible for telework. It also requires agencies to designate a telework office and ensures that telework is part of planning for continuity of business operations.

Although this measure does not apply to private employers, it reflects an endorsement of the benefits of telework and illustrates its appeal. As more employees require flexible work options and the economic and environmental benefits of workplace flexibility become even more apparent, federal and state proposals to encourage telework and other flexible work arrangements are likely to gain momentum.

Legal issues impacting flexible work must be carefully considered if efforts to encourage these practices are to be successful. FLSA has failed to keep pace with technological advancements that have transformed the 21st century workplace. This gap has, in some cases, inhibited the workplace flexibility that technology now enables. Some policymakers are attempting to remove impediments in current wage and hour laws in order to advance work flexibility. The Family Friendly Workplace Act, for one, seeks to extend "comp time" arrangements to the private sector. The legislation, introduced by Representative Cathy McMorris Rodgers (R-WA) in February 2009, would amend the FLSA to allow private sector employees to opt for paid time off at the same time-and-a-half rate as they get for overtime hours.

There is hope that technological advances and the realities of the modern workforce and workplace will drive employers, employees and policymakers to reexamine the impact of wage and hour and other laws on work flexibility. The call for promoting workplace flexibility amid an ever more competitive global economy is expected to grow louder. The prospects for legislation advancing this practice improve as trends toward flexible work environments are increasingly seen as both an employee-friendly practice and a business necessity.

Recommendations issued by Workplace Flexibility 2010 may inform the direction future legislation will take. This five-year, cross-constituency policy analysis concludes that the goal must be to integrate flexible work practices into the workplace as standard operating procedure. The organization recommended policies that would, at a minimum, support innovation by funding projects to test new models and measure results; facilitate model practices by the federal government; establish minimum labor standards to ensure that flexible work arrangements are available; provide technical assistance and training for employers; create public education campaigns; and develop an infrastructure of federal, state and community players to execute the policies. In short, it recommends policies that would offer incentives, supports and models to stimulate the growth of flexible work from the perspective that it is in the best interest of businesses and individuals alike and a critical component of any new economic thinking.

Conclusion

Employers can avoid difficulties with flexible work policies — including potential litigation — by setting up legally compliant flexible work practices early on and ensuring that their company remains compliant. Employers should apply the same care and attentiveness to developing their flexible work policies and practices that they apply to their other human resources and personnel policies and practices. Both employers who are considering implementing flexible work practices and those who have already done so should consult knowledgeable partners regarding legal and policy issues pertaining to flexible work.[10]

"Flexible working is being shaped by new organizational partners whose perspectives and involvement will change the direction and velocity of its growth, as well as how it is viewed and implemented," says Neil Alexander, a shareholder with the labor law firm Littler Mendelson. "These partners will be an important force in the creation of the workplace of the future. As a result, the cost savings, morale boost, and productivity are undeniable in virtually all industries. The increased use of contingent or project workers will rise to help reduce labor costs during the peaks and valleys of production. Those organizations that do not embrace the concept will be left wondering why their costs are higher, and their morale is lower."

Julie Schwartz Weber, a lawyer and policy specialist on work-life issues, agrees, noting that companies need to understand the legal issues involved in this new paradigm. "Increasingly, more and more companies are involving lawyers in the crafting and management of their flexible work initiatives. Where today, companies are regularly recognizing that flexible work arrangements are beneficial for numerous reasons — such as improved recruitment and retention of a more diverse workforce, greater productivity, reduced absenteeism, the ability to work across time zones, work continuity in the case of disasters, and saved real estate costs — companies are also aware that there are a host of federal, state and local laws that they must carefully navigate when implementing and managing flexible work arrangements. These laws are varied and complex, and include statutes concerning employment discrimination, labor, tax and benefits, and leave."

Only with the ongoing participation of legal partners and flexible work specialists will employers be equipped to take advantage of the strategic and practical value that this new, agile way of working and managing can bring to the 21st century workplace.

Legal/Compliance

TIP SHEET
Tips for Flexible Work and Legal/Compliance Issues

The labor law firm Littler Mendelson suggests the following steps to ensure that the day-to-day behaviors practiced by employees, managers and leaders are aligned with what is legally required:

- ❏ The organization's legal counsel and HR department should work closely together so that after legally compliant policies and protocols are established, they are communicated, understood and followed consistently across the enterprise.
- ❏ The working relationship between the legal and HR departments should be oriented toward facilitating, rather than restricting, flexible work, albeit in a legally compliant manner.
- ❏ Managers, employees, leaders and work teams should be trained as new policies and protocols are rolled out. Guidance should be ongoing, and can be provided via live or online training, internal resource personnel, or other means.
- ❏ Policies and guidelines, procedures, and guidance about how to use and manage flexible work options should be available broadly to all employees and managers. Such a system can help promote transparency, consistency of practice and accountability.
- ❏ Managers and employees should be held accountable for following the recommended policies and protocols; assessments can be done in performance reviews, 360 evaluations, and annual reviews of flexible work agreements between managers and employees.
- ❏ Methods and mechanisms should be established for accurately and efficiently tracking access to and use of flexible work options among employee subgroups and work units in order to identify discriminatory issues, note areas in need of improvement, and measure success.
- ❏ Regular legal audits can be helpful in determining whether further modifications in policy or practice are needed as changes take place in the company or in the legal environment.[11]

REFERENCES: CHAPTER 7

1. (2009) SHRM.
2. (2009) "Managing Flexible Work Arrangements," SHRM.
3. (2009) Wendy Bliss, J.D., SPHR, and Gene R. Thornton, J.D., PHR, "Employment Termination Source Book: A Collection of Practical Samples," (SHRM).
4. The Center for WorkLife Law, http://www.worklifelaw.org/
5. The Center for WorkLife Law, www.worklifelaw.org
6. (2010) Littler Mendelson PC.
7. Thomas Benjamin Huggett, Morgan, Lewis & Bockius LLP.
8. Philip Gordon and Chris Leh, Littler Mendelson's Privacy Data Protection Practice Group,
9. William Hays Weissman, Littler Mendelson PC.
10. http;://workplaceflexibility2010.org/index.php/laws_impacting_flexibility/FEFCWA
11. (2010) Littler Mendelson PC.

Chapter 8 Trends in Flexible Work

Trends

Organizations are leveraging flexible work in a variety of ways as they compete to attract, retain and engage diverse talent. Certain trends are emerging that provide a glimpse of what the agile workforce and agile workplace will look like. When participants in a 2010 FlexPaths and LinkedIn series of global focus groups were asked for their vision of the workforce of 2015, the majority of participants said they expected significant increases in the proportion of their workforces that would be engaging in flexible work. Some forecast a flexible workforce as high as 80 percent; a majority predicted it would be about 50 percent. Most participants struggled to say what portion of workers were on flexible arrangements today, and those who could cited numbers around 25 percent. The majority of CEOs acknowledged that embracing flexible work would be critical in remaining competitive. In terms of the future, without exception, all participants agreed that buy-in from senior leadership would be crucial to the success of a flexible work initiative and suggested that in the future companies will focus on:

Sending a Consistent, Legally Compliant Message
- ✔ To create clear and well-thought-out and legally compliant flexible work policies.
- ✔ To communicate those policies, along with internal case studies that recognize successful flexible work practices, to all staff, in a place where they are sure to find it and in a way that will resonate with them.

Educating to Keep the Focus on Results
- ✔ To educate individuals about how to create a results-oriented business case for a flexible work proposal.
- ✔ To educate managers thoroughly about why the company is engaging in flexible work, how to leverage it as an asset, and how to

manage flexible workers in a way that allows them more freedom without sacrificing results.

Simplifying the Process
- ✔ To enroll all employees — not just those with formal flexible work arrangements — in a work style, the same way employees are enrolled in medical, pension and other programs. There is no need to create separate cultures if flexible work is just treated as "part of how we do business."
- ✔ To make the administrative process for enrollment as automated, straightforward and flexible as possible.

Measuring Return on Investment
- ✔ By enrolling all employees and automating the process, to create detailed reporting on the true utilization of different types of flexible work. This can be used to make decisions around physical space requirements. By measuring productivity and staff turnover, a return on investment can be determined.

Leveraging Technology and Redefining "Face Time"
- ✔ To arm all employees with the tools they need to collaborate both on- and off-site, and provide them with opportunities and spaces to meet face-to-face.

These recommendations are a preview of the future of flexible work. But there's more in terms of trends that will impact the expansion and shape of flexible work in organizations and the role that various internal stakeholders will play in the future of flexible work.

In Chapter 8, we will explore the following questions:

- How is the changing nature of workforce planning related to flexible work?

- How is the growth of remote work changing the employment landscape?

- How do hourly workers work flexibly?

- How does the contingent workforce relate to flexible work?

- In what ways is flexible work becoming part of career planning?

- What is the impact of flexible work on the multiple generations in the workforce?

- How can caregivers benefit from flexible work options?

- How is public policy influencing flexible work?

- What are some of the global issues related to flexible work?

Workforce Planning and Flexible Work

Flexible work options are becoming part of overall workforce planning for many organizations. As organizations look at their current and future talent needs, they are beginning to take into consideration the fact that employees will be changing the ways they work, with some transitioning to reduced schedules from full-time ones and others working from remote locations as opposed to relocating. These flexible work options are becoming part of strategic workforce planning, a management process that involves analyzing and forecasting the talent that companies need to execute a business strategy. Strategic workforce planning is being used increasingly to help control labor costs, assess talent needs, make informed business decisions (e.g., where to open new facilities or whether it's cost effective to add full-time employees or contractors), and to assess human-capital needs and risks as part of overall enterprise risk management. It is essentially aimed at helping companies ensure they have the right people in the right place at the right time.[1] Creating a flexible workforce is critical to a company's ability to adapt and adjust to changing business needs.

Many factors are driving companies toward a more strategic approach to workforce planning. A study from the Conference Board, *Strategic Workforce Planning: Forecasting Human Capital Needs to Execute Business Strategy*[2] found that the forces driving strategic workforce planning include current movement and projected labor shortages; globalization; the growing use of contingent, flexible workers; the need to leverage human capital to enhance return; mergers and acquisitions and the evolution of workplace technology and tools.

Companies are changing the way they plan for workforce needs because, as Mary B. Young, senior research associate, The Conference Board, and author of the report, says, "In many companies traditional workforce planning was an onerous process that HR imposed on management. Too often, the net result was a humongous report, blinding spreadsheets, and a dizzying amount of data that provided very little value to the business."

In addition, methodology is rapidly advancing in response to changing business needs and the development of new tools and technology. This Conference Board study found, in fact, that some organizations have enhanced the simple gap analysis (workforce demand vs. supply) that constitutes traditional workforce planning by adopting the logic and analytical tools of other corporate functions, such as finance, strategic planning, risk management, and marketing.

There is greater opportunity for effectively creating and managing a flexible workforce with strategic planning. "Strategic workforce planning enables the organization to slice and dice its workforce data to discover critical issues, compare different groups, understand patterns and trends, home in on critical segments of the workforce such as mature workers and top performers, and customize its approach to managing different segments of its workforce," says Young. "By enabling leaders to see across lines of business, workforce planning can more effectively leverage the talent within a company. Ultimately, the same workforce planning database tools will enable employees to shop for new jobs, assess their own developmental needs, and prepare for career moves inside the organization."[3]

Flex and Hourly Workers

There is a serious misperception that flexible work is not appropriate for hourly workers. According to a 2009 study by Corporate Voices for Working Families, a nonprofit organization, workplace flexibility initiatives for hourly employees are as successful as those designed for professional staff.[4] Businesses that offer hourly employees flexible work options, in fact, find that they are critical management tools that enhance recruitment, retention, engagement, cost control, productivity and financial performance. Donna Klein, executive chairman of Corporate Voices, says the organization's study, *Innovative Workplace Flexibility Options for Hourly Workers*, demonstrates that, when available, flexibility can be as beneficial or even more beneficial to hourly workers and the businesses that employ them.

Key findings from the Corporate Voices report include:
- Managers and employees agree that flexibility adds value for the business and for the individual employee in key areas involving productivity, customer service, employee work-life effectiveness, stress and well-being.
- For businesses, flexible schedules are an effective means of managing personnel costs, in particular overtime costs, which is a win-win for employees and employers.
- More than 80 percent of employers and employees surveyed say flexibility is important to recruitment and retention.
- Companies have found that offering flexible schedules and innovative time-off policies contribute to being considered an "employer of choice" by younger workers.
- For positions in customer service and sales with typically high turnover, companies find that flexibility is a way to retain high-performing employees. These companies use flexibility to respond to the changing needs of workers at various stages of their lives and careers.
- Flexible work options are being used in businesses with continuous operations that need weekend coverage or whose business hours extend beyond the standard 9-to-5 day. This includes voluntary part-time positions as well as flextime and compressed work schedules.

"In this study, we find that it is not only formal flexible arrangements that produce these impressive results, but progressive personnel policies and a work culture supportive of occasional flexibility that give workers access to a variety of time-off options and control over their work schedules," says Klein. "When companies provide employees with an array of flexibility and time-off options and an environment in which it is possible to access flexibility opportunities without barriers, employees develop strategies that best meet their individual needs and satisfy business requirements."

This trend is supported by the findings of the Working Mother's Best Companies for Hourly Workers.[5] According to the initiative's findings, Best Companies provide hourly workers:

- Access to advance notification of monthly work hours, volunteer overtime and extended unpaid time off without penalty.
- Access to guaranteed scheduled time off, trading of shifts, pickup shifts and episodic time off.
- Access to schedule preference bidding, trading of partial shifts, floating holidays and downtime leave.
- Access to drop shifts and shift time off that can be made up during the pay period.
- Opportunities for split shifts.

Organizations with large hourly populations will find great advantages from leveraging flexible work options in terms of their ability to attract, retain and engage diverse talent and reduce overhead costs, particularly in terms of real estate.

Flex and Career Paths

With changing employee demographics and work and life styles, the definition of a career is evolving as well. No longer is there just the "up or out" model of career development. Today's careers are as unique as each individual employee. More and more employees today are moving in and out of the workforce and choosing to slow down or speed up their careers in order to meet personal work and life needs.

The corporate workforce has, in a few short generations, completely transformed. Yet, the expectations of the traditional workplace and the one-size-fits-all corporate ladder model of career progression has not changed in many companies. Deloitte's Mass Career Customization™ (MCC) is an example of one organization's attempt to redefine the notion of a career. According to Deloitte, MCC enables a more adaptive approach that responds to the realities of how work gets done and careers are built, reflecting the career shifts of climbs and lateral moves. In contrast to the more limited options provided by the corporate ladder, Deloitte believes that the corporate lattice makes it possible for employees to customize careers — to the benefit of both the individual and the company. The result is an adaptive model of career progression that offers employees career-long options for keeping their work and personal lives in sync and employers the long-term loyalty of their best and brightest talent.[6]

Today, many employees are already building their own lattice-like careers by moving in and out of organizations, dialing up or dialing down — or, as Sylvia Hewlett, president of the Center for Work-Life Policy, calls it, off- and on-ramping. However, these employees are making these adaptations often without support or structure from their employers. Organizations can gain a significant competitive advantage by both recognizing this reality and addressing it by creating a more flexible work culture. The Center for Work-Life Policy's latest research on on- and off-rampers says that organizations are at risk of sidelining or losing nearly three out of five of their most talented workers by not supporting their need for more flexible career paths.[7] According to this study, some 58 percent of a company's high-echelon female talent experience career interruptions that sidetrack them from traditional lock-step linear career paths, penalize their earning power, sabotage their long-term promotional prospects, sap their ambition and cause many women to switch employers or quit work altogether.

But that's not all. More than one-quarter of the women in the sample were single and 38 percent of them were childless. Yet, even without the additional tug of child care, these women still chose to off-ramp in significant numbers, with 14 percent of single, never-married women reporting having taken a break at some point during their careers, as did 31 percent of childless women. Moreover, 44 percent of childless off-rampers cited an unsatisfactory or disappointing career as a major factor in their decision to depart, while 28 percent said they felt stalled. No matter what their reason for taking a break, the vast majority of highly qualified women want to return to work.

Further, the long-term penalty for women taking a timeout from their career has worsened since the recession, according to a new study from the Center for Work Life Policy.[8] Since the recession, the study found, timeouts or "off-ramping" from a career for child care or other reasons have become increasingly unaffordable to women whose income has become even more important to family budgets. And getting back into the workforce after a timeout has become even more difficult. Seventy-three percent of women trying to return to the workforce after a voluntary timeout for child care or other reasons report trouble finding a job. Those who do return report losing 16 percent of their earning power, while more than a quarter saw a decrease in their management responsibilities, and 22 percent had to step down to a lower job title. Unless companies facilitate off-ramping and on-ramping more effectively, over the long term, they will lose out on the valuable contributions of women, who represent 58 percent of the highly credentialed talent pool.

The Center for Work Life Policy found that almost 70 percent of participants in the survey said they would not have left if their companies had offered one or more specific flexible work options, such as reduced-hour schedules; job sharing; part-time tracks; short, unpaid sabbaticals; and/or flextime. And yet, even when companies offer such options, they often fail to adequately publicize them to their employees: 54 percent of women said they left without discussing their options with their supervisor. Many companies also fail to adapt their incentives to accommodate the high value women place on such things as flexible work arrangements, the chance to collaborate with others, an opportunity to give back to the community, and recognition — all of which they rate higher than compensation. Clearly, with more effective career planning that incorporates options to dial down or up, off- or on-ramp without penalty, organizations will be able to retain valuable talent more effectively.

Flexibility and the Multigenerational Workforce

For the first time ever there are four generations working at the same time — in some cases, in the same organization. Stanton Smith's book, *Decoding Generational Differences: Fact, Fiction, or Should We Just Get Back to Work?*, details a cultural learning exercise at Deloitte, a Big Four accounting and consulting firm[9] that has four generations of employees at work: veterans (those born before 1946), baby boomers (born between 1946 and 1964), Generation X (born between 1965 and 1980) and Generation Y (born after 1980). Smith found that while there are differences, there are also similarities between generations. One thing they all have in common is their interest in more control over how, when and where they work. They may be interested in flexibility for different reasons — some for child care, others to exercise, volunteer or go back to school — but regardless of the reason, more flexibility is part of the solution.

Clearly, there are different motivators for the different generations. According to the Sloan Center for Aging and Work's recent study, the notion that "one size fits all" when it comes to the steps that employers could take with regard to employee engagement no longer exists. The findings also suggest that employers might want to focus on specific drivers of engagement for some employees in particular age/generational groups and other drivers for some of those in other groups. For example, having access to the flexibility that employees need to fulfill work and family responsibilities was one of the factors related to higher levels of employee engagement among the Gen Ys in its study.[10]

Supporting this point is a 2008 PricewaterhouseCoopers study, where more than 4,200 university graduates from around the world who either worked for or were about to work for PwC were surveyed.[11] They found that while only 3 percent of respondents expected to work mainly at home, 66 percent expected to work regular office hours with some flexible work. Presumably, most of these workers do not yet have family responsibilities competing with work responsibilities, yet they want to incorporate flex into their working lives from the beginning of their careers.

A number of studies have further highlighted the value of work/life benefits and flexible workplaces. Although these benefits have often focused on women, they increasingly include men and consider other factors, especially age, race and ethnicity. A survey on the "Bookends Generations" by the Center for Work Life Policy's Sylvia Ann Hewlett found that 87 percent of baby boomers and 89 percent of Gen Y said flex time was important to them.

Winners of the Alfred P. Sloan Award for Business Excellence in Workplace Flexibility demonstrate how they use workplace flexibility as a strategy to make work better for both the employer and diverse, multi-generational employee populations.[12] For example, Blue Gecko, a Seattle-based database services company that has won the award four years running, promises hair-trigger responses when client computer systems go awry. An observer might assume that Blue Gecko's pledge to have someone respond to a customer emergency within 30 minutes, regardless of the time of day, might preclude flexibility, but the company claims the opposite is true. Most of its work requires only an Internet connection and focus, the company says, asserting that technology allows great flexibility with staff time and location. To date, Blue Gecko claims to have been able to respond to every reasonable schedule request any staff member has proposed. "Our people get called in for emergencies," says a representative. "We need to give them the same level of flexibility we expect from them."

"Two of the biggest issues for employers in today's economy are recruitment of top talent and retention of valued employees," said Greg Roth, senior manager of programs for the U.S. Chamber of Commerce's Institute for a Competitive Workforce. "The business community sees workplace flexibility as a vital piece in a broader plan to develop the strongest possible workforce. As a strategy to stay competitive, workplace flexibility can be a sound business decision for employers no matter the size or industry sector."

Kathleen Christensen, program director of the Workplace, Workforce and Working Family Program at Alfred P. Sloan Foundation, believes that the aging workforce will be one of the major drivers for increased flexibility in the future. As employees reach retirement age, organizations will realize that they may be facing a major talent shortage with a smaller, less-skilled workforce. These factors may force employers to consider flexible ways for mature workers to phase into retirement by reducing their schedules, which is the way many older workers want to — and, for financial reasons may need to — end their careers.

Flexibility and Caregivers

Working mothers were the first group to push for more flexibility in the work place as they struggled (and continue to be challenged) with trying to meet the needs of their families and their employers. As the demands from work and family grew women began to ask their employers to consider programs such as child care support. From there, efforts started to focus on getting more flexibility in how, when and where they worked. Women are also most frequently the caregivers for aging relatives. And, while the needs and demands are significantly different than those of taking care of children, both types of caregiving require flexibility.

Healthways Center for Health Research, a global Disease Management and Well-Being provider,[13] examined the impact of caring for a loved one while holding outside employment. The study, found that 52 million Americans currently provide care for an ailing or disabled loved one, while one in five U.S. households provide support to an aging or disabled loved one for 18 or more hours each week.

Multiple demands on the Sandwich Generation and other caregivers will only increase the need for flexible work arrangements, according to Joseph Coughlin, Director of the Massachusetts Institute of Technology Age Lab and author of the study. The research found that stress increases and happiness decreases markedly as caregiving demands grow. Employed non-caregivers report the least stress and most happiness, while employed caregivers reported the highest levels of stress and least happiness. Given that the fastest growing segment of the population is those over 85, and the children of this cohort are still working toward their own retirement means that regardless of gender, elder care is going to effect the workforce in dramatic ways and caregivers will need a range of flexible work options to address these issues.

Even caregivers of loved ones who reside in assisted living communities or nursing homes can experience caregiver stress, accompanied by guilt. Families often still carry much of the responsibility for scheduling appointments and managing medical care and finances. Some make daily visits, contributing to their own stress in the process. In terms of working caregivers, stress can be eased with social and financial support, but also with flexible work arrangements. Coughlin identified several factors that can help companies retain caregivers as employees while boosting caregiver well-being including:

- Flexible hours
- Unpaid family leave
- Paid sick or vacation days
- Workplace wellness programs

Almost one in five companies say that in 2011 they plan to add or increase the amount of flextime options they offer employees to accommodate employees' caregiving responsibilities, according to a survey by executive search firm Amrop Battalia Winston.[14]

Public Policy and Flexible Work

There is a new focus on flexible work from not just public policy leaders and the White House, but a broad range of organizations, as well. According to the Georgetown Law School report, "Workplace Flexibility 2010," making workplace flexibility the norm will require development of innovative employer and employee practices in the public and private sectors and thoughtful public policy by all levels of government. The first policy platform in this report focused on flexible work arrangements. It argues that while flexible work arrangements alter the time and/or place that work is conducted, it can be done in a manner that is as manageable and predictable as possible for both employees and employers.

The report went on to recommend that flexibility be voluntary and that it be requested by employees. Flexible work arrangements should not be imposed by employers in order to reduce costs. Employees may need flexible work arrangements for any number of reasons, including child care, elder care, medical treatment, education and training, volunteering, or faith-based practice. It was therefore recommended that integrating flexible work arrangements into the workplace should be done as standard operating procedure. The commitment must come from all levels of government, as well as the private sector, in a comprehensive campaign.

The report specified a three-pronged approach to create a comprehensive flexible work public policy strategy as follows:

1. Make the adoption of flexible work arrangements compelling to the general public by explaining in persuasive terms why flexible work arrangements deserve to be the "new normal" in the workplace. A successful media campaign should reach into all sectors of society, deploying strategic public education and awards.
2. Support employers and employees in integrating flexible work arrangements into their workplaces as standard operating procedure.
3. Invest government money and ingenuity in piloting on-the-ground innovative flexible work arrangement approaches, learning from those efforts, and then disseminating the

lessons learned. Establish laws that require employers to have a process through which supervisors and employees discuss requests for flexible work arrangements.

Workplace Flexibility 2010 also suggested that a Presidential Committee on Workplace Flexibility could be created by executive order that would not administer any programs, but would provide visibility in advising federal agencies about the direction, coordination and content of workplace flexibility policies and programs. A Citizens' Advisory Council could be created by executive order as well, composed of employee and employer interests, as well as other stakeholders, to advise the Presidential committee.

In a separate but related activity, on January 30, 2009, President Obama announced the creation of a White House Task Force on Middle Class Working Families. Chaired by Vice President Joe Biden, the Task Force is a major initiative targeted at raising the living standards of middle-class, working families in America and has the following goals:
- ☆ Expanding education and lifelong training opportunities.
- ☆ Improving work and family balance.
- ☆ Restoring labor standards, including workplace safety.
- ☆ Helping to protect middle-class and working-family incomes.
- ☆ Protecting retirement security.

According to President Obama, "Workplace flexibility is about attracting and retaining top talent in the federal workforce and empowering them to do their jobs, and judging their success by the results that they get — not by how many meetings they attend, or how much face-time they log, or how many hours are spent on airplanes. It's about creating a culture where work is what you do, not where you are."

In an effort to use the federal government as an example of how flexible work can positively impact business outcomes, the federal Office of Personnel —the HR arm of the government — instituted a flexible work pilot initiative in 2010 to support working flexibly in ways that focused on results instead of face time as the measure of performance. Other state and local government agencies are also involved in various pilot projects to explore the use of and demonstrate the value of a variety of flexible work options.

The power of shining a spotlight on government agencies is also apparent in the Working Mother/Corporate Voices for Working Families Best of Congress Award. The purpose of this award is to elevate the discussion and policy debate on working family issues and to demonstrate that many members of Congress are tireless advocates for improving the lives of working families. The recipients of the Best of Congress Award serve as models for what can be accomplished through legislation and a personal commitment to policies that benefit working families. Organizations like the Society for Human Resource Management (SHRM) and AARP, among others, have also taken active roles in public policy and flexible work issues before Congress that impact their members.

Global Issues and Flexible Work

Many companies are examining global issues related to flexible work practices in the regions where they operate. But while employees' needs for flexibility may be universal, the social norms and legal issues that relate to flexible work are not the same in every country. In some cases, employers are creating a common framework for their approach to flexible work on a global level, while other companies are providing flexible work information and resources that relate specifically to local issues.

Some countries, like the United Kingdom, Singapore and Australia, have established laws that govern the way employers must offer flexible work options. However, in most countries, flexible work is left up to the employer. That said, many international companies realize that there are employee issues around fairness and equity regarding who has access to flexible work options. And, in fact, there is the potential for serious discrimination as different organizational policies and practices become known in various parts of the world. Even as companies try to disseminate benefits and communicate to employees around the world, there are challenges in making sure that there is clarity and consistency regarding the way flexible work issues are handled. Given that the interest in flexible work on the part of employees is fairly universal, employers need to address these issues in a consistent way.

The Corporate Voices 2011 report, "Business Impacts of Flexibility: An Imperative for Expansion," includes information on how flexibility policies are being adopted globally. The global expansion of flexibility is more complex due to prevailing work cultures and local laws governing work hours and provision of parental and personal leaves. Companies have found that they have succeeded by establishing strategic flexibility objectives and guidelines at the global level coupled with actions and implementation at the local level, including specifics of flexibility offerings, communications and training. The experiences from leading organizations demonstrate best practices in incorporating flexibility into business processes and work culture. In particular, the involvement of employee resource groups as stakeholders, advances in the use of online flexibility management systems, tracking of flexibility arrangements in Human Resource Information Systems (HRIS), conduct of global employee surveys, and incorporation of flexibility into performance management discussions and metrics have vastly improved the availability and accessibility of information about flexibility both to support global implementation as well as to provide invaluable data on the business impacts of flexibility. The report includes examples from several global companies, including the following.

IBM

Flexibility is a key component of IBM's global work/life strategy to create a workplace where employees can thrive on and off the job in what is called the "New Normal" work environment. As part of this "New Normal" way of business, the enterprise never stops and results in global interdependencies at all levels of the business. Flexibility is an essential tool that enables employees at IBM to adapt to when and where work gets done, and to maintain sufficient time and energy to enjoy a satisfying personal/family life. It also enables the company to attract, motivate and retain key talent. IBM's creation of a Workplace Indicator Code in its global HRIS system is evidence of the integration of flexibility as a business tool. Each employee is assigned one of six global work location types: Customer/Alternate Location, Work at Home, Mobile, Traditional Non-Office, Traditional, or Extended Office. A Workplace Indicator Guide provides guidance for considering and effectively managing employees who work in IBM's unique individual work environments. Thus, basic information on the use of flexibility is as readily available as other talent management information for different geographies and business divisions.

Merck

"If you give the flexibility, if you give the responsibility to the employee, if you say, 'Here's the work that needs to be done; the way you do it is irrelevant to me,' it improves productivity," says Dick Clark, chairman and CEO of Merck and also the winner of the Families and Work Institute 2010 Work Life Legacy Award. "I actually see better productivity from employees who use flextime because they are dedicated to the company, they know they have that responsibility and they're thankful for what the company did to be able to give them the flexibility of deciding when and how to do [their work]. The empowerment aspect of these programs is just fantastic."

Merck's 10 Global Constituency Groups (senior leadership teams that set the global diversity and inclusion strategy) were formed in 2007 and 2008 and play an important role in presenting a powerful case to the executive team and promoting flexibility globally. For example, Merck's 2008 global flexibility baseline survey revealed some limitations in how flexibility was utilized, and strengthened the business case for expanding flexibility by demonstrating the strong relationship of flexibility to higher levels of engagement and retention. Now, two years after the global rollout, semi-annual culture and engagement surveys continue to document the impact of flexibility: As of March 2010, roughly 80 percent of employees globally reported feeling they had the flexibility they needed and the engagement level rose significantly as a result of an increased use of flexibility. Merck's global flexibility website and tracking tool, available in 10 languages, is a hub for flexibility information and resources.

Procter & Gamble

Over the past five years, Procter & Gamble's internal research has consistently validated that on a global basis, flexibility, energy and simplification of work demands are the three drivers of work-life effectiveness and personal well-being that in turn drive personal business performance and the company's ability to remain an employer of choice.

The Central and Eastern Europe, Middle East and Africa (CEEMEA) region's experience highlights how Procter & Gamble translates data on flexibility into action in a large and complex international region, representing 16,000 employees in more than 20 countries. The business case comes from its internal survey data and the ability to tie flexibility to energy and work simplicity, along with other issues such as retention and generational needs. P&G's annual

Employer of Choice survey measures flexibility both qualitatively and quantitatively. Survey results are used in communications to employees so that they not only know what is available to them, but also understand the broader implications of flexibility and work-life effectiveness, the linkages between flexibility and key business drivers, such as intent to leave and performance.

As a result of the 2009 implementation of flexible work options, more than 2,500 employees (57 percent of survey respondents) report using some form of flexibility. The 2009 survey showed a 12-point improvement in favorable ratings on the statement, "I have sufficient flexibility to effectively manage my work and personal life," for the CEEMEA region as compared with 2008. Employees participating in flexible work arrangements report higher work-life effectiveness scores (personal well-being and work simplification) as well as Employer of Choice survey scores.

Although Procter & Gamble had supported flexible work policies for many years, the global expansion of flexibility was facilitated by the introduction of the web-based Flex Management System, a powerful online infrastructure rolled out in 2007, which has legitimized and leveraged the business value of flexible work in a proactive way. The Flex Management System is the central repository for all flexibility information specific to Procter & Gamble, housing flexible work policies, forms, philosophy, tool kits and success stories. Each region has its own section for region-specific policies and practices. The system equips line managers, employees and human resources to apply flexibility specifically to their role and educates each stakeholder about the importance, implications and implementation of flexibility.

American Express

For American Express, competition for diverse top talent, retention of top talent and real estate factors drive the business need for flexibility. Formalized flexibility policies and programs are in place and are being expanded upon across the company's global network. American Express' flexibility infrastructure consists of a three-pronged foundation supported by Human Resources, Global Real Estate and Global Technology. The flexibility program combines work styles, work arrangements, workspace and workplace technology to offer several innovative options including reduced hours for up to three years, compressed work-week schedules, part-time roles, telework and home office setups.

Flexibility leaders understand the importance of valid, usable data as they continue to implement flexibility globally. Showing the return on investment and business value for flexibility is crucial for adoption. Through company enterprise resource planning systems, internal surveys and focus groups, American Express captures global, business unit and location-specific data. It is able to track the utilization of flexibility options globally and to connect flexibility usage with employee engagement, productivity, collaboration, connectivity, decision-making, employee satisfaction and retention. Flexibility also offers corporate financial benefits by creating real estate cost savings and reinvestment opportunities. The global economic recession has helped spark a sense of urgency to promote flexibility within American Express and other companies. No longer something that is just nice-to-have, flexibility has become an organizational requirement as the need for employees to work more effectively and productively increases, and as competition for the multi-generational and diverse workforce escalates.

Conclusion

There are numerous trends that impact, or are impacted by, flexible work. As social and economic conditions change, organizations will need to continuously adapt, and one of the tools they will use is increased flexibility in how, when and where work is done. In terms of these trends, a look at what is currently happening in the workplace may provide some sense of what we can expect in the future. Writing in Working Mother, Life Meets Work's Kyra Cavanaugh noted that in January 2011, with economic conditions still tight, employees weren't stepping up to ask for flexibility. Indeed, they still aren't asking for much of anything. But if ever there was a time when the words "pent-up demand" meant something, 2011 is it. Businesses are already seeing an uptick in voluntary quits. With three years of corporate belt-tightening and hard work behind them, workers are looking for new opportunities. According to one study, as many as 81 percent of employees may be lured away.

Here are Kyra's prediction for the top five flexible work trends expected in 2011:

1. **Employee exodus.** It takes a lot to overwork a nation of chronic workaholics, but we finally did it. Productivity dropped for the first time since late 2008, and the recessionary mindset of doing less with more is starting to give way. The Department of Labor recently revealed that even with our current unemployment rate, the number of voluntary departures has risen since August 2009. According to Right Management, a talent management consultancy, 54 percent of companies have already lost top talent involuntarily in the first half of 2001. Workers will continue to leave in bigger and bigger numbers, citing work/life, a need for flexibility, and too much stress as the causes.
2. **Greater shift in gender roles.** Women match men in workforce participation and are beginning to outpace them in educational attainment. Thanks to a recession that hit men especially hard, more women are also finding themselves in the role of primary breadwinner. That's just one reason men are stepping up and taking on more child care responsibility. Proof? Men now win primary custody in 50 percent of contested divorces. But no matter who the primary caregiver is, we're going to see greater parity as both mothers and fathers take responsibility for the work/child care juggle.
3. **Telework leads the way.** Of all the flexible work strategies, telework will have the greatest acceptance rate. The explosion of tech tools, real estate cost cutting, and other financial benefits means telework will continue to increase in American corporations, whether or not it's tied to a bigger flexible work strategy. The government is modeling the way: President Obama signed the Telework Enhancement Act in December 2010, mandating that government agencies step up their use of telework. This is not just a U.S. trend: Technology analyst TechCast predicts 30 percent of the industrial world will telecommute two to three days per week by 2019.
4. **Focus shifts to hourly workers.** While the workplace flexibility discussion is well entrenched in our country's top offices, only 13 percent of American families are led by

professional or managerial parents. Forward thinking companies recognize that flexibility is achievable, but different, for hourly workers. To minimize work/life stress for their hourly workers, organizations are finding success with tactics like predictive scheduling, shift trading, and new strategies for staffing unexpected overtime.

5. **Look beyond flex policy.** HR leaders are increasingly aware that policy is not enough to achieve the business benefits of flex. Award-winning companies and newbies alike are rethinking their approach to flex implementation in order to address middle manager resistance. Even in organizations where executives support and encourage flexible work practices, middle managers steeped in traditional ways of working (think: face time) still resist alternative work strategies. Organizations are realizing that official flex policies mean little if managers won't get behind them.

Life Meets Work's Kyra Cavanaugh goes on to say that work-life issues will be a driving force behind attrition. Companies that have already built supportive, flexible work cultures will rise to the top. Meanwhile, companies that insist flexible work strategies are impossible — that "flex could never work for us" — will find themselves handling the bulk of future quits.

The significance of the trends in flexible work will vary for each organization. However, there will be some trends that are important to every organization. By monitoring current trends, each organization can stay ahead of the curve and identify information relevant to their unique business needs. Identifying the trends that support their organization's ability to create a more flexible workplace and workforce will position the company to attract, retain and engage the most productive workforce and be able to face the future with greater confidence of success.

TIP SHEET
Trends in Flexible Work

- ❏ Examine your organization's policies and practices in various geographies where you operate to ensure there is consistency in terms of flexible work messaging.

- ❏ Make sure that your flexible work policies and practices are legally compliant in all geographies.

- ❏ Ensure that your labor relations and legal staff are up to date on laws and issues related to flexible work and aware of potential compliance requirements.

- ❏ Provide your lobbyists with information about flexible work and make sure they are aware of the company's initiatives.

- ❏ Know your company's position on contingent workers and provide appropriate flexible work information.

- ❏ Create a holistic strategic workforce plan that includes the way flexible work practices will impact and support these efforts.

- ❏ Consider the needs of multiple generations in the workforce and leverage flexible work options to appropriately address them.

- ❏ Ensure that when people need to work flexibly — permanently or occasionally — that they are not at risk of being marginalized.

- ❏ Protect employees from being penalized by receiving less challenging assignments or growth opportunities when they work flexibly.

- ❏ Plan for employees who work flexibly — permanently or occasionally — to advance as easily as others. It can be at a prorated pace, however, in the case of people who take time out of a career or work less than full-time.

- ❏ Choose and develop leaders from among a pool that includes flexible workers.

- • Make sure that flexible careers are possible and truly viable and that they include off ramps, detours or side streets.

- ❏ Include flexible workers among the mentored, and specifically coach them on career flexibility.

- ❏ Identify the information you need relative to the specific trends that will impact your organization's ability to attract, engage and retain diverse talent.

REFERENCES: CHAPTER 8

1. (2007) "Flex and Strategic Workforce Planning: A New Way to Boost Productivity," American Management Association.
2. (2008), "Strategic Workforce Planning: Forecasting Human Capital Needs to Execute Business Strategy," The Conference Board.
3. (2010) Elsdon, R. "Building Workforce Strength," National Career Development Association.
4. (2009) "Innovative Workplace Flexibility Options for Hourly Workers," Corporate Voices.
5. (2010) "Best Companies for Hourly Workers," Working Mother Media.
6. (2010) Hewitt, S., "As Careers Paths Change, Make On-Ramping Easy," *Harvard Business Review*.
7. (2010) "Time-Outs Take an Increasing Toll on Women's Careers," The Center for Work-Life Policy.
8. (2008) Smith, S. "Decoding Generational Differences: Fact, Fiction, or Should We Just Get Back to Work?"
9. (2004) Koeppel, D. "When 'Job' Means Part Time, Life Becomes Very Different," The New York Times, October 4, 2004.
10. (2010) "Engaging the 21st century multi-generational workforce Findings from the Age & Generations Study," Sloan Center for Aging and Work.
11. (2008) "Millennials at Work," Research from PricewaterhouseCoopers.
12. (2011) "Flexible Work: Bringing the Work to People Rather than People to Work," Microsoft,
13. (2009) "Guide to New Ideas for Making Work Work," Families and Work Institute.
14. (2010) Tom, J., "Caregiver Demands Call for Flexible work arrangements," Seniorhomes.com.

Chapter 9

The Process: How to Plan, Implement and Manage Flexibility

The Process

For many years flexibility was viewed as a special privilege for a select few employees, or an initiative that required just a few guidelines for managers in order to be successful. Today, flexible work is part of an organization's approach to culture change. It requires a comprehensive plan involving a number of key stakeholders, including diversity/inclusion, technology, facilities, business continuity and health/wellness. Regardless of who is responsible for the planning, implementation and management of flexible work, there are some basic components that should be included.

Strategies for implementation vary depending upon whether the company is just beginning to develop its flexible work initiative or if it is expanding an existing policy. In both cases the process is similar. Keep in mind that creating a more agile workplace and workforce requires continuous attention to what's working and what's not; it is not necessarily a linear approach to change.

In Chapter 9, we will explore the following:

✔ How do you plan a flexible work initiative when the organization is initiating, enhancing or advancing flexibility?

✔ How do you develop an effective communication/marketing plan?

✔ What is the best approach to implementing a flexible work initiative?

✔ How do you handle challenges to creating and implementing a more flexible culture?

✔ What role do managers, employees, HR or the flex "gatekeeper" play?

✔ What are possible guidelines to help managers and employees manage flexibility?

✔ How do you evaluate the effectiveness and ROI?

Planning a Flexible Work Initiative

The best initiative in the world won't accomplish its goals if it is not designed and managed effectively. Whether you're initiating, enhancing or advancing your organization's flexible work program, the key to success is having a consistent message across marketing/communications, implementation and evaluation plans and processes.

Workplace flexibility is an ongoing initiative, not a one-time program. Because it requires such extensive culture change — scheduling, employee face time, methods of supervision and performance evaluation will undergo vast reworking — it should be implemented in stages as part of an overall, long-term strategy. The goal should be to maintain current levels of productivity as opposed to boosting it; creating a flexible work environment should not be held to a higher standard than other organizational change initiatives.

Here is a blueprint for planning, implementing and managing a flexible work initiative:

Gain support for the initiative.
Introducing a workplace and workforce flexible work initiative requires the ability to manage basic change because it will likely affect all aspects of the company's systems, policies and practices. Support for managing more flexibly needs to come from the top of the organization in order for it to be more than just a one-time effort. Making the business case for the use of flexible work arrangements is a way to lay a solid base of support. Support from internal "customers" is an important aspect of satisfying external customers.

Appoint a cross-functional planning group or task force.
If a task force is formed, it is important to include members who represent diverse groups or positions within the company. Be sure to include representatives from such departments as IT, facilities, diversity/inclusion, talent management, health/wellness and business continuity. If possible, a high level champion should function as the leader or spokesperson of the group. The goal of the task force is to define a direction for the company regarding flexible work issues. Individual issues must be handled in such a way that they can be easily explained and related to the overall business strategy of the organization.

In some companies, the first job of a flexible work task force is not to solve a particular problem, but to position flexible work as part of a larger effort of culture change. In this way, the value of flexible work is clear and the mission of the flexible work task force is seen as relevant to the organization's success. Even companies that have a flexible work initiative in place can benefit from the formation and work of a task force.

The task force should approach obtaining the necessary information on flexible work issues just as it would for any other business issue it may be investigating.

The task force may be responsible for the following:
- Investigate what similar organizations have done
- Inventory existing flex-related experiences in the organization
- Define objectives and desired results
- Develop a draft policy statement or guidelines for review
- Develop an action plan and timetable for evaluating the new initiative
- Devise a system for gathering input and generating feedback during the initial phases of the initiative
- Revise the policy and action plan as appropriate
- Determine the initial scope of the initiative: Will it start out as a pilot? Will it be companywide or apply only to select units? Will it be introduced incrementally?
- Plan how the initiative will be evaluated
- Set up a process to provide ongoing support for those charged with implementing the change and reiterate top management's commitment to increasing flexibility

Set up an administrative plan
- Implement specifics of the initiative devised by the task force
- Coordinate and develop technical assistance for HR, managers/supervisors and employees

Design the initiative
- This could be the responsibility of the task force or a subgroup created by the task force
- Review current policy/guidelines for compatibility with new objectives and form new policy/guidelines where necessary
- Consider issues such as eligibility, application process, approval/denial, effect on employee status, and measurement/metrics

Develop resource materials
- Create materials for employees, managers and HR representatives
- Include description, educational and technical assistance materials, and training to explain new options and policies and provide support and guidance
- Use intranet and other technology support to disseminate and share resource information

Announce the initiative
- Take an assertive posture rather than waiting for employees to request a flexible schedule
- Cascade information about the flexibility initiative down the organization so that leaders and managers are aware of the plans and have the appropriate tools and resources to support it at every level

Promote the initiative
- If an organization and its employees are to take full advantage of any of the new work arrangements, flexibility must be promoted on an ongoing basis. From management's perspective, the benefits associated with most of the options come from a multiplier effect; that is, the more employees who use flexibility on a voluntary basis, the greater the benefits to the organization

- Promote on a regular basis and in a variety of ways
- Reassure employees that participating in flexibility will not have an adverse effect on their career or earning potential
- Encourage managers to model flexibility
- Reward managers who effectively use flexibility

Evaluate the initiative
- Build the end evaluation process into design of the initiative from the beginning
- Consider whether the initiative has had the desired effect. If not, why not? What are the problem areas? Any unexpected benefits? How have employees and managers reacted?

Fine tune the initiative
- Use information from the evaluation process to modify the tools, resources, messages, etc.
- The task force should present results and recommend next steps to senior management
- Develop a process for obtaining feedback from managers, employees and HR representatives as a component of the ongoing flexibility initiative

Flexible Work Communications Plan

The goal of the communications plan is to provide a thoughtful, culturally appropriate, step-by-step guide to promote the flexible work initiative over time. The communications plan should take into consideration the work that has already been done and involve the appropriate internal stakeholders. Typically, the flexible work communications plan will include the following steps:

- Determine the audience(s) and assess their needs
- Know the culture
- Create a message map with consistent terminology and themes
- Define the process for decision making and dissemination
- Identify the communication vehicles/media outreach
- Involve key stakeholders
- Outline timing and deliverables

Let's look at each element in more detail:

Determine the audience(s) and assess the needs. It is important to decide who needs to know about the flexible work initiative, what they need to know, and when they need to know it. There may be one audience, like senior leaders, or there may be several audiences — human resources, managers and employees — and for each audience there may be a different communication strategy, process and messages. The focus may be on getting a buy-in, or on educating certain populations about their roles in creating a more flexible culture. So, first, determine the audience for the communication plan.

Conduct an informal or formal needs assessment. Identify the key audiences and separate those groups in terms of their different needs. For example, identify the employee segments that a new initiative is most likely to benefit. Then estimate the size of the segment and project the benefits to the company that are expected from the initiative. Quantify the benefits as much as possible. Always include ongoing market research — ask end users what they like, dislike, want, don't want, etc.

Know the culture. What works in one company may not work in another. Companies are like families — similar to each other in some ways but different in many other ways. That is why it is often difficult to replicate another company's successful flexible work initiative. Consider what has been effective in your organization in the past and why. Develop a flexible work communication plan that takes into account the personality of your organization. Know current hot issues in the company, where the pain is (recruitment, retention, absenteeism, facility costs, etc.). Involve someone in the process who really understands the corporate culture. Be aware of the image the company wants to project.

Create a message map with consistent terminology and themes. The purpose of the message map is to provide a common vocabulary for the flexible work initiative. Are the key messages centered on the role of flexible work in solving business challenges? Attracting diverse talent? Avoiding business interruptions? Reducing costs? Establishing a competitive advantage? What are the terms the organization should use when referring to aspects of flexible work? Whether you call it telework, telecommuting, virtual work, work at home, or remote work, the messaging must be consistent. Is the goal to create a brand or special identity for the flexible work initiative? Some organizations give their initiative names such as "Working Smart" or "Work Well." The flex brand might relate to the organization's business brand. So, if being adaptive and resilient is part of the company's brand recognition, "Flex Agility" may be a good name for the flex initiative. It can be fun to make a contest out of creating the right identity for the initiative and maybe involve marketing/communications folks in the decision making process.

Define the process for decision making and dissemination. Because flexible work tends to touch on all aspects of the organization — from technology to benefits, from HR systems to external branding and recruiting — it is important to consider who needs to sign off on the communication process and messages. In terms of dissemination, some companies cascade the communication starting at the top and moving down through the organization. Typically, the more senior person introduces the flex initiative, explains the why, what, etc., either in face-to-face meetings, a webinar format or by email. Some organizations target a specific population and focus exclusively on that group. A word of caution, though: Flexibility tends to be highly valued and word of the initiative can travel fast. It is important to control the message, rather than to be forced to do damage control. So, cast a broad net when thinking about the decision-making and dissemination processes.

Identify the communication vehicles/media outreach. There are many ways to get the message out, but care must be taken to determine the most culturally appropriate methods of communication. Clearly, technology plays a big part in planning the communication vehicles and outreach. Leveraging email, webinars, social media, internal websites and newsletters, etc.

are all good ways to maintain awareness. It is also a good idea to connect the dots wherever possible, linking and aligning the flexible work messages with other communication. For instance, you might take the opportunity during a benefits enrollment period to include a message about the flexible work initiative. Manager training activities, workshops held by the Employee Assistance Initiative or health screening assessments all represent good opportunities to reinforce flexible work messages.

Involve key stakeholders. As the saying goes, keep your friends close and your enemies closer. That is also true when it comes to creating the right messages and process to communicate about flexible work. Be sure to get input from the naysayers, as well as supporters. Consider the areas that will be impacted by the flexible work plans — technology, communications, talent management, HR generalists, benefits, policy, legal, health/wellness, facilities — and include them in the process. It could entail just alerting them to what is being planned or actually asking them to take a role in the communication planning and dissemination. It can be extremely valuable in the communication process to involve a senior leader who is willing to speak publicly about the initiative, become the champion or advisor, and/or actually pilot the effort in his/her department or division.

Outline timing and deliverables. Timing is everything. Careful planning will pay off. It's wise to map out the entire process, even if it means looking ahead several years. The short-term plans should be as specific as possible, while, longer range, the information can highlight general next steps and what-if scenarios. Be sure to include a timeline that describes what is expected to happen and when, what materials are needed, and who needs to be involved. As the plan evolves, the timing can always be adjusted. Be sure to keep all stakeholders informed as things change, but also tell them about results and success stories along the way.

Marketing the Flexible Work Initiative

Once the plan has been created, it is time to get started. The process of internally marketing flexible work initiatives requires creativity and perseverance on the part of all of those involved. It also requires considerable knowledge about the organization, its culture and the relevance of flexible work issues to the company's goals and concerns. In terms of marketing the flexible work agenda, it is important to know who to target and the likely obstacles or resistances that will be encountered. Effective marketing is necessary if a culture change initiative is to survive. In many ways, marketing flexible work initiatives is similar to marketing any other human resource initiative. The key to getting a company to adopt flexible work initiatives and making them successful is to take a basic marketing approach: Sell the ideas as part of an overall business strategy to meet corporate objectives. Promoting flexible work is an ongoing process that requires constant feedback and communication. Packaging the flexible work message, customizing communication for different target audiences, and involving employees all contribute to the long-term success of a flexible work agenda.

Some basic principles that apply to flexible work are:

Attach the flexible work agenda to business needs
Position the flexible work initiative in terms of its benefits to the target audience(s) and to the organization's short-term and long-term goals. Find out if the company is concerned about quality, diversity, productivity, morale, cost savings, or downsizing and use this to promote the flexible work agenda.

Check out the competition
Benchmark the activities of the competition. This competition can be across companies or within the company or division. Consider ways flexible work initiatives can help define the organization as different/better than the competition. Find ways to keep people informed about what the competition is doing on flexible work issues. Also, assess competing issues or products that may draw needed resources and attention away from the flexible work agenda.

Identify key decision-makers and their preferred influence style
Know who has to be convinced and find out how s/he likes to be influenced. Consider visual, verbal, written, face-to-face, phone, notes or blogs, as well as the content of the presentation. Identify objections that will be raised and develop tactics to proactively address those objections.

Position flexible work in its broadest context
Develop a sequential or staged approach for focusing on different audiences and/or objectives. Try not to compartmentalize each flexible work initiative; instead, package the message. Flexible work is not one thing (i.e., telework) but many combinations of when, where and how work is done. Consider the life cycle and career cycle of employees and include the diverse needs of employees and business units in your plans.

Use internal and external resources
Explore a wide range of methods and approaches to communicate about flexible work initiatives. Internal resources might include newsletters, email messages or websites. External resources might be the local press, community organizations, applications for awards and recognition.

How to Implement Flexibility

Implementing a flexible work initiative involves understanding and addressing business and employee needs and wants and getting feedback. Initiatives have failed when they were implemented for the wrong audience and/or the wrong reason. In many companies the decision-maker for flexible work issues is senior management. The person who is often responsible for selling initiatives to senior management may be the head of human resources or IT. Remember, everyone has his own agenda. The flexible work strategy must take into account the interim decision-makers as well as the final decision-maker.

The word strategy is taken from the Latin word meaning "battle plan," and that is what is required when developing a flexible work initiative strategy. Too often, flexible work initiatives are undertaken because someone thinks they are "nice to do." Flexible work initiatives can be implemented for many reasons — to keep up with the competition, to recruit and retain the desired workforce, to reduce facility space — but how flexible work initiatives will serve the needs of both the employees and the business must always be clear.

In developing a flexible work initiative, it is important to determine where support will come from and where there might be resistance. In some cases the support or restraint will be a person, but in other cases it might be an organizational issue or resource. Whatever the case, successful implementation requires that you make the best use of supportive forces while coping with or minimize the restraining forces.

In the best of all possible worlds, the organization's values dictate its mission. Strategies evolve from the mission and result in tasks that need to be accomplished. When this kind of organizational structure is in place, the strategies used to plan and implement flexible work initiatives can be clearly determined. However, in most organizations, there is not such a clear definition of purpose or direction. This makes it somewhat more difficult to determine the appropriate strategy for creating and marketing flexible work initiatives. Deciding the appropriate course for marketing flexible work initiatives involves research, advertisement, public relations and communication.

Source of Commitment

Obviously, the more senior management support for flexible work issues, the better. The reasons why a company wants to create a more flexible culture vary greatly. The reasons may be organizational, personal or the result of some external influence. In some companies, unions are influential in getting flexible work on the agenda. In some organizations there is an informal network, often of mothers, that may work for years trying to determine the needs and presenting ideas to management. In some cases a flexible work agenda surfaces when the company realizes it has recruitment and/or retention difficulties with a particular segment of the workforce, perhaps highly skilled females.

Some companies respond to their competition's activities and create initiatives and/or policies in an attempt to stay competitive. In some cases, a company initiative receives positive press that encourages more flexible work development. There have been examples of companies that have implemented a particular flexible work initiative, such as job sharing or part-time work, for a highly prized employee, and then learned that other employees want to take advantage of the same benefit. In some companies flexible work initiatives are implemented because they are consistent with the organization's philosophy or culture. In still other cases, when the CEO experiences a flexible work problem personally, the organization then develops a response. Whatever the source in implementing flexible work initiatives initially, once started they tend to expand. Often, one area of the organization — such as facilities or IT — is working on an initiative to reduce space or improve technology support for remote work independent of any coordinated flexible work effort. The goal should be to identify what other departments' priorities are and create a more integrated approach to flexible work.

Anticipating Challenge

It is important to be prepared to respond appropriately to challenges to the flexible work initiatives. There are many messages that are heard within organizations that may or may not be accurate, but are often given as the reason why a particular flexible work initiative cannot be undertaken or expanded.

Despite all the documented success, resistance to flexibility continues. Potential obstacles lie in many different areas — an unsupportive culture, skepticism on the part of management, concern about productivity and client satisfaction, the need to comply with state and federal laws, and administrative difficulties and work overload.

Corporate Culture

There are many ways in which the culture of a company can be unsupportive of flexibility. It may be in a value system that holds (explicitly or implicitly) that employees' personal issues do not — and should not — have anything to do with the company. It may be a belief that employees who cannot manage their work and personal lives effectively are at fault.

Sometimes the culture is dominated by control: Achieving business goals means keeping a tight watch on how, where and when people work. And yet, controlling behavior works against the team autonomy, self-directedness and empowerment that characterize successful flexible environments. Too often company cultures reward the heroic behavior that causes stress rather than change the work processes so they won't be stressful.

Corporate culture can be an intangible thing, but workplace values have a dramatic effect on the effectiveness of flexible work initiatives. To understand the values that form a company's culture, it is important to observe what behavior is rewarded or encouraged and what is not. Does senior management support flexibility? Do any executives model it? Do managers view employees who use flexible work arrangements as less serious, less committed to their jobs? Do employees perceive that to be the case, whether or not it is true? Other common assumptions intrinsic to many company cultures include the feeling that long hours are necessary to get the work done, as well as time at work is an indicator of the extent to which an employee is committed and productive.

If values exist that undermine flexibility, they will have to be addressed — and changed — before a flexible environment can be truly successful.

Management Skepticism or Lack of Support

An organization's unwillingness to offer flexibility to employees is often due to misconceptions about flexible work arrangements. The following are examples of common misperceptions.

Flexibility is inequitable. Flexible work is designed to meet the needs of a few employees and has no impact on business goals.
Fact: In an increasingly diverse workforce, not everyone has the same needs. Equity no longer means that every employee must have the same options; it means everyone should have access to the options they need. As flexible work becomes more commonplace, these policies are

being used by employees in all strata of organizations to meet a wide variety of needs: people with child or elder care responsibilities, those with educational or community commitments, employees who interact with people in other time zones, and those who wish to reduce commuting time.

Flexibility has a domino effect. If we let a few employees flex their time, telecommute or job-share, everyone will want to do it.
Fact: Research and experience have shown that this has not been a problem. The fact is, most people already work flexibly – from home or in transit – some of the time. Many actually prefer a full time job and a regular schedule and they cannot afford to significantly reduce their work time. However, even in situations where large numbers of employees opt for some form of flexibility, the needs are generally so varied that schedules can be worked out through collaboration and negotiation. In addition, organizational policy always gives managers control over whether or not to allow flexible work arrangements and it is the manager's role to make sure that business needs are addressed.

Flexibility only works in low level or routine jobs, not in positions with a lot of responsibility.
Fact: Flexible arrangements work successfully for workers in a variety of functions, including supervisors, employees who have clients and those who travel on a regular basis. Some work part-time in top-level jobs, some work at home several days a week and others work on flexible schedules.

Flexibility is disruptive.
Fact: Most change is disruptive unless it is well managed. Losing good people because they need more flexible schedules is disruptive. Layoffs are disruptive. Using new forms of flexibility requires planning and communication — in other words, good people management skills that can actually facilitate more effective work practices and reduce disruption.

Most supervisors dislike flexibility — it makes more work for them.
Fact: Supervising flexible work arrangements requires a new kind of management style, one that emphasises results rather than oversight. Some managers are more comfortable with this change than others; indeed, many supervisors report they have less work once they have some experience managing flexible scheduling arrangements. Working flexibly often enhances self-management. Managers of job sharers comment that partners tend to supervise each other and to compensate for skill deficiencies.

Unions are against flexible scheduling and staffing arrangements.
Fact: Unions vary in their positions; some oppose part-time and work-at-home across the board, others do not. Unions try to represent their members' interests. When members express a need for more flexibility, labor representatives try to include that issue in their negotiations. There is no doubt that unions will look very hard at the fairness of any flexible arrangement.

Flexibility works best if it is limited to a "ring" of contingent employees so that benefits and salary costs can be cut.
Fact: Higher energy and improved morale are the productivity gains most often cited in relation to flexible work practices. Supervisors' major criticism of contingent workers is their lack of energy or commitment to organizational goals, with lower productivity as the result. The short-term gains of reduced benefit and salary costs must be weighed against the longer term and less obvious gains derived from an energetic, motivated workforce.

Concerns about matters related to supervision and impact on clients
It is true that supervising in a flexible work environment requires a new set of management skills. Training can help managers learn this style of managing — variously called results-oriented, performance-based or managing by objective — which helps managers feel comfortable supervising people they can't see. Recent research indicates that supportive managers are key to the ability of employees managing their work and life conflicts.

Work Overload
Many people believe that work overload is the number one barrier to creating a work environment that supports flexibility. Increased hours are a source of burnout and have a circular effect on both work and personal life. There's a growing trend toward 70-hour weeks; companies blame it on pressure to stay lean and a lack of skilled employees. But workers are getting tired. The cost of absenteeism has jumped and stress is beginning to show up as a significant cause. Personal and family issues have replaced illness as the leading reason for employees' unscheduled absences. People who are giving 110 percent sometimes feel they need to take a break. Many researchers say that if employers want to retain talent, they must create an environment that allows employees some control over their schedules.

More and more companies are measuring the link between employee satisfaction and the bottom line and finding that employee attitudes drive customer satisfaction and revenue.

Roles and Responsibility

To be successful, flexible work initiatives require the cooperation of all involved: the organization, human resources, facilities, technology, health/wellness, business continuity, as well as managers and employees. All of these partners have roles and responsibilities. Employees should not expect to be granted flexibility without being accountable to supervisors and colleagues. And the company has the responsibility to ensure that the culture of the organization supports this new, more flexible work environment.

The Role of the Organization
In addition to ensuring that the culture of the organization supports flexibility in how, when, where and how much work is done, the employer must also provide tools, training and guidelines for managers, supervisors and users of flexible work options. Specifically, responsibilities of the organization include the following:

The Process

- Communicate support of flexible work initiatives clearly and often.
- Review and, if necessary, revise policy and/or administrative systems to support flexibility (e.g., headcount policy, benefits eligibility, definition of workday/workweek, etc.).
- Provide guidelines, eligibility criteria and procedures for managers to ensure equity, consistency and clarity.
- Provide guidelines for employees, including sample proposals, sample flexible work options and possible manager responses to proposals.
- Provide training in managing flexibility as part of overall manager training. It can be online, just in time learning, an e-learning course, webinars, face-to-face training or a combination of all of these approaches. Good training in flexibility should be ongoing — not a one-shot effort — and should include examples and case studies from the company: successful situations as well as challenging ones provide excellent learning models.
- Provide information and support for employees to plan, request and work flexibly.
- Recognize and reward managers who effectively implement and manage flexible work arrangements.

Policy, Administration and Systems Issues

The policies and systems of an organization — regarding issues like head count, performance evaluations, benefits eligibility, etc. — may serve as invisible barriers to managing work flexibly.

- The head count system may need to be changed from the traditional system of counting one person as one employee, regardless of time worked, to a full-time equivalency (FTE) system that counts individuals based on the percentage of time worked. Some companies use a combination of both systems, with a code to indicate who is on what system.
- Managers must be encouraged to use flexibility and rewarded when they use it well. Performance evaluations may need to be revised to provide a way to evaluate managers on their use of flexibility and their supportiveness to employees.
- The workweek or workday may have to be redefined to allow for employees working shorter days across a six-day week, or longer days in a 3- or 4-day week.
- Job descriptions may need to be defined in terms of work requirements rather than in terms of a formal schedule; client billing systems may need to be adjusted — e.g., from hours to job. Work can be spread evenly across the year in some cases.
- Benefits decisions can stall the implementation of flexibility, particularly with regard to reduced-time options. It is important to create equity in benefits around issues such as the company's contribution to the medical plan, the employee's cost of coverage, eligibility for benefits, vacation and holidays. Pension policies also may need to be examined and possibly revised to prevent senior employees from being penalized for reducing their work time.

Responsibilities of Human Resource Managers or Flexible Work 'Gatekeepers'

Human Resource managers or flex 'gatekeepers' provide an interface between the big-picture goals of the organization and the specific needs and goals of individuals and departments. They are often directly involved in developing guidelines and procedures for managers and employees as well as communicating them. In addition, HR representatives and flex gatekeepers are often involved in examining all of the systems — benefits, policies, technology, facilities, etc. — that need to be evaluated and possibly redesigned to support workplace flexibility.

Responsibilities of Managers/Supervisors

Managers and supervisors are vitally important to successfully implementing flexibility. Managers must consider any reasonable request for flexibility and evaluate its viability based on the needs of the department; the requirements of the employee's job function; the likely impact, if any, on productivity and workload of the department and an assessment of the employee's skills and ability to work effectively in the new arrangement. Managers must:

- Address the business needs of the company and the department.
- Consider each proposal on its own merits.
- Present options to employees/encourage employees to make requests.
- Listen, be open minded, think creatively.
- Consider the advantages, possible obstacles, resources, customer needs, staffing needs, cost, employee's skills and past performance, and whether or not eligibility criteria have been met.
- Seek advice from Human Resources and colleagues with experience in managing flexibility.
- Review the plan with the requesting employee and modify it.
- Accept or reject the proposal (and understand that it is OK to say no, for the right reasons).
- Communicate with the flexing employee, other members of the department, peers on a regular basis.
- Pilot the agreed-upon plan.
- Monitor and modify the plan, assuming fine-tuning will be required.
- Evaluate and give regular feedback.
- Communicate successes and challenges that result from the new arrangement.

Responsibilities of Employees

It is the employee's responsibility to satisfy all requirements of the job, both in terms of quality and quantity of results as well as meeting the business objectives of his or her job function. Specific employee responsibilities include the following:

- Know what flexible work options are available.
- Analyze your personal needs and determine what flexible work option(s) will meet your needs.
- Consider how the arrangement will impact your work, your colleagues and their work, the department, the organization.
- Talk to other employees who work flexibly.
- Talk to your manager.
- Write a proposal.
- Iron out details of proposal.
- Address your own and your manager's concerns in discussions with your manager.
- Be flexible.
- Be willing to compromise, try new ideas, pilot initiatives.
- If a flexible arrangement is initiated, communicate the new arrangement to co-workers.
- Evaluate the arrangement periodically with your manager.

Guidelines for Managers

Not an entitlement. Many managers are relieved when they realize that flexible work arrangements are not an entitlement. Requests for flexibility are evaluated on a case-by-case basis and decisions are based on the business needs of the department, the applicant's ability to perform under the proposed work arrangement, the past performance of the applicant and whether he or she meets eligibility criteria. When this is understood, it becomes clear why managing flexibility does not mean losing control over one's workforce.

Managing by results. This approach is consistent with current management goals of flattening the organization and requiring more responsibility and self-management of all employees. It is critical for managing employees who are not on site all the time or not within line-of-sight supervision.

Communication. Regular communication between employees, managers, co-workers and clients is vital to managing flexibility, and it is equally important to communicate about successes and challenges as it is to communicate about concrete details such as schedule changes.

Observe, adjust, observe. Since these are new ways to work and manage, flexibility requires fine-tuning. Guidelines will require further adjusting as situations and demands change. This should be viewed as a normal part of the process.

Some Do and Don't Tips for Managing Flexibility:

DO

- ✓ Reflect flexibility in your management style; communicate and model your support for flexibility.
- ✓ Take time to think through your reasons for approving or disapproving a request for flexibility.
- ✓ Keep your employee's work goals and tasks, as well as your business goals, in mind as you seek ways to support his or her need for flexibility.
- ✓ Consult with other managers who have had similar flexibility challenges.
- ✓ Encourage employees to form problem-solving support groups with other employees in similar non-traditional arrangements.
- ✓ Reward performance and productivity, not the amount of time spent in the office.
- ✓ Inform employees of any potential impact a flexible work arrangement will have on rank, pay and benefits, training and advancement.
- ✓ Encourage communication about the need for flexibility and its impact after implementing it.
- ✓ Build relationships based on trust and respect.
- ✓ Recognize that an employee has a right to a life outside of work.

DON'T

✗ Limit your thinking about solutions to a flexibility problem — what is proposed is not the only possibility.
✗ Ask more about an employee's personal reasons for wanting more flexibility than you need to know or that s/he is comfortable sharing.
✗ Assume that you have to agree to all requests similar to one you have approved.
✗ Agree to an arrangement that would diminish an employee's rights, violate labor laws, or risk safety or security even if the employee requests it.
✗ Let your personal biases or values influence your decision. Live by your values and encourage others to live by theirs.
✗ Use flexibility as a reward to top performers.
✗ Try to solve problems of competence or irresponsibility by using flexible work arrangements.
✗ Focus on hours of work time or location rather than output.

When evaluating a proposal for a flexible work arrangement, consider work processes that are critical for achieving business objectives and cannot be compromised. Determine what the business parameters are for your department. Some examples include:
- Regular department/team meetings, which all members must attend.
- Ongoing informal communication among co-workers.
- Travel requirements.
- Face-to-face customer interface.
- Required telephone coverage.
- Extended hours during certain business activities such as financial close.
- Availability to customers and co-workers.

Budget/cost

Salary, benefits, travel and training may require adjustments depending on the proposed flexible work option. Typically, a compressed work schedule will not affect costs, but other flexible options can either lower costs (e.g., part-time) or increase costs (e.g., job share where the total scheduled hours for the two employees exceeds 40 hours/week).

Equipment/Office set-up

Some flexible work options require an investment in equipment (e.g., computer, modem, fax, printer, cell phone, etc.). These expenses may be absorbed by the company/department, the employee or shared by both. Sometimes a change is also required to the configuration of the office. Such expenses might be one-time costs (such as moving furniture) or ongoing (phone line charges).

Vacation, sick days, holidays, overtime

For part-time arrangements (including job sharing), vacation and sick days are typically prorated. Therefore, a person who works four days a week, if entitled to two weeks of vacation, would be entitled to two *four-day weeks*. For employees on compressed work schedules, vacation and sick days are calculated according to hours rather than days. For example, two weeks of vacation for a regular full-time employee would be 10 8-hour days. If working a compressed work schedule, the employee is still eligible to receive 80 hours of vacation, but it might be calculated as eight 10-hour days.

Typically, employees on flexible work arrangement are compensated for holidays when they fall on their regularly scheduled workdays. However, some companies require that employees working a compressed work schedule modify their schedules during holiday weeks so that they work a regular schedule and take off the holiday. These are details that must be worked out in advance and clearly communicated.

Skills Assessment

Part of the evaluation process includes determining whether or not the employee has the skills and personal characteristics necessary to work effectively in the proposed flexible arrangement. The skills assessment should be done by both the employee and the manager. The following questions can be used as a guide.

- Does the employee have the flexibility to adjust the arrangement to meet specific short-term business needs should they arise?
- Can the employee work independently? This is particularly applicable to telecommuting situations, where employees must be self-directed and work without a supervisor in close proximity.
- Can the employee be productive when working extended hours? (Applies particularly to compressed work schedules.)
- Does the employee communicate well with others?
- Can the employee document and catalogue information in a way that is accessible to others?
- Does the employee have good organization and prioritizing skills?
- Can the employee effectively cooperate with others?
- Does the employee have the ability to ignore distractions if working off-site?
- Can the employee function effectively without having a single, direct influence over outcomes? (Relevant to job-sharing.)
- Can the employee accept not being present at all meetings and social functions?
- Can the employee deal personally with recognition of group performance rather than individual performance?
- Does the employee perform better as part of a group or as an individual contributor?
- Does the employee understand financial cutbacks, if any, that may result? Can the employee's situation tolerate these reductions?
- Will the flexible option affect the employee's existing career development plan? Does he or she understand and accept any changes that are likely to result?

Guidelines for Employees

Employees need to understand that flexibility is not an entitlement. Each proposal is evaluated on its own merits, with decisions based on the past performance of the employee, the ability of the employee to work effectively under the proposed arrangement and the ability to continue to meet the job requirements and business needs of the department. Nor are flexible arrangements a cure-all. Employees must carefully assess their own situations and match them up with flexibility that can *realistically* help them meet their needs.

Often employees have misconceptions about flexible work options. Those with young children frequently think that working at home will solve all of their child-care problems. However, it is often necessary to have child care coverage in order to work at home. Some employers even require it. But while telecommuting may not solve all child-care problems, it can reduce commuting time significantly, thereby reducing the number of required child-care hours and increasing the number of hours parents can spend with their child(ren). The important thing, then, is to understand both the advantages and drawbacks of each arrangement, so employees know how it will affect them.

Typically, the process for planning a successful flexible work schedule would follow this outline for an employee:

Understand the options
Obtain information from the company that describes options that are available and what their impact is on things like salary, benefits, vacation, holidays and career advancement.

Carefully assess your own situation
What do you want to accomplish by working flexibly? What are your skills and strengths? Do you have the skills to work in this new way?

Make a proposal
The initial request should be prepared like any other business request. It should consider advantages and disadvantages from both management's and the employee's perspective, and a time frame in which the flexible schedule will be followed.

Have an open discussion
There should be an exchange of ideas about the proposal that considers the individual's and the department's needs. Discuss potential advantages and obstacles. Don't think of this first conversation as the time to make final decisions. It is an opportunity to exchange ideas and get more information.

Decide how you will demonstrate that the work is being done
Plan how this will fit in with the department's goals. Is the work load easily measurable?

Problem solve
Use business skills (e.g., negotiation) to work toward a mutually acceptable plan.

Discuss how you will continue to communicate
Modify the plan as necessary. Be prepared to make changes and adjustments at any time.

Explain plans to other employees
Involve them in decision making, if appropriate.

Employee Proposal
Although there may be times when a flexible work arrangement is proposed by the manager, it will generally be the responsibility of the employee to draft a proposal. This is an important process because it helps the employee organize his or her thoughts, spells out the specifics that can be agreed upon (or negotiated), and allows the employee to address potential problem areas and offer possible solutions. It also provides a written document that can serve as the basis of understanding between the managers and an employee, as well as a record to present to senior management if the need arises.

The following guidelines and proposal questions can be used for an employee's request for any flexible work arrangements. All proposals will be different, but most should include the following:

- How will your new work arrangement benefit customers/clients, other employees, the company? How will this maintain or improve the business, and how will you overcome any obstacles?
- What is your proposed work schedule? Number of hours per day and per week? Where will work be done? How long do you expect the arrangement to last? Are peak periods adequately covered?
- How will the flexibility affect your work priorities? Will it improve dealing with them, or will it require adjustments to your work and that of others?
- What, if any, job redesign will be necessary? Will all tasks now done continue to be accomplished?
- How will availability issues be dealt with? If there is less face-to-face contact, how will the employee 1) attend meetings, 2) stay in touch with others in the department, including the manager, 3) attend to client/customer needs and 4) handle emergency situations?
- Will working a different schedule affect your dealings with clients? Other employees?
- What impact will the flexible schedule have on salary/benefits?
- What other facts will help your proposal? Provide examples of other successful flextime arrangements within the company or your division if possible.

General Proposal Checklist
Managers and employees need to consider the same issues when evaluating or creating a proposal. The following checklist can be used to ensure that the important issues are being addressed. Additional considerations that are specific to particular work arrangements can be found in the following sections.

The following issues should be reviewed when a flexible work arrangement is being considered:

- Effect on Department/Company. How will the change affect the department? Are there business advantages to the department/company? What are they? Do they justify implementation of the plan?

- Coverage/Staffing/Workflow. What is the proposed arrangement? How will staffing and workflow requirements be affected? Are peak periods covered? Does the plan ensure that minimum employee coverage is provided at all times?
- Job Responsibilities. What impact, if any, will the new arrangement have on employee job responsibilities? How will problem areas be addressed? How will work continuity be maintained? Does the employee have the skills to handle the proposed arrangement?
- Communication. How will employees communicate with management and each other? Clients/customers, other departments, etc.? What time will be set aside for this? How will attendance at meetings and functions be handled? How will the change in schedule/work arrangement be communicated to other employees? Clients?
- Contingencies. How will sick days, holidays and vacation be covered? What about increased workloads, seasonal requirements? Can employees be asked to work on days off?
- Compensation, Benefits, etc. Will there be any effect on compensation, benefits, overtime, career advancement? Does employee understand what the effects will be?
- Time Frame. Is this a time-limited arrangement or is it open-ended? If time-limited, what is the plan for terminating it? If open-ended, what will happen if it doesn't work out?
- Supervision. Will the proposed arrangement change the way supervision is handled? In what way? How will the employee's performance be evaluated?
- Monitoring and Evaluation. Will there be a trial period? For how long? How will the arrangement be evaluated? When and how will the success of the arrangement be measured?

Evaluating the Flexible Work Initiative

As implementation plans are being made, it is a good idea to also plan how the initiative will be evaluated. A plan for evaluation should be an integral part of the recommendations for any flexibility initiative or service. This system for tracking and measuring the outcomes and costs of the flexibility initiatives and policies should be developed with the company's goals and objectives in mind. The tools for evaluation might include checklists, written or oral reports, observations, interviews, surveys and comparison of data before and after the service was initiated. A combination of approaches might be used to obtain the best results.

Ongoing monitoring allows the company to refine and improve its flexibility initiative to best meet its objectives and employees' needs. If possible, personnel records should be modified to include such factors as absenteeism and to identify those who benefit from the flexibility initiative. Periodic employee surveys and focus groups can be conducted to validate record keeping. Additionally, accounting systems can be modified to include relevant cost and benefit data.

In determining the effectiveness of flexibility initiatives, it is important to match the initiatives' performance with the original objectives for the initiative. Assessment by users of the initiative or service is essential. During the early months of an initiative, it may be valuable to solicit feedback more frequently. Feedback should be designed to be constructive, not merely positive

or negative. For example, employees can be asked for suggestions rather than complaints. Some questions may include the following:
- How did you hear about the initiative?
- Why did you choose to use it?
- What did you like most about the initiative? Least?
- What suggestions, if any, do you have?

Another way to assess the effectiveness of the flexibility initiative is to start with a restatement of what the company hopes to achieve and set up a before-and-after comparison. If the company hopes to demonstrate improved recruitment, lower turnover rates or decreased absenteeism as a result of initiative use, there must be prior documentation for comparison. Even if statistics show change for the better, it will be necessary to interview employees to confirm that the initiative is responsible for the changes. For example, if one objective is improved recruitment, new hires should be asked if they knew about the initiative and if so, how it influenced their decision to take the position. It is also possible to compare certain variables such as absenteeism and tardiness among employees using the service and those not using the service.

"Last things first" should be your motto when it comes to evaluating the impact of flexible work initiatives. In other words, evaluation plans should be determined before the initiative even gets off the ground. Knowing what you want to accomplish and how you will know if you get there are integral parts of the initial planning.

Evaluation should address:
- What are the flexibility initiative goals and objectives? These should be the goals and objectives that are most crucial to management and employees.
- What specific measures or outcomes will be used to track the accomplishment of these goals and objectives?
- How will you evaluate the flexible work initiative? What methodology will you use?
- Why do you want to evaluate the flexibility initiative? What will happen with this information?

The following suggestions for initiative evaluation are for employers who want to conduct their own pragmatic evaluation. Whatever method you use, it is important for you to understand the limitations of evaluation. Other initiatives or organizational changes such as downsizing may also be affecting employees. Therefore, it is important to measure the effectiveness of your flexible work efforts, but be careful about making definitive claims.

How to Measure
There are a number of practical tools to evaluate flexibility initiatives including:
- Employee surveys
- Management surveys and interviews
- Return-on-investment analysis
- Focus groups
- Organizational profile

The Process

It is possible to simply describe flexibility initiative activities in terms of cost, number of events, and participation by employees.

Additionally, current initiative status can be compared with the goals articulated in the original initiative proposal or plan:

- Accomplishment of overall goals and objectives
- Specific initiative, budget and utilization goals
- Inventory of current training initiatives and gap analysis
- How closely the plan was followed
- Problems encountered
- What worked/didn't work

It is possible to apply accounting measures to the evaluation of flexible work initiatives. These measures can include: Return on Investment (ROI), Cost/Benefit Analysis, Break Even Analysis, and Productivity Measures, among others. Regardless of the approach, it is important to specify the goals and expected outcomes, select financial (or some equivalent) measures for the outcomes, collect the data and make calculations, and then make recommendations to maximize the financial benefits.

Flexible work initiatives can be viewed as an investment in helping the company's most valuable asset (its employees) better manage their work and personal lives and as an effective approach to business outcomes. The ROI compares the relative profitability of an initiative with the investment required to implement and maintain it. A cost/benefit analysis compares all costs (direct and indirect) associated with the development and implementation of an initiative with the cost savings (direct and indirect) or increased profits associated with the use of the initiative.

Some questions that might be asked regarding these approaches are as follows:

- What are the goals for the flexible work initiative?
- What financial measures can be used to document the extent to which flexible work policies and initiatives meet financial objectives?
- Which non-financial outcomes for flexible work initiatives can be translated into monetary equivalents?
- What level of investment has the company made in flexible work initiatives?
- What are the costs associated with the company's flexible work initiatives?
- What are the savings/expenses associated with the company's flexible work initiatives?
- What are the financial gains/losses associated with the company's flexible work initiatives?
- What should the company do to maximize the financial contributions that flexible work initiatives can make to the bottom line?

It is important to note that there are many areas that are likely impacted by flexible work initiatives that are difficult to measure quantitatively, and yet may have very high value, including a reduction in health care costs (less stressed employees) and the organization's carbon footprint (fewer commuters and reduced office space).

ROI information can be collected on a variety of areas including: turnover, absenteeism, productivity, stress related health care, morale/commitment and job satisfaction. Some of the sources of the data used for ROI include: HR information systems, business unit revenue, health insurance enrollment and claims, salary, survey results, and performance and promotion data.

The following is an example of ROI calculations based on survey results:

Annual Cost: Flexible-Work-Related Turnover

Of 2,727 survey respondents, 42.4% report actively looking or considering looking for a more flexible job at a different company to better manage their work and personal life.

Assuming 1/3 of those looking or considering looking actually leave, the estimated annual replacement cost of flexible work related turnover at Company X is $22,440,000.

Calculation:
- Assumption: Average salary (exempt) = $50,000
- Assumption: Average salary (non-exempt) = $28,000
- Assumption: 70% of the population is exempt, 30% non-exempt
- 42.4% of 2,727 employees = 1,156 employees
- Assuming 33% of the 1,156 employees looking to leave actually leave = 382 employees leave. Replacement cost* per exempt employee = ($50,000 X 1.5) = $75,000
- Replacement cost* per non-exempt employee ($50,000 X .75) = $21,000
- 267 separated exempt employees X $75,000 = $20,025,000
- 115 separated non-exempt employees X $21,000 = $2,415,000

*Source: Using research indicating that employee turnover costs a company roughly 150% of an exempt employee's annual salary (finding a replacement, getting that person up to speed, etc.) and 75% of a non-exempt salary as a guideline.

Conclusion

Today successful companies realize that flexibility is vital to their corporate culture. And yet, real flexibility is not something that happens overnight. Key stakeholders from across the entire corporation must be involved in the planning, implementation and management of flexible work.

Whether just getting started or expanding an existing policy, all companies must have a clear strategy in place for flexibility to be truly impactful and successful. As stated at the beginning of this chapter, keep in mind that creating a more agile workplace and workforce requires continuous attention to what's working and what's not. It is not necessarily a linear approach to change.

Chapter 10 | Assessing the Value of Flexible Work

Assessment

For many years, the return on investment (ROI) for flexible work focused on the fact that increased flexibility in how, when and where work is done has a positive impact on employees' ability to manage their work and life needs more effectively. More recently, however, employers have focused on a business case for flexible work that considers business outcomes when assessing the success of the initiative.

When leaders can see the results of a well-designed, implemented and managed flexible work initiative, they begin to understand its value. Most businesses need to improve performance and shareholder value, get the best work from current employees, and compete for future talent. Flexibility is not only a powerful tool to drive businesses toward these goals, it is a key component of successful management practices. This shift to business outcomes (versus personal ones) is driven in large part by new stakeholders in areas like technology, facilities, health/wellness, diversity/inclusion, real estate, legal, and business continuity and is significant as it positions flexibility as a must-have for any size organization in every industry.

There are many ways to assess the value of flexible work today. Previous chapters discussed data that can be used to form your organization's business case for flexible work, whether you're initiating, enhancing or advancing your initiative. In Chapter 10, we will look more specifically at the value and impact of flexible work for organizations as we explore the following:

✔ What are the main areas of focus to create the right ROI for an organization?

✔ How are organizations documenting the value and impact of flexible work?

✔ What internal information is needed to assess the value of flexible work?

✔ What is the best way to report to management on the value of flexible work?

✔ What specific data is needed for a company to report on a flexible work pilot project?

✔ What are unique ways to communicate the impact of flexible work?

Areas of Focus for the Impact of Flexible Work

According to a 2011 Corporate Voices for Working Families report, the positive impacts of flexibility can be summarized as:[1]

Talent management: Organizational research presents compelling evidence of the positive impact of flexibility on talent management, especially retention of key talent. Based on their internal research, organizations conclude that flexibility has saved individual companies millions of dollars in expenses from employee turnover.

Human Capital Outcomes: Internal organizational studies find that individuals who have even a small measure of flexibility in when and where work gets done have significantly greater job satisfaction, stronger job commitment and higher levels of engagement with the company, as well as significantly lower levels of stress. As demonstrated in profit value chain research, these human capital outcomes translate into innovation, quality, customer retention and shareholder value.

Financial Performance, Operational and Business Outcomes: Organizations find that flexibility is a driver of financial performance and productivity and is correlated to increased revenue generation, as well as having positive impacts on cycle time and client service.

It is interesting to note, however, that the return on investment (ROI) for workplace flexibility is still not measured by most organizations. According to WorldatWork's 2011 Survey on Workplace Flexibility, only 7 percent of organizations attempt to quantify the ROI of flexibility programs by measuring productivity, customer satisfaction or product quality.[2] This means there's a great deal of opportunity for organizations to connect flexible work outcomes to other measures of performance to truly demonstrate the value of flexible work to leaders.

That said, companies do document the value of flexible work in a variety of ways. In some cases, they use external data to document specific business outcomes that can be achieved by creating a more flexible culture. Other organizations conduct internal research that specifically asks employees and managers about their perception regarding the impact of and satisfaction with flexibility. Regardless of the approach, it is important to make sure the data collected will resonate with the organization's leaders and decision makers.

When documenting the value of flexible work, it is important to know whom you will be presenting the information to. The best research in the world may not be convincing to your company's CEO. Find out what keeps him up at night — retention of top talent, reducing overhead costs, business continuity in an emergency, high health care costs, legal exposure — and focus on those issues.

Flexible work can mean many things to many people, which is often a challenge, but it can also be an opportunity. Focus on those areas that are most important to your leaders. It is not only formal flexible arrangements that produce impressive results; indeed, creating a culture that supports occasional flexibility can also have a significant impact. Positive outcomes such as retention, employee engagement, job satisfaction and financial performance have been found to be consistent across different industries. Moreover, the positive effects of workplace flexibility have been documented in hourly, non-exempt environments as well as those for salaried, exempt employees.

Consider these findings from the WorldatWork 2011 report:[3]

- Organizations with an established culture of workplace flexibility that includes training, policies and use in recruitment are significantly more likely than organizations with a developing workplace flexibility culture to:
    1. Provide training to employees and management on how to be successful with flexible work schedules.
    2. Have a formal written flexibility policy.
    3. Market or feature the organization's flexibility program as a key benefit when attempting to attract new talent.

- The higher an organization rates itself on the flexibility scale, the lower the organization's voluntary turnover rate. However, no correlation was found between the number of flexibility options offered and turnover.
- As many as eight out of every 10 respondents believe their workforce would say there is a positive or extremely positive effect of flexibility programs on employee engagement (72 percent), employee motivation (71 percent) and employee satisfaction (82 percent).
- Organizations that rated themselves as having an established flexibility culture also report overwhelmingly that workplace flexibility is having a positive or extremely positive impact on motivation (90 percent), engagement (90 percent) and satisfaction (98 percent).
- Companies with the highest turnover (11 percent and higher) are less likely to report that the effects of flexibility on motivation, engagement and satisfaction are positive.

Making the Business Case

Organizations that value and invest in human capital and use the full talents of their workforce grow revenues and profits and generate substantially more value for shareholders. Certainly, the flexible human capital strategies are not a cure-all. Organizations must understand their customers, target the right market with the right products and services for that customer, execute strategies to attract them, price and promote their products appropriately and produce their products efficiently. They must also have access to financial capital and attend to risk management, changing regulations and technological innovations.

Still, the research is unequivocal; Flexible cultures and flexibility practices make a significant and measurable difference in organizational performance. They contribute to a workforce that is more skilled, stable, enthusiastic and free of distractions. These talented and focused employees are more likely to be committed to the organization's goals and deliver superior value to customers, who in turn are more inclined to be satisfied and loyal, generating strong sales. The organization is more efficient in the short run, and more profitable. It is better situated for long-term success, able to innovate, continually improve processes and minimize overhead. Its investments are in constructive, future-oriented assets — human capital, innovation and customer relationships — all leading indicators that analysts use to evaluate stock price.

In other words: Fulfilled Employees = Satisfied Customers = Happy Shareholders. We use the image below to demonstrate that progression.

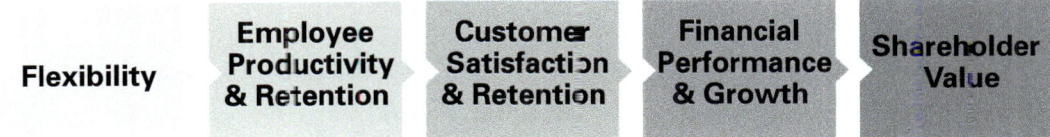

Though flexibility may require a substantial investment of time and financial resources, it translates to stronger financial results, generating significantly greater performance from employees and for customers. This process is best exemplified by the landmark work First Tennessee did in the 1990s to create a more flexible culture.

Assessment

FLEX IN-DEPTH: First Tennessee

Flexibility at the Heart of Results-Driven Culture Change

The 10-year transformation of the culture of the First Tennessee National Corporation had significant measurable results. It grew assets from $8.9 billion to $24.8 billion, retained an amazing 95 percent to 96 percent of customers, and was the most profitable banking institution in the United States for five straight years (1999-2003). Flexibility was at the core of the cultural change.

In 2006, First Tennessee National Corporation (FTN) was a 143-year-old, diversified financial institution with $3.6 billion in sales and more than 12,000 employees; it was one of the 30 largest banking companies in the United States in asset size and market capitalization.

To remain independent in the highly competitive financial services market of the early 1990s, FTN needed to close the $5 to $6 million gap in earnings between the retail commercial bank and industry high performers. It used a data-driven route to its goal.

Strategy Identification: Customer Retention = Profitability

First Critical Step: Gather data to indicate course of action
- Most organizations believe that retaining customers increases profits, but few actually collect the data to know the extent to which it does. FTN was unusual in documenting that connection; it knew precisely the impact of retaining customers.

Second Critical Step: Make data-driven decisions to create loyal customers
- Knowing that measurable relationship, FTN focused on measuring the drivers of customer satisfaction and loyalty. It learned that whether customers stayed or not was directly related to whether employees stayed. Branches with the highest customer retention were those with the highest employee retention. What customers said they wanted most was a relationship with the people who handled their money.
- At FTN branches with an employee tenure rate of two years, customer retention rates were 83 percent. When employee tenure increased to four years, customer retention rates shot to 92 percent (Flynn 1997).

Strategy Identification: Reordering Priorities and Following Through

First Critical Step: Decide that employees come first.
- A reordering of priorities for key stakeholders was initiated by chairman Ralph Horn. He decided that the change must begin with putting employees first. An employee-centered culture would create value for customers, loyal customers would lead to profitability, profitability would benefit shareholders and the company would be able to invest in the community.

Discovering Employee Success Factors
- Employees said, "When you don't respect me, when you don't treat me like an adult, you take away my incentive to help make this a better company." Employees said they needed:

Assessment

- Empowerment on the job — the ability to make decisions about how to better serve customers.
- Empowerment to manage their responsibilities outside of work — in short, flexibility.

Strategy Identification: Reinventing the FTN Culture

First Critical Step: Create Firstpower — an employee-centered culture
- The new FTN culture was philosophically grounded in an attitude of ownership and teamwork, and that, as owners, employees:
  - recognize that a job well done is the first order of business.
  - are empowered to take care of customers (internal and external).
  - create a flexible work environment so they can embrace both personal lives and professional responsibilities at work.
  - know that what they create at work is a reflection of themselves and as such, only the absolute best is good enough.

Second Critical Step: Create a Real Organizational Commitment
- The change was to be long-term and involved every employee at FTN; it was not a cosmetic re-statement of corporate values.
- It was reinforced by the CEO and all leaders were trained on the importance of embracing the change, understanding that it was critical to achieving FTN's goals.
- In 2003, more than 90 percent of employees were working flexibly. One option, "Prime Time," allowed employees to work 20 to 35 hours a week with benefits and advancement.
- New employees were told at orientation, "Flexibility is the foundation of our culture. We encourage you to talk with your leaders about how to flex your schedule." FTN staffed with floaters and cross-trained work groups to accommodate the inevitable last-minute changes in schedules.
- Employees were in fact owners. All employees received stock, including part-timers

First Tennessee National - Results of *FirstPower*[4]

FTN maintained its goal of remaining independent and executed a number of important business strategies including significantly increasing customer satisfaction. Not only did FirstPower, the newly branded FTN culture, create a better work environment, it created a better business from every perspective: customer loyalty and satisfaction, productivity and profits and employee recruitment and retention.

Increased Customer Satisfaction
- 34 percent of customer loyalty was associated with employee factors; with an overall customer satisfaction rating of 95.3 percent in 2002
- Customer retention increased 9 percent above the banking industry average in consumer and business markets; from 95 percent in 1995 to 97 percent in 1998 (Casner-Lotto 2000)[5]

Productivity & Growth
- From 1990 to 2000, FTN had a 17 percent growth rate — one of the highest in the industry.
- FTN was among the top 10 fastest growing bank holding companies (14 percent in earnings per share over two years) and among the top 10 in Bloomberg's ranking of total underwriting volume in U.S. agency bonds for 2001.

- One-third of the $350 million in fee income produced by FTN Financial was generated by new products and services not offered before mid-year 2000. (2001 first quarter report)
- 15,000 work days of productivity were gained in one year, valued at $1.5 million
- A micro-analysis of the loan operations department found that it more than doubled its volume between 1992 and 1998 with no increase in staff.

Recruitment/Retention and Employee Satisfaction

FTN received national and regional recognition, which allowed it to attract top talent:
- 100 Best Corporate Citizens in 2003 (*Business Ethics* magazine).
- *Fortune* magazine's 100 Best Companies to Work for in America, six years running.
- 100 Best Companies for Working Mothers 1994 through 2002 (*Working Mother* magazine).
- *BusinessWeek*'s number one family friendly company in America.

An internal measure of how FTN employees perceived their experience continued to rise:
- 92 percent of employees considered their overall compensation to be of greater value because of the family friendly benefit programs and resources.
- 94 percent of employees had flexibility in completing their job duties and tasks.
- 94 percent reported that someone at work cared about them as a person.
- 93 percent of employees were likely to recommend FTN as a great place to work.
- 89 percent of employees reported that their leader was supportive of their ability to embrace both work and personal responsibilities.

Turnover is low and recruitment is strong:
- By 1997 FTN took on average just 20 days to fill an open position; competitors took nearly twice as long. "Recognition as one of the best companies to work for has led to the filling of positions at more than 40 percent of the industry rate." (Casner-Lotto 2000)

Profitability and Shareholder Returns

- In 2001 FTN ranked as the most profitable banking company in the United States for the fourth consecutive year, according to *Forbes* (2001), and it made the *Forbes* list of the 400 Best Big Companies in 2000, 2001, 2002 and 2003 with an 18 percent five-year-average return on capital, as well as the *Forbes Platinum* list of profitability in January 1999.
- In 2002, FTN ranked third among the top 50 bank holding companies, with an annual revenue per share growth rate of 15.3 percent over the previous five years. Total return to shareholders for FTN was 24.03 percent, compared to the Top 50 at 18.64 percent and the S&P 500 at -2.84 percent. Dividends increased annually from 1998.
- FTN outperformed market expectations each quarter in 2001 and 2002, and the first quarter of 2003.
- Earnings of $376.5 million in 2002 represented an 18 percent growth from 2001 earnings of $318.2 million. Return on the average shareholder's equity was 24 percent for 2002 compared with 22.7 percent in 2001 (2003 annual report). Five year annual growth rate of earnings per share was 14 percent and continued to be 11 percent for dividends. (Wall Street Research Net 2003)
- By the end of 2002, FTN had total shareholder returns higher than its peer group and significantly higher than the S&P 500. (FTN Proxy Report 2003)

Assessment

Collecting Data

According to Corporate Voices' *Business Impacts of Flexibility: An Imperative for Expansion* report, one of the most common approaches to collecting data is for companies to embed two to three questions about flexibility in their annual employee opinion survey or employee pulse survey. These questions usually measure: 1) the perceived availability of flexibility, and 2) the relative importance of flexibility in a person's decision to stay at the company. Analysis of survey responses allows the company to see how the profile of people who have flexibility differs from those who do not on factors such as job satisfaction, level of commitment, intent to stay and perceived effectiveness in one's job. The organization can also consider the weight given to flexibility compared with other motivators such as compensation and advancement. For organizations that measure flexibility issues in more general employee surveys, these flexibility findings are usually considered against the backdrop of information about changing workforce demographics, particularly the increase in dual earner couples and employees with significant responsibilities in both the job and personal spheres.

Another common approach is to ask about flexibility within the context of a specialized work-life, diversity or total rewards survey. This approach has the advantage of allowing the employer to ask more questions about flexibility than could be included in a more general survey. For maximum impact the survey can also include items related to employee productivity, personal effectiveness and performance, to permit analysis that measures the correlation of flexibility to performance and behaviors. The additional probes permit deeper understanding of employees' attitudes about flexibility, ability to use flexible work options without career jeopardy; the role of flexibility in alleviating stress; and the dynamics of flexibility in work groups and between managers, co-workers and clients.

Some of the most compelling business case data has come from flexibility evaluation surveys that focus entirely on employees' experience of and perceptions about flexibility. The in-depth analysis that is possible in this kind of survey sheds light on both formal and informal types of flexibility at different career and job levels and describes patterns and implications of utilization of different kinds of flexibility. These surveys also examine in depth the barriers and enablers of flexibility, the role of managers and co-workers in achieving flexibility impact, and the influence of flexibility on career progress, as well as anticipated patterns of future flexible arrangements.

Qualitative information that is more subjective is also a part of corporations' measurement of flexibility's effects. Qualitative information can be collected in surveys with write-in comments and also through interviews and focus groups, as well as online communities. For example, one company determined that there is a relationship between "manager supportiveness and sensitivity" and successfully implementing flexibility and with positive employee outcomes of discretionary effort and retention. The company used the survey data to pinpoint those business units that were high scoring in flexibility implementation and then conducted focus groups with managers in those units to identify the behaviors that contribute to employees' perception of manager sensitivity. These behaviors were translated into company-wide "workplace flexibility standards of excellence." Another company found that interviewing managers for success stories about individuals and groups who have used flexibility successfully also generated influential data and posting good stories on the intra-company website has proven to be effective in demonstrating flexibility effects for the business and individuals.[5]

Assessment

SAMPLE: Assess Your Organization

The following questions will help you determine how flexible your organization is:

1. Is flexibility integrated in the culture?
- ❏ Is flexibility considered to be the rule, rather than the exception?
- ❏ Is flexibility applied broadly and found in a wide variety of forms?
- ❏ Is flexibility included in more than just practices (flexible schedules, remote work, customized careers, etc.)?
- ❏ Is flexibility also included in the cultural conditions that make these practices legitimate?
- ❏ Are the people working flexibly considered equal in terms of their access to advancement, status, integration into the business and quality of assignments?
- ❏ Does the company's climate recognize and respect that employees have lives outside of work? Can people set boundaries on work time and/or accessibility, as long as they accomplish their work?
- ❏ Is flexibility considered not just beneficial for employees, but also a means to accomplish strategic business objectives, such as better customer service?
- ❏ Are leaders committed to making flexibility viable?
- ❏ Are your flexibility principles part of the organizational communications on corporate objectives, mission, vision and values?

2. Is flexibility used to attract and retain employees?
- ❏ Are your talent acquisition processes and messages designed to appeal to people who value flexibility? Are you clearly communicating that flexibility is possible?
- ❏ Do recruiters know how to present the job to candidates who value flexibility and how to evaluate a fit with them?
- ❏ Do recruiters and managers reduce roadblocks to attracting, hiring or retaining people who require flexibility?

3. Is flexibility part of your employment brand?
- ❏ Is flexibility incorporated into the internal and external employment brand?
- ❏ Is flexibility used to gain public recognition?

4. Is flexibility incorporated into you talent management processes?
- ❏ Is flexibility incorporated into performance management, leadership development, career development, health and wellness efforts and manager training?

5. Is flexibility incorporated into the diversity function?
- ❏ Is it understood how flexibility can help achieve diversity goals?
- ❏ Is flexibility being used to reduce barriers and achieve full inclusion?

6. Are your operational systems aligned with flexibility?
- ❏ Do your systems/tools/business processes, such as technology, staffing, reporting, etc. facilitate flexibility and eliminate barriers to its success?
- ❏ Is flexibility incorporated into health and wellness processes?
- ❏ Is flexibility incorporated into change management processes?

7. Are the outcomes of flexibility measured?
- ❏ Are internal measures of use, satisfaction and success tracked?
- ❏ Are benchmarks with peers tracked?
- ❏ Is the impact of flexible practices on business performance and talent goals measured?

Using a Flexible Work Pilot Program to Collect Information

Piloting a flexible work initiative can be an effective way to obtain management support and buy-in. The pilot is for a specified period of time — usually six months — and is conducted within a controlled environment, often in a business unit or select group within the organization. Care must be taken to clarify the goals of the pilot, whether it is, for instance, to test a specific approach or product to support flexible work or to determine the impact on managers, employees and/or customers. The advantage of a pilot is that data are easier to collect, the local manager is usually motivated to create change, and evaluation is usually targeted to a well-defined objective or problem. For example, most of the data collected at PNC Financial Services Group and Cardinal Health has been of this type, resulting in several dramatic stories that pinpoint the impact of flexibility in specific situations. Eli Lilly has also used pilots and demonstration projects to measure how flexibility affects a range of business outcomes.

When designing and implementing a flexible work pilot, developing a strategic communication plan is critical. While the pilot may only involve a small segment of the population, word will get out. Because flexible work is often highly desirable, it's important to control the messaging content and process. Organizations often cascade information about the initiative, its purpose, the process and expected outcomes, alerting senior management first and then moving down the organization. In addition, employees and managers not directly involved in the pilot should be made aware of it and what the process will be, how they will be notified about the results, and expected next steps.

The following are sample results from one organization's six-month flexible work pilot:

Sample Flexible Working Pilot Study Report

Goals of Flex Study

1. To implement flex Web portal to educate managers and employees re:
    - Flex options.
    - How to request and work flexibly.
    - How to manage a flexible workforce.
2. Document impact of flexible work from manager and employee perspective/Company Barriers/Obstacles to flexible work:
    - Face time culture
    - Different rules in different departments
    - Lack of connectivity and remote access
    - Limited understanding of what flexible work means
    - Customer needs/demands
    - Lack of tools/resources to understand and manage flex including:
    - Self and job assessments to determine what will work
    - Clear guidelines, helpful hits, FAQs for managers and employees

Assessment

- Senior level support
- Improved technology/connectivity

Resources Implemented
- FlexPaths' *Educate* Web-based platform for managers, employees and flex administrators
- Kickoff and continual webinars to introduce and demonstrate available resources
- Communication campaign including periodic email messages and collaborative touch-base sessions to discuss successes and challenges

Results: Based upon survey of 100 participants after six months of program usage

Productivity:
- 57 percent of managers reported a "strong positive impact" on productivity, up from 26 percent previously (119 percent improvement).
- 71 percent of employees reported a "strong positive impact" on productivity, up from 47 percent (51 percent improvement).

Effectiveness:
- 57 percent of managers report a "strong positive impact" in employee effectiveness, up from 39 percent previously (46 percent improvement).
- 67 percent of employees report a "strong positive impact" in their own effectiveness, up from 47 percent previously (43 percent improvement).
- Other areas that displayed significant improvements:
  - Quality of work
  - Stress level
  - Energy level
  - Retention
  - Loyalty
  - Job satisfaction
  - Resilience (ability to adapt to situations as they arise)
  - Ability to get enough rest
  - Coworker support for using flex model
  - Employee engagement

Tracking Flexible Work Arrangements

Documenting use of specific flexible work — both formal arrangements and occasional use — can serve as a significant dimension of measurement. In some cases, tracking and administration is done through flexible work Web-based products designed specifically for this purpose, while some organizations rely on existing human resource software, benefits records, and/or employee survey data. The purpose for most organizations is to study the utilization of different types of flexible arrangements in order to determine the penetration of flexibility in various parts of the business and to assess patterns of use among different demographic groups and job types. While most formal work arrangements can usually be identified, organizations acknowledge that utilization statistics probably underestimate the true reach and impact of flexibility. In some cases they cannot accurately determine the extent of informal flexibility, as in the case of employees who occasionally alter their work schedule or location. Today, many organizations want to improve tracking mechanisms as a way of measuring the extent and impact of flexibility and, depending on the approach, are using newly created systems to document both formal and occasional flexible work. Having access to the data produced by flexible work tracking and administration tools can be used to demonstrate consistency, which can be useful to protect the organization from any risk in terms of compliance issues.

Companies like American Express are using flexible work administration systems that allow employees to register for flexible work arrangements. These systems include detailed information about individual employee arrangements and also provide real-time reports for managers, HR or flexible work gatekeepers. Each group can then use the information in their strategic and workforce planning, as well as compare it with other information regarding performance management and turnover. Once implemented, such systems generate extensive data regarding various aspects of flexible work.

Comparing Flexibility with Other Data

Understanding the value of flexible work is enhanced by the ability to leverage the information about flexibility and compare it with other data. For instance, evidence can be obtained from employee surveys about how the availability of flexible work arrangements influences an employee's decision to stay in an organization. According to Corporate Voices, a recent work-life survey found that approximately 80 percent of Accenture employees said that their ability to successfully manage work and home life roles had an impact on their career choices and their desire to stay at Accenture. The survey also found a strong correlation between the ability to achieve balance in one's work schedule. Of the employees who report that it was easy to balance work, career and home life, approximately 75 percent say they have the flexibility they need in terms of when work gets done. When asked to compare flexibility relative to other benefits or rewards, flexibility ranked as one of the top three factors on the list at Accenture, challenging the notion that compensation and advancement are employees' primary motivators. The findings provided motivation to make flexibility more available across the organization.

Sample In-Depth Assessment Report

The Impact Of Flexible Work Arrangements: A Survey Of Managers

Adapted from a report by Dr. Sandy Burud, principal, Flex Employment Services, FlexPaths

Introduction

The objective of the survey was to capture feedback, quantify results and identify consistencies and differences. The report is organized by categories that were measured: productivity, manager/team functioning, satisfaction/engagement, absenteeism, lateness and scheduling, health, and facilities/space.

The Impact on Productivity

Nearly half (45 percent) of surveyed managers report that productivity has increased as a result of flexible work arrangements (FWAs). The rest report no impact[1] (41 percent) or are unsure (13 percent), and less than 1 percent report a decrease. This increased productivity is in both the

Assessment

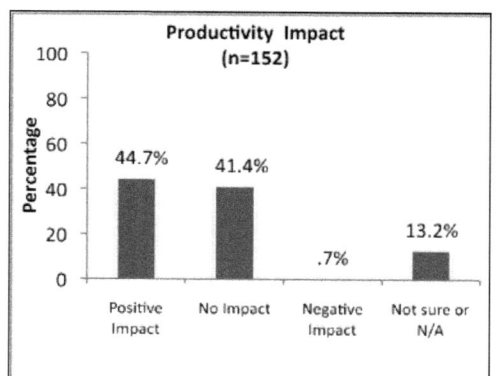

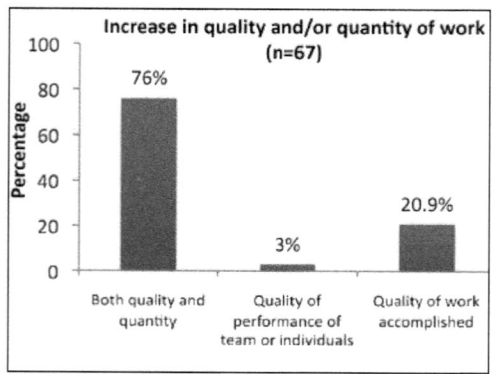

quality of the performance of the team or individuals and in the *quantity* of work accomplished, according to the 76 percent of managers reporting increased productivity.

Among those who quantified the increase, nearly half reported an increase of 11 percent to 35 percent.

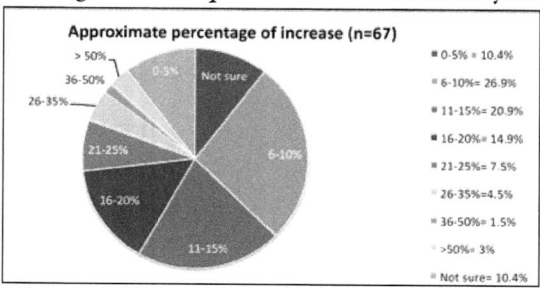

Asked, "To what do you attribute the increase?" managers' comments had the following recurring themes:
- Fewer distractions and greater ability to focus
- Reduced commuting time (resulting in more work time, less stress and a more positive attitude)
- Flexibility of hours worked provides better coverage and more job satisfaction
- Longer days can improve focus and continuity of work/attention
- Improved morale leads to increased productivity

Sample Comments: Productivity

Quality is also increased because of continuous focus on the task at hand (i.e. less time spent stopping/starting since work days are longer).

[Improved productivity results from]"the opportunity to proactively manage work projects in a systematic, orderly manner without office distractions. Also, the stress reduction that results from telecommuting one day a week translates to higher energy, increased work output, and a calmer approach to a formidable workload and deadlines."

"Improved employee retention; decrease in commuting time; off-hours coverage for on-call support; happier employees — happier manager."

"Finishing a task in one go — less set-up and wind-down time."

"Ability to reach participants and ability to work in environment that better facilitates what one needs to get done."

Assessment

The Impact on Manager/Team Functioning

Manager Functioning. One often-heard concern from managers is that managing employees with alternative schedules will make things more difficult, both for them and their team's ability to work with other departments. This survey showed the opposite. Forty-one percent of managers found that working with team members with FWAs had a positive impact on their own ability to focus; the remainder reported no impact (55 percent) or not sure (3 percent). (Less than 1 percent reported a negative impact.)

Team Functioning. Additionally, 36 percent of managers found a positive impact on team functioning (i.e., planning, communication, relationships); 5 percent reported a negative impact. The remainder found no impact (53 percent) or were unsure (7 percent).

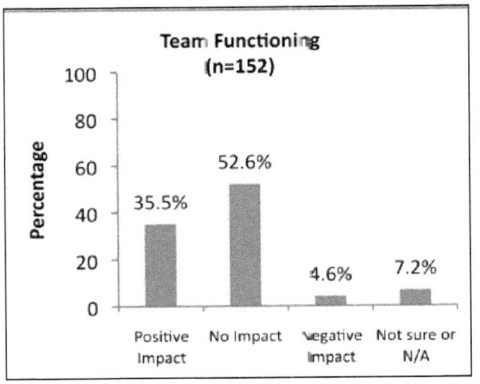
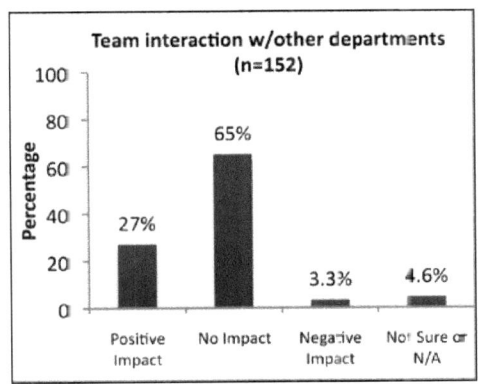

Cost Savings. More than half of managers (55 percent) reported that cost savings had been achieved as a result of FWAs enabling more efficient operations.

The Impact on Satisfaction/Engagement

Responses to the question about satisfaction and engagement reinforced the finding that there is little negative impact on teams when some work flexibly. A large proportion of managers report an overall positive impact for employees currently on FWAs, and some even report a positive impact on other employees' satisfaction. While there is some negative impact on others, there is a net positive for the rest of the team's engagement and satisfaction.

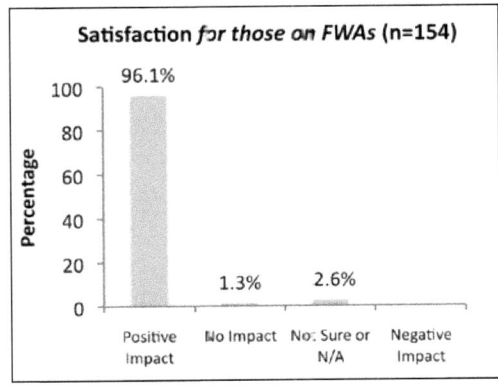
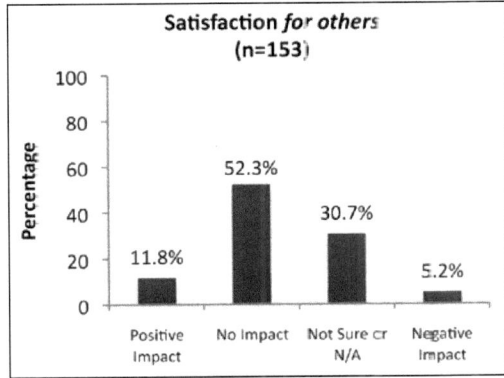

Assessment

Satisfaction: 96 percent of managers report a positive impact on job satisfaction among employees on FWAs and 12 percent report a positive impact on *other* employees' satisfaction; 52 percent report no impact on other employees' satisfaction and 5 percent report a negative impact.

Engagement: 77 percent of managers report a positive impact on engagement among employees using FWAs; 14 percent report a positive impact on other employees' engagement; only 2 percent report a negative impact on others. The remainder report no impact on others.

Sample Comments: Satisfaction/Engagement

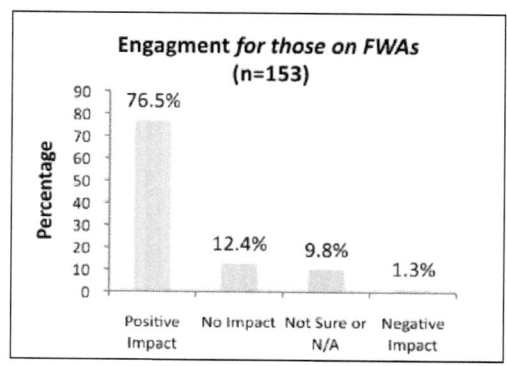
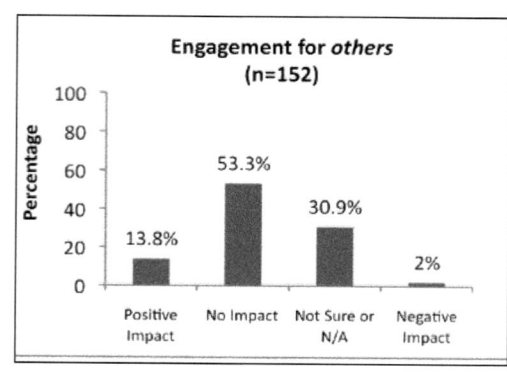

"Many of our senior managers have taken advantage of FWAs. They have expressed how much the new schedule has added to their appreciation of their work."

"Our employee satisfaction and retention levels are positively impacted by our ability to offer FWAs."

"Overall, I feel my staff are a much happier group with so many options available to them. This is obvious to me by their attitude and their productivity, and their expressed appreciation of having the option of telecommuting and flex hours. I have been able to keep experienced, seasoned employees within my department due to these work options, allowing for consistency in workflow, [which gave] me the opportunity to work on projects other than training. I…also have the option of telecommuting and of a compressed workweek; that FWA has immensely improved the quality of my life, which, in turn, makes me a much more appreciative and productive employee."

The Impact on Absenteeism, Lateness and Scheduling

Absenteeism. One-third (34 percent) of managers credit FWAs with reducing absenteeism in their departments (65 percent reported no change or were not sure). Only one manager found absenteeism to increase. Of the 49 managers who estimated the rate of the decrease, 72 percent report decreases up to 20 percent, 4 percent reported a 36 percent to 50 percent decrease and 6 percent noted a decrease of more than 50 percent.

Lateness/Early Departure. Nearly half of managers (47 percent) see a positive impact on the incidences of lateness and early departures; another 47 percent report no impact. There were no reports of a negative impact, and 6 percent were not sure.

Several themes recur in managers' comments about the decrease in absenteeism:

Assessment

- The ability to get work done during both short-term and long-term illnesses has value to both employee and manager.
- In addition to getting work done, an ill person working from home is less likely to infect coworkers.
- Staff have more flexibility in setting doctor and other appointments for times outside of their standard work hours.
- Employees are healthier when they are less stressed.
- Increased morale and job satisfaction leads to increased commitment.

Sample Comments: Absenteeism, Lateness & Scheduling

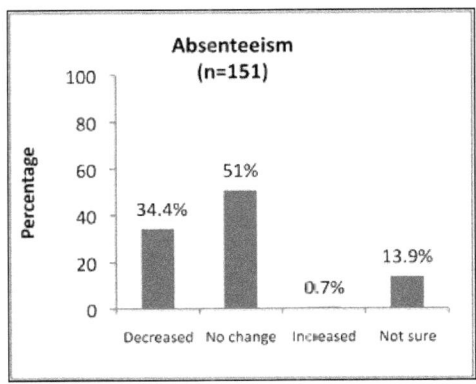
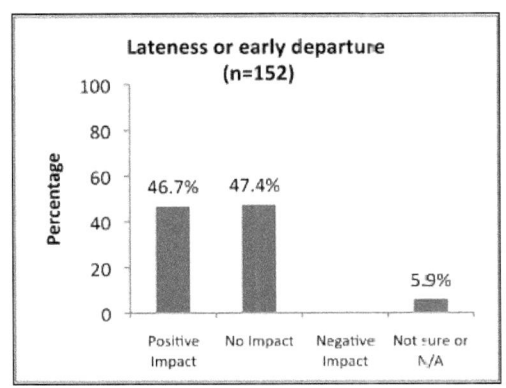

"Many employees work four 10-hour days, which provides them with 52 days off a year that they do not normally have. This dramatically reduces sick calls."

"We had a couple of long-term illnesses and injuries that would have required long absences if the staff hadn't had the ability to telecommute."

"Flexibility with work hours allows staff to go to doctor's appointments rather than calling in sick for the whole day."

"Because the workload can be completed anytime between 7 a.m. and 11 p.m., staff are able to reschedule their work day. ...This allows them to attend to other commitments ... and still meet their productivity for the day."

"[E]mployees are happy (less stressed) due to having this benefit, but also very committed to performing their work responsibilities."

"[I]f one is not feeling well enough to travel, that does not mean they are not well enough to work ... especially in the line of work that my staff does, which is mostly data entry."

Scheduling. FWAs have also helped managers fill schedules more predictably, with 35 percent reporting a positive impact, less than 1 percent reporting a negative impact, and the remainder no impact or unsure.

Cost Savings. More than half of managers (55 percent) reported that cost savings had been achieved as a result of FWAs reducing absenteeism and enabling more predictable attendance. One in six (17 percent) report costs savings achieved from reduced overtime associated with FWAs.

The Impact on Retention and Recruitment

Many managers believe that flexibility helps retain and attract not only those who are currently

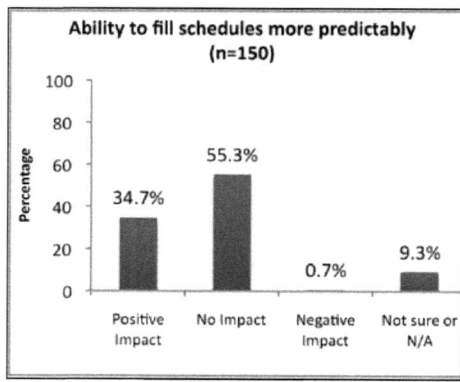

using FWAs, but those who might be interested in using them in the future.

Asked to estimate the impact on retention and recruitment considering not only those currently using an FWA but also those who might be interested in the future:

- 54 managers reported retaining an average of 2.8 exempt employees, and 42 reported retaining an average of 3.1 non-exempt (hourly) employees *at least partially due to FWAs*.
- More than half the managers reported that those retained were "top talent" and/or "hard-to-fill" positions.
- One-third of managers (33 percent) reported that cost savings had been achieved because FWAs had facilitated recruitment.

Recurring themes:

- Managers repeatedly noted how important it is to retain employees once they have been trained, given how much training they go through. The often-repeated comment, "It's hard to find good/experienced people" was said about a broad range of skilled experts.
- Telecommuting can retain the talents of highly valued employees who move far away.
- Telecommuting enables those with short- and long-term medical conditions to continue to work.

Sample Comments: Retention & Recruitment

"Some employees have been courted by the outside, and I believe FWAs were one of the reasons they stayed."

"Telecommuting is definitely an incentive when hiring new staff. In addition, those who have chosen not to use FWAs at this time appreciate the fact that it is an option they may still choose in the future."

"We have a long-term employee who was considering retiring ... and was considered a valuable asset both to her team and this department; her absence would have been greatly felt. We were able to keep her and keep consistency in [the department]."

"By allowing flex-time to attend school, employees stay within our department longer and can then move on/up within the company."

"The system we support requires years of training. Both of my [FWA] employees have been trained internally. It would be quite difficult to replace them if they were to leave."

Cost Savings. Given the breadth of the question, and the fact that the cost of turnover varies depending on the position, it is difficult to calculate specific savings. However, based on the following assumptions, we can estimate potential savings:

- Assuming a non-exempt (hourly) salary of $50,000 and full cost of turnover at 75 percent, retaining 10 positions could save $475,000.
- Assuming an exempt salary of $80,000 and full cost of turnover at 150 percent, retaining 10 positions could save $1.2M

The Impact on Health

FWAs had a positive impact on the health of employees, their managers' health, and even their co-workers' health. Four in five (81 percent) managers report a positive impact on the health and stress of employees using them. Nearly two in five managers (38 percent) report a positive impact on their own health; 4 percent report a negative impact; the balance report no impact or are unsure.

One in six (16 percent) report a positive impact on the health of other team members; 4 percent report a negative impact; the balance report no impact or are unsure.

Stress reduction and improved morale are mentioned many times throughout the survey as positive effects of FWAs.

Sample Comments: Health

"In general, I believe FWAs make for a much healthier and better work environment. All of those who I work with seem extremely dedicated to their work and would never allow their work to suffer."

"[T]he stress reduction that results from telecommuting one day a week translates to higher energy, increased work output, and a calmer approach to a formidable workload and deadlines."

"Reducing the long hours of commute alleviates a huge burden on employees and creates a loyal and positive environment."

Cost Savings. Two-thirds of managers (68 percent) reported that cost savings had been achieved as a result of FWAs reducing stress of the team overall.

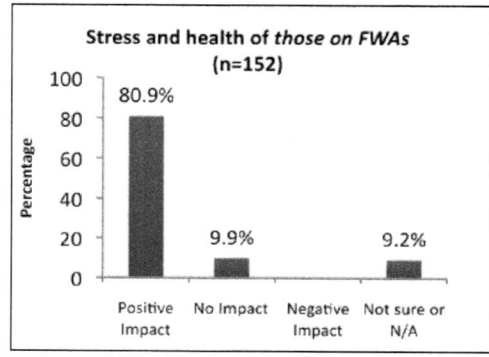
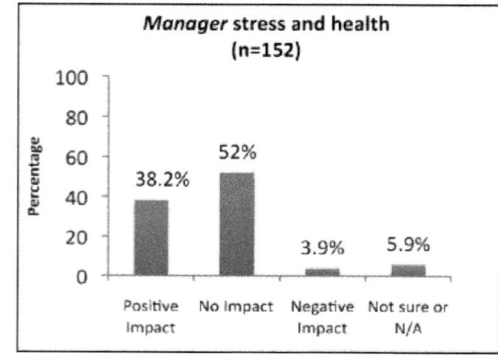
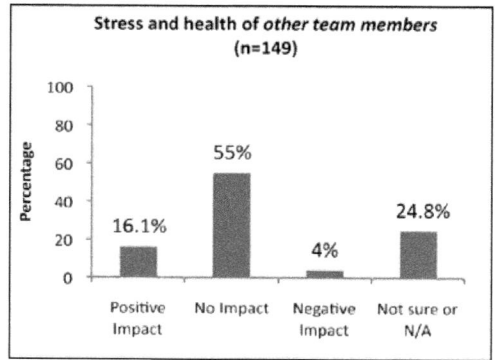

The Impact on Facilities/Space

Nearly half of managers (49 percent) found FWAs helped their department make better use of space or reduced space needs. They reported that FWAs have had the following impact in the time FWAs have been in effect at the company:

- The number of offices needed was reduced by: 1
- The number of cubicles/work stations needed was reduced by: 3
- The number of offices now shared: 1
- The number of cubicles/workstations now shared: 3

Cost Savings. If every space "saved" (i.e., not needed) was used for another purpose, the saved office space would yield a net savings of more than $2M. However, because not all saved spaces are used for other purposes, it makes more sense to calculate the savings for one office or cubicle, then use that as a unit of measure to estimate actual or potential savings for a particular situation.

Based on the assumptions and calculations below (Assumptions based on information from Facilities and Information Systems Departments — cost per square foot: $400; office size: 11 x 10; cubicle size: 5.5 x 5; average cost of standard telecommuting workstation: $2,850 [includes configuring/testing workstation, training, setup, travel, hardware, and cable. Calculations — office cost: 11 x 10 = 110 x $400 = $44,000; cubicle cost: 5.5 x 5 = 27.5 x $400 = $11,000; one cubicle saved: cost of one cubicle ($11,000) less the cost of one telecommuter set-up ($2,850) = $8,150; one office shared: cost of one office ($44,000) less the cost of two telecommuter workstations ($5,700) = $38,300]), two people sharing an office could save $38,300 in expenses, and one cubicle saved could yield $8,150. Therefore:

- Ten people sharing five offices could save or avert $191,500 in annual expenses.
- Ten people working from home instead of an onsite cubicle could save $81,500 annually.

If the space saved is due to telecommuters who don't require a home workstation, or several people on compressed work weeks sharing space, the savings would be even greater.

Cost Savings Data

Cost savings data that appears throughout this report represents responses to the following question: *Overall, have FWAs resulted in cost savings for your department?* The graph below shows all responses to that question.

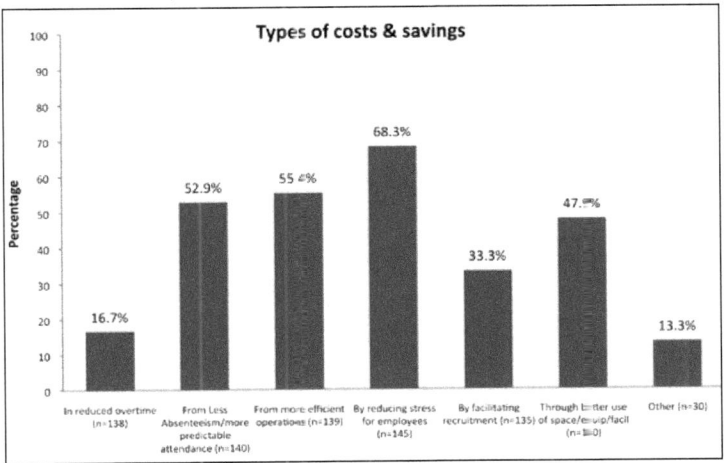

Unique Approaches to Documenting the Value of Flexible Work

As part of the new normal, companies are finding different ways to document the impact of flexible work in their organizations, often using real-time communication techniques that require a push/pull approach of providing information while also collecting information from users. American Express, for example, uses a web portal to provide information about the scope of the organization's BlueWork initiative and demonstrate the interconnectedness of real estate, technology and HR resources while also connecting the dots for the user regarding work and personal life.

FLEX IN-DEPTH: Ernst & Young

Using Social Media to Gather Information

During the recent economic downturn, the efforts of Ernst & Young's people in the marketplace were increased as it sought to serve clients and build business. E&Y's commitment to work flexibility was put to the test as the work-life "balance" tipped temporarily toward the need to quickly respond to difficult economic conditions. When the firm inaugurated a series of formal and informal discussions with its people across ranks and practices, it heard some of the firm's busiest people say they wanted to be sure E&Y's commitment to flexibility was intact. The firm set out to drive local, team-based conversations on flexibility as widely as possible, with encouragement from the voices of both senior leaders and from work teams already successful at practicing flexibility during busy times.

The initiative was developed by leaders and managers chiefly in human resources, inclusiveness and communications groups. The design for the project was pitched to and approved by E&Y's Americas managing partner, its vice chair for people, its Americas inclusiveness officer, and its Americas communications and marketing leader, all partners. Once the initiative was approved, our strategic messaging and planning leader oversaw the efforts of a team comprised of the Americas inclusiveness officer, a communications consultant, a communications senior associate, an inclusiveness center of expertise (COE) director and a COE assistant director; the last two roles were specialists in the area of our flexibility efforts.

Process:
E&Y knew that the overriding goal of the initiative was to be sure that its commitment to flexibility felt real to its people. The firm knew that social media platforms would encourage a candid and lively tone from participants and could allow it to elevate the voices of its people. E&Y also wanted to ensure that regional and local offices and teams would find the initiative engaging and would seek to leverage it on behalf of their own flexibility initiatives. The firm circulated an outline of the design to team members in key groups for review and comments before launching. It went to inclusive and flexibility leaders, selected members of sub-area people teams, sub-area communicators, and a focus group of junior staff from different teams. Most importantly, E&Y fixed the timing of the initiative to occur during the annual busy season for its audit teams. E&Y knew it risked diminished attention and participation of those professionals at that time, but felt it was critical to communicate flexibility options from and for busy teams at a time when it was most valuable to put them into practice.

Solution:
E&Y launched an online social-media campaign, called "Making It Real: Team Flexibility When Teams Get Busy" by dedicating a Lotus Connections workspace to collect ideas from people on how flexibility works best for them. The Americas managing partner launched the campaign

with a personal invitation to people to visit the campaign site and participate, and noted there would be a competition, with recognition awards for the best ideas submitted.

A weekly online newsletter followed up with links to the site over a five-week period, each week announcing a new weekly winner from the "Flex Team Challenge" competition; the winning teams received a recognition event that allowed them time as a team to gather and celebrate. During the last week of the campaign, people firmwide were able to vote on the team with the best idea; that team received both recognition and a seat on a new council that would advise the Americas managing partner and other leaders in the area of social media use at the firm.

During the weeks of the campaign, the site featured:

- Blogs (started by identified authors) on topics including a dad's parental leave, a marathon runner's training regimen, and team entries to the competition.

- Discussion forums (able to be started by anyone) on topics such as current concerns of working mothers, community volunteering during busy season, and use of our additional days off program.

- Videos, including comedienne Anita Renfroe's "Mom's Advice" song, and a summary of the business case for flexibility from Life Meets Work, Inc.

- Team photos and video clips submitted by teams themselves.

Results:
Judging from the tone of the submissions and the fun, positive buzz created in regions and offices through local promotion, we clearly were able to quickly enhance the tone of the conversation on flexibility on our teams, from one of concern to one of engagement and excitement.

- The majority of team competition submissions came from the audit-practice teams in the midst of their busy season, signaling that flexibility was indeed a hot topic for them and that they worked to carve out time from deadline demands to respond.
- Local flexibility champions and communicators were strongly interested in the campaign topic and the social media approach, resulting in continuing viral interest both during the campaign and in subsequent months.
- E&Y was able to achieve an Americas-wide approach to discussing flexibility across many countries' borders and cultures. In some locations, the pick-up for the campaign was low, but local flexibility champions and communicators were eager to participate and look ahead to what could be done after the campaign closed.
- E&Y learned a lot as it went along about what it would ideally need in a technology platform to support internal social media activity. Users accustomed to Internet platforms like Facebook and YouTube will expect ease of use from internal platforms as well if they're going to participate fully.

Assessment

Measurement/Metrix:

Across the entire site, more than 7,500 page views were logged over the time the campaign was actively promoted, a number that well outpaced expectations during the audit busy season. Nearly 800 ballots were received for the final vote for overall team winner, with 285 completing write-in questions about the campaign; of those, one-quarter said they would be "taking new actions regarding flexibility" as a direct result of the campaign; that was a significant number of teams affected. E&Y also received dozens of comments on the site that illustrated some of the values and enthusiasm our people associate with flexibility, including:

- "We all understand that flexibility is a two-way street ... we measure our success through the recognition of our clients and the success of our employees to develop and have balance."
- "Our [action plans] were all posted in the audit room so that the team was reminded that we weren't just talking about flexibility — we were going to live it."
- "Does all this flexibility make us a happier team? I like to think so. Does it mean we are a more productive team than we were in previous years? That answer is an unequivocal Yes!"
- "Fun and flexibility are not typically words associated with busy season, but at our account, we strive to make these words a reality every single day."

Modifications:

The campaign began and ended, and the intent now is to leverage both the tone and content aggregated on the campaign site to seed ongoing activities in regions and offices. The contributions from each location will be distributed to those locations so that local teams can be held as examples to others and so that leaders can have specific, working ideas to promote.

The social media approach used for the topic of flexibility will be used again to generate ideas and input on other topics of interest, such as recognition and entrepreneurship.

Conclusion

When people ask what the return on investment is for flexible work, Dr. Sandy Burud, principal of Flex Employment Services at FlexPaths, says it is sizable, as evidenced by an avalanche of research. Still, she says, if you are focusing on the ROI alone, you may be asking the wrong question. Instead, leaders should ask what flexible work is worth potentially to the organization in order to:

- Expand the range of ideas and problem solvers
- Achieve an alignment of purpose and culture
- Create new knowledge in an atmosphere of mutuality (where employees openly contribute their best ideas)
- Increase the sense of loyalty, affiliation and ownership throughout the organization
- Attract and keep a higher level of knowledge capital and increase the workforce's ability to focus, create and build relationship capital
- Replace the sense of a "transactional relationship" (e.g. "I will get mine") between managers and employees with a mutual commitment to common goals
- Increase the proportion of employees who are fully engaged, motivated by the work itself and require minimal oversight
- Reduce waste, errors, mishires, disengagement, turnover and burnout
- Have the nimbleness to respond quickly to market forces and increase efficiency
- Enhance customer experience and increase customer satisfaction and retention

Becoming a more flexible organization is not simply a new initiative tacked on to the normal way of doing things. It asks leaders and managers to summon the personal and organizational courage to examine what they believe and how they operate, and to change from the inside out. But in return, it offers the opportunity to leverage this new human capital for all it's worth. For those who make the effort, the dividends can be enormous. With the introduction of new stakeholders into the flexible work arena has come an increased focus on business outcomes from flexible work initiatives. Most organizations recognize that in order to meet today's workforce and workplace needs, flexible work has become a culture game changer. How flexible work is defined, who champions it, how it is leveraged and managed, the tools and resources provided to employees and managers — all will determine the ultimate success of an organization's effort to create a more agile workforce and work environment. This is truly a journey and not a destination. But, it is one that all organizations must embrace if they are to survive and thrive in the 21st century.

Assessment

TIP SHEET
Assessing the Value of Flexible Work

- ❏ *Position flexible work as a strategic business tool.* Can flex allow your organization to proactively respond to changes in the workforce and work place?
- ❏ *Change labels.* Forget about work-life balance. Consider work-life effectiveness as your positioning to employees and their managers. It is about each individual defining what it means and making it work for the business and themselves. There is no one-size-fits-all when it comes to flexibility.
- ❏ *Evaluate current and future workforce demographics.* What impact can flexible work have on workforce planning?
- ❏ *Assess the organization's current flexible work offering.* Is it positioned as a right or a privilege? Is there a penalty for using flex? Are only women using it? What messages does senior management send about the value of flex workers?
- ❏ *Document and measure the current state of flexible work.* Know how it works; who's eligible; what the utilization is of various options, in what departments, by men/women or length of service.
- ❏ *Involve managers and employees.* It's not enough to provide information and resources to only one side of the equation. Flex is a shared responsibility and both managers and employees need to be held accountable.
- ❏ *Collect the data.* Anything can be measured, but not everything should be measured. Pick your battles carefully and create a compelling case using both external and internal data.
- ❏ *Involve a variety of stakeholders.* Include leaders from IT, real estate, diversity/inclusion, facilities, health/wellness, legal, business continuity. Clarify the WIIFM — What's In It For Me? — for each role/responsibility.
- ❏ *Pilot.* Pick your target carefully. Look for influential partners whose voices and opinions will be respected by the business.
- ❏ *Make your partners look good.* Give them the ammunition they need to show that their investment of time and resources in flex have paid off.
- ❏ *Leverage technology.* Technology is the key to many successful flexible work options, but it has to work for the individual and the business. It is also the primary means to communicate, educate, administer and track flexible work.
- ❏ *Consider the importance of boundaries between work and the rest of life.* Burning out employees results in costly mistakes, higher health care costs and greater turnover.
- ❏ *Stay informed.* Be aware of changing laws and public policy related to flexible work.
- ❏ *Market, market, market.* At the end of the day, creating a more flexible culture is like launching a new product or service. It requires creative marketing and communication and constant and consistent attention.
- ❏ *Brand your flex initiative.* Call it something that relates to your business objectives. Make flex stand out, but also make it make sense inside your organization. If health is important, maybe call it "healthy lifestyles." For example, if the focus is on productivity, maybe "Work Smart."
- ❏ *Tell your story internally and externally.* While data is necessary, it's often the human-interest stories that change behavior and opinions, even at the executive level. Create a flex community and collect employees' and managers' stories about their experiences

Assessment

- with flexible work. Apply for awards and recognition that keep raising the bar on flexible work.
- *Remember sibling rivalry is alive and well in the c-suite.* Make sure you use it to encourage naysayers to get with the program.
- *And finally, don't give up.* Change takes time. Take baby steps if you have to. It's like skiing down a hill. If you stand at the top of the hill and look all the way down, it may be hard to get started. But if you slalom a little to the left and a little to the right and keep going, before you know it, you'll make it all the way to your end goal.

REFERENCES: CHAPTER 10

1. "Business Impacts of Flexibility: An Imperative for Expansion," Corporate Voices, researched by WFD Consulting, 2011.
2. Survey on Workplace Flexibility, A Report by WorldatWork, 2011.
3. Survey on Workplace Flexibility, A Report by WorldatWork, 2011
4. "First Tennessee Bank's story" adapted from © Copyright 2004 by Davies-Black Publishing, a division of CPP, Inc. Adapted from "Leveraging the New Human Capital: Adaptive Strategies, Results Achieved, and Stories of Transformation", S. Burud & M. Tumolo. All rights reserved.
5. Casner-Lotto, J. (2000). "Holding a Job, Having a Life: Strategies for Change." Scarsdale, NY, Work in America Institute. Flynn, G. (1997). "Making a Business Case for Balance." Workforce: 68-74.
6. Previous section adapted from Corporate Voices, "Business Impacts of Flexibility: An Imperative for Expansion," 2011.

About the Sponsors

Cardinal Health is a Fortune 19 healthcare services company that improves the cost-effectiveness of healthcare. Cardinal Health helps pharmacies, hospitals and ambulatory care sites focus on patient care while reducing costs, improving efficiency and quality, and increasing profitability. As one of the largest healthcare companies in the world, Cardinal Health provides pharmaceuticals and medical products to more than 60,000 locations each day and employing more than 30,000 people worldwide. For more information, visit cardinalhealth.com.

Today's Merck is a global healthcare leader working to help the world be well. Merck is known as MSD outside the United States and Canada. Through our prescription medicines, vaccines, biologic therapies and consumer care and animal health products, we work with customers and operate in more than 140 countries to deliver innovative health solutions. We also demonstrate our commitment to increasing access to healthcare through far-reaching policies, programs and partnerships. For more information, visit www.merck.com.

NOVARTIS

Novartis Pharmaceuticals Corporation (NPC) researches, develops, manufactures and markets innovative prescription drugs used to treat a number of diseases and conditions, including cardiovascular, dermatological, central nervous system, bone disease, cancer, organ transplantation, psychiatry, infectious disease and respiratory. The company's mission is to improve people's lives by pioneering novel healthcare solutions. Located in East Hanover, New Jersey, NPC is an affiliate of Novartis AG, which provides healthcare solutions that address the evolving needs of patients and societies. Headquartered in Basel, Switzerland, Novartis Group companies employ approximately 121,000 full-time-equivalent associates and operate in more than 140 countries around the world.

 **STATE STREET.**

State Street Corporation (NYSE: STT) is one of the world's leading providers of financial services to institutional investors, including investment servicing, investment management and investment research and trading. With $22.8 trillion in assets under custody and administration and $2.1 trillion* in assets under management at June 30, 2011, State Street operates in 26 countries and more than 100 geographic markets worldwide. For more information, visit State Street's website at www.statestreet.com.

*This AUM includes the assets of the SPDR Gold Trust (approx. $58 billion as of June 30, 2011), for which State Street Global Markets, LLC, an affiliate of State Street Global Advisors serves as the marketing agent.

About the Authors

Karol Rose is a Principal, Advisory Services at FlexPaths, a women-owned business that has provided flexibility software solutions to companies like Procter & Gamble, Cardinal Health, John Deere and American Express. In her past role as FlexPaths' Chief Knowledge Officer, Rose's work and subject matter expertise formed the foundation for many of the online tools and resources in FlexPaths' software products.

Rose has worked at the forefront of the work-life effectiveness field – a term she coined – for more than 25 years. She led the work-life practice at such major organizations as PricewaterhouseCoopers and TimeWarner Inc., and created many "firsts" in the work-life field, including developing one of the first on-site back-up child care centers in the country. As a consultant, Rose has developed, designed and implemented innovative flexible work practices and culture change initiatives for numerous Fortune 500 companies. Her work has impacted the work and lives of managers, employees, and human resource leaders.

Lori Sokol, Ph.D. is an industrial psychologist and work-life consultant to organizations large and small. She teaches businesses how to integrate work-life resources and services into their corporate culture to increasingly attract and retain the most talented, productive and loyal employees regardless of gender, age, sexual orientation, marital status or geographic location.

In addition to on-site consulting, Dr. Sokol's work has been profiled on MSNBC, Fox 5 News, and CNBC. Her writing has been published in the Baltimore Sun, The Huffington Post and The New York Times Business Blog; and she was the host of the radio show, Juggling Act, on 1490AM WGCH, where she provided listeners with work/life tools and strategies to help them achieve more effective career and personal goals. Dr. Sokol is also the Founder and Publisher of Work Life Matters magazine, a national publication that provides businesses with news and analysis about the latest trends in the work-life arena.

About the Foreword Author

In August of 2006, *J.T. (Ted) Childs, Jr.,* retired from IBM after a 39-year career, the last 15 spent as the executive responsible for the company's Global Workforce Diversity Programs. In the July 2000 issue of FastCompany magazine, Keith Hammonds wrote that "Ted Childs is perhaps the most effective diversity executive on the planet." Ted's goal has been to be the Workforce Diversity thought leader, strategist, catalyst for change and key executive partner of this generation. The role of Ted Childs® LLC is to serve as a "Global Strategic Advisor" to Senior Management and Workforce Diversity teams, leading them in the examination of their culture. The goal is to move a company from "spinning your wheels, politically correct behavior" to execution that reflects performance and leadership.

About the Working Mother Research Institute

The Working Mother Research Institute (WMRI), a division of Working Mother Media, is home to the Working Mother 100 Best Companies, Working Mother Best Companies for Multicultural Women, Working Mother Best Companies for Hourly Workers and the National Association of Female Executives' Top Companies for Executive Women, among other initiatives. WMRI produces insightful benchmarking reports as well as important research papers studying work life and the advancement of women and conducts surveys, such as *What Moms Choose: The Working Mother Report,* to further corporate culture change nationwide.

Working Mother Research Institute

President	Carol Evans
Director	Jennifer Owens

Senior Research Editor	Krista Carothers
Senior Manager, Editorial Research Initiatives	Kristen Willoughby
Senior Manager, Corporate Research Initiatives	Michele Siegel
Primary Research Associate	Kaisa Filppula
Contributing Editor	Katherine Bowers
Creative Director	Ebelinda Antigua
Production Designer	Brett Sonnenschein

Sales & Marketing

VP, Group Publisher	Joan Sheridan LaBarge
Executive Account Directors	LaQuanda Murray
	Kim Sealy
	Jennifer Smyth
Senior Account Directors	Takita Mason
	Alisa Nadler
Director, Marketing and Public Relations	Nancy Intrator
Marketing Manager	Jessica Goldman
Assistant Marketing Manager	Carolina Pichardo
Art Director	Helena You

Workingmother.com

Director, Digital Media	Helen Jonsen
Manager, Online	Kelli Daley